Building
MINIATURE HOUSES
and
FURNITURE

Dorie Krusz

ARCO PUBLISHING COMPANY, INC.
219 Park Avenue South, New York, N.Y. 10003

Published by Arco Publishing Company, Inc.
219 Park Avenue South, New York, N.Y. 10003

Copyright © 1977 by Doris J. Krusz

All rights reserved. No part of this book may be
reproduced, by any means, without permission in
writing from the publisher, except by a reviewer
who wishes to quote brief excerpts in connection
with a review in a magazine or newspaper.

Library of Congress Cataloging in Publication Data

Krusz, Dorie.
  Building miniature houses and furniture.

  Includes index.
  1. Miniature craft. 2. Doll-houses. 3. Miniature
furniture. I. Title.

TT178.K78   745.59'23   77-1525
ISBN 0-668-04184-6 (Library Edition)

Printed in the United States of America

To Arthur, Jim, Tom and Tracey

Contents

List of Plates

Introduction

This book deals with building and furnishing miniature houses, with emphasis on a Georgian house similar to the one shown in the photographs, because I know it best. Suggestions and directions are given for building other types of houses, also, using the same basic technique.

There are many books on building "doll" houses, simple projects for children to play with. There are also some books for advanced builders showing very sophisticated projects and how to handle complex tools and work with the finest materials.

This book fills the gap between the two. The materials and tools are inexpensive and easily obtained. The techniques are simple, suitable for beginning and intermediate builders. Some lovely results can be obtained by the miniaturist who wants more than a child's plaything but doesn't feel ready yet for a masterwork.

Chapter 1
Tools and Materials

TOOLS

There will be many small tools and building materials listed here. They are generally inexpensive and though the list seems long, let me assure you, all the tools I own can be kept in a shoe box.

Most of what you need you probably have already: scissors, glue, pins, emery boards, etc. The only things you will probably have to buy are tools to cut and drill with.

For long straight cuts and cutting thicker wood, an X-acto razor saw is good. This is a metal blade about 6″ long with tiny teeth for making fine cuts. It fits into a wooden handle (Fig. 1A). Single-edged razor blades are good for cutting thin wood. For cutting and carving, a utility or mat knife is useful (Fig. 1B). This is basically a metal handle in two halves, held together by a screw. The handle holds replacement blades. The mat knife can be used for making long straight cuts, or can be held like a penknife for carving. A ruler with a metal edge and small, straight fingernail scissors will also be needed.

For drilling holes, a pin vise is needed (Fig. 1C). This is a small drill which holds tiny bits. It is held in the hand and rotated with the fingers. I have two of these; one holds bits up to $\frac{1}{32}$″ diameter, the other holds bits from $\frac{1}{32}$″ to $\frac{1}{16}$″

diameter. These two seem adequate for most needs.

As for miscellaneous tools, emery boards are invaluable for sanding and shaping wood. Straight pins or the smaller lill pins are used to strengthen glued joints. A small wire clipper to cut off the excess pin is handy. Round toothpicks are essential for many things because of their strength and shape.

One tool you might like is a miniature miter box. X-acto makes one including the saw, though you can make your own easily enough. I have a set of Swiss pattern files, various shaped small files—oval, flat, triangular, etc.—which are especially useful in furniture making. Tweezers and needle-nose pliers complete my personal tool list, but as you work you will find many others. Tools should be chosen for your own comfort in working.

MATERIALS

For making house walls, floors, and ceilings, you need two basic materials: $\frac{1}{16}$″ thick poster board and wood strips (see Plate 1). Poster board is a smooth-surfaced, multi-ply cardboard, available at art supply stores. It makes a good base for everything.

For wood, basswood is best. It is harder than balsa, softer than pine, and does not seem to warp, though it can be soaked in water and bent into curves when needed. Basswood comes in a great variety of sizes from $\frac{1}{32}$″ × $\frac{1}{32}$″ to $\frac{1}{4}$″ × 2″. Most sizes are available at hobby shops but the complete range can be ordered through Model Shipways (see Source List).

For making furniture, I use a method of building-up rather than carving out, because I'm not good at carving. The techniques are explained fully later in this book, but let me say here that shapes ordinarily beyond the beginning

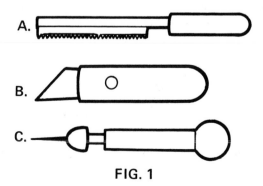

A.

B.

C.

FIG. 1

13

builder are obtainable with this method. For materials I use basswood of many sizes, dowels of various diameters (see Source List: Model Shipways), beads, sequins, many types of string, etc., all inexpensive and readily available. Pins can be used for hinges on some furniture. For other hinges (for drop-leaf tables, etc.) silk mesh, 40 to the inch, is used (see Source List: Woolcraft Ltd.).

Glue is another important material. For gluing wood to wood, or wood to poster board, two glues are most used. Elmer's glue or similar white glues are excellent. They are strong, dry quickly, can be used to fill in cracks where wood is joined and even build up decorative details on furniture. They are, however, water soluble and sometimes cause large pieces of thin wood used in wall paneling and floors to curl a bit at the edges. For these and other thin woods, use Weldwood cement. This is a very strong glue somewhat like rubber cement. It is a contact cement, which means that once two glued surfaces meet they are permanently joined, but some adjustments can be made before it sets up. Excess white glue can be removed with water, excess Weldwood with lacquer thinner.

"Super Glue" sold under various brand names is good for gluing metal, as is silicone glue, a cloudy glue which dries clear and has more body than super glue. "Stickum" is another useful substance, also sold under various names. This is a very sticky plastic material, good for holding candlesticks on mantles, vases on tables, etc.; it holds firmly but can easily be pulled off or removed completely with turpentine should you wish to change your accessories around.

Paints and varnishes have their own properties. Basically, they are either oil- or water-based. The oil or polyurethane based paints, stains, etc., dry slowly, but many prefer them for their permanence and luster. The water-based latex and acrylic paints, stains, etc., dry quickly, are fun to work with, and are really quite permanent. All paints, varnishes, etc., can be used in combination and the general rule is: you can use oil base over water base but not water base over oil base.

Metallic paints and rub-on finishes are useful, but delicate and slow to harden. However, Treasure Jewels metallic brass with a bit of oil base varnish and a touch of yellow Testor's

enamel paint gives a hard, fast-drying brass finish.

One thing I always find use for is antiquing ink. This is an oil base fluid, rather like a furniture stain, but heavier. It can be brushed on, then wiped off to soften and accent. I am personally fond of antiquing as a technique.

Water base antiquing can be made of thinned down acrylic tube paints, brown and a bit of black.

Generally, you can get the same results with oil base or water base paints, stains, and varnishes. You just have to play a bit with both kinds to see what's comfortable to work with.

Although the following is not strictly a tool or material, you might find it useful in working to the standard miniature scale of $1'' = 1'$.

$$1'' = 12''$$
$$1\tfrac{5}{16}'' = 11\tfrac{1}{4}''$$
$$\tfrac{7}{8}'' = 10\tfrac{1}{2}''$$
$$1\tfrac{3}{16}'' = 9\tfrac{3}{4}''$$
$$\tfrac{3}{4}'' = 9''$$
$$1\tfrac{1}{16}'' = 8\tfrac{1}{4}''$$
$$\tfrac{5}{8}'' = 7\tfrac{1}{2}''$$
$$\tfrac{9}{16}'' = 6\tfrac{3}{4}''$$
$$\tfrac{1}{2}'' = 6''$$
$$\tfrac{7}{16}'' = 5\tfrac{1}{4}''$$
$$\tfrac{3}{8}'' = 4\tfrac{1}{2}''$$
$$\tfrac{5}{16}'' = 3\tfrac{3}{4}''$$
$$\tfrac{1}{4}'' = 3''$$
$$\tfrac{3}{16}'' = 2\tfrac{1}{4}''$$
$$\tfrac{5}{32}'' = 1\tfrac{7}{8}''$$
$$\tfrac{1}{8}'' = 1\tfrac{1}{2}''$$
$$\tfrac{3}{32}'' = 1\tfrac{1}{8}''$$
$$\tfrac{1}{16}'' = \tfrac{3}{4}''$$
$$\tfrac{1}{32}'' = \tfrac{3}{8}''$$

I've given a few 32nd of an inch measurements which are useful in furniture making. For others, on a ruler, measure between the 16th of an inch measurements given. For example:

$$\tfrac{3}{4}'' \text{ or } \tfrac{24}{32}'' = 9''$$
$$1\tfrac{1}{16}'' \text{ or } \tfrac{22}{32}'' = 8\tfrac{1}{4}''$$
$$\text{Therefore}$$
$$\tfrac{23}{32}'' = 8\tfrac{5}{8}''$$

If you want to get picky, you can figure out 64ths of a inch.

And since we're talking about teeny sizes, let me recommend one last tool: magnifying glasses. They come in many styles and magnifications. Some are mounted on a table, some worn around the neck or on the head. They are sold at hobby shops, needlework stores, and optical companies. Get some!

Chapter 2

The Modular Structure

Modular building is suited to everyone, but especially to those with only simple tools and those who hate sawing wood as much as I do. In modular building, the floors, walls, and ceilings are constructed as separate units (see Plate 1), then put together to make a room (see Plate 2). The rooms are then put together to make a house (see Plate 3).

Modular building has many small advantages and one *big* one. Since everything is made in separate units, there is easy access to everything. Each unit can be completely constructed, decorated, and furnished right down to the last detail before the house is assembled . . . no hanging wallpaper in impossible corners, no lying on your back painting ceilings like Michaelangelo, no working in cramped spaces at all; and if you mess up one unit, the whole house is not spoiled.

The separate units are made in a hollow wall construction, as shown in Plate 1, much as in a real house. That is, there are two sides to each unit, like walls, and wood framework in between, like studs and joists in a real house. This is the basic modular "sandwich." The walls are made of 1/16" thick poster board which can be cut with a mat knife. The framework is made of basswood strips which are cut with a razor saw. Most of the major construction will be done with these two tools.

Plate 1 shows a basic wall unit of two pieces of 1/16" poster board for the sides and 1/4" × 1/8" wood for the studs. Floors and ceilings are made basically the same way, but with thicker framework, which will be explained later. This hollow wall construction is not only easy to do, but gives space for wires for a lighting system.

You will notice in Plate 1 that the framework extends, in places, past the poster board sides. When the units are assembled (see Plate 2), these extensions add to the strength of the room and later, the house. The extensions need not interlock, but it does not hurt if they do (Fig. 2).

At first glance this "cardboard" and wood construction may not seem strong enough to you. Let me assure you that it is not only strong but much lighter in weight than a house built of solid wood. You will notice in Fig. 2 that the side wall unit overlaps the floor unit. The ceiling unit will overlap the wall unit. True, this is only a 1/16" overlap now, but when the walls are finished, with ceiling and baseboard moldings in place, the overlap will be 3/16", which is a lot in miniature. This adds much strength to the whole structure. My miniature house which is quite large (6' long × 3' high × 2' deep) is carried up and down stairs and travels, lying on its side, in a station wagon without undue stress.

FLOOR PLANS

Once the separate units are made, they are assembled to form a house. The basic house shown in Plate 3 has the side and front walls stable and the exterior completely finished. The back is open for viewing the interior and the back side of the roof lifts off for access to the lighting system. This is just one example of how the units

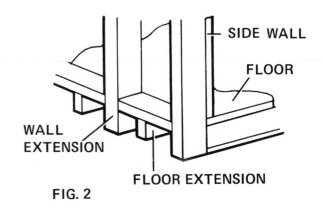

SIDE WALL

FLOOR

WALL EXTENSION

FLOOR EXTENSION

FIG. 2

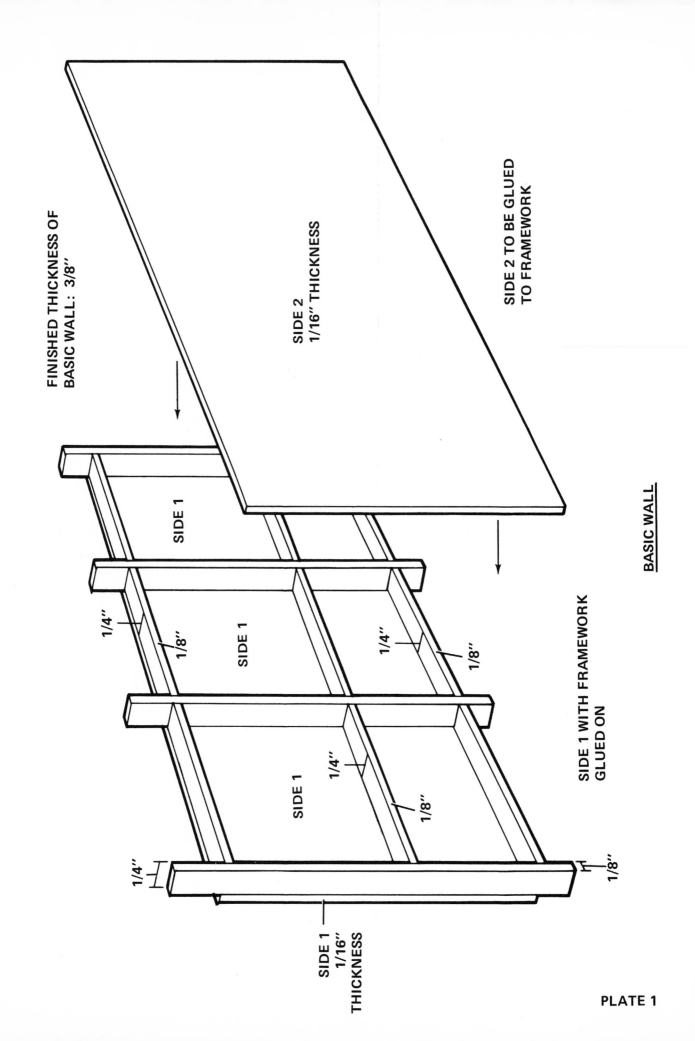

FINISHED THICKNESS OF
BASIC WALL: 3/8"

SIDE 2
1/16" THICKNESS

SIDE 2 TO BE GLUED
TO FRAMEWORK

BASIC WALL

SIDE 1

SIDE 1

SIDE 1

SIDE 1

1/4"

1/8"

1/4"

1/8"

1/4"

1/8"

1/4"

1/8"

SIDE 1 WITH FRAMEWORK
GLUED ON

SIDE 1
1/16"
THICKNESS

PLATE 1

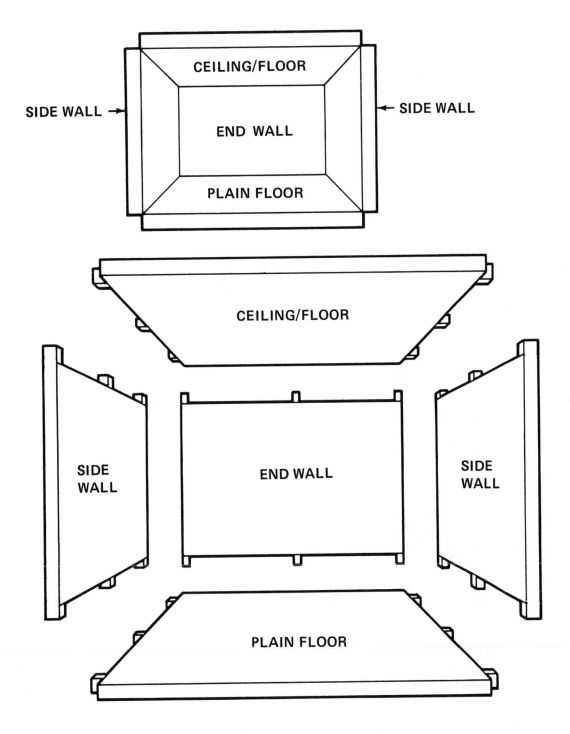

BASIC PARTS FOR ONE ROOM

PLATE 2

BASIC PARTS OF THE MODULAR HOUSE

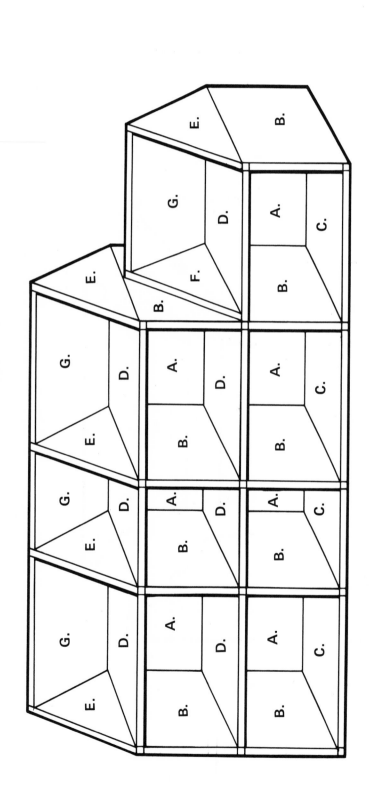

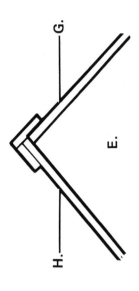

A. END WALL
B. SIDE WALL
C. PLAIN FLOOR
D. CEILING/FLOOR
E. PEAK
F. EXTRA PEAK FOR ROOF ON WING
G. FIXED ROOF
H. LIFT-OFF ROOF

PLATE 3

LR - LIVING ROOM
H - HALL
DR - DINING ROOM
BR - BEDROOM
K - KITCHEN
LIB - LIBRARY

3 SUGGESTED PLANS

BR	H	BR
LR	H	K

BR	H	BR
LR	H	DR
		K

LIB	BR	H	BR
	LR	H	DR
			K

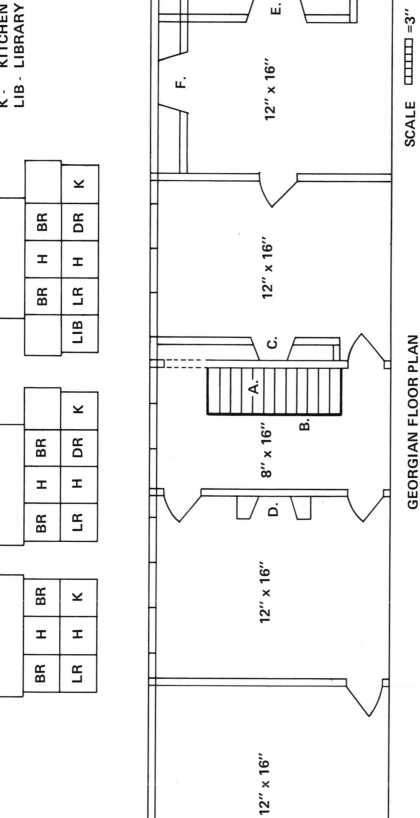

12″ x 16″

12″ x 16″

8″ x 16″

12″ x 16″

12″ x 16″

E.

F.

A.

B.

C.

D.

GEORGIAN FLOOR PLAN

SCALE ▯▯▯▯▯▯ =3″

A. STAIRCASE SHOULD BEGIN AT FRONT OF HOUSE BUT CAN START AT BACK TO BE MORE ATTRACTIVE.

B. DARK LINE SHOWS SECOND FLOOR HALL CUT OUT FOR STAIRWELL.

C. FIREPLACE INSET INTO FALSE WALL, EARLY GEORGIAN.

D. FIREPLACE EXTENDING INTO ROOM, LATE GEORGIAN.

E. PROPER PLACEMENT OF FIREPLACE IN ADDED WING.

F. POSSIBLY MORE ATTRACTIVE PLACEMENT OF FIREPLACE IN ADDED WING.

PLATE 4A

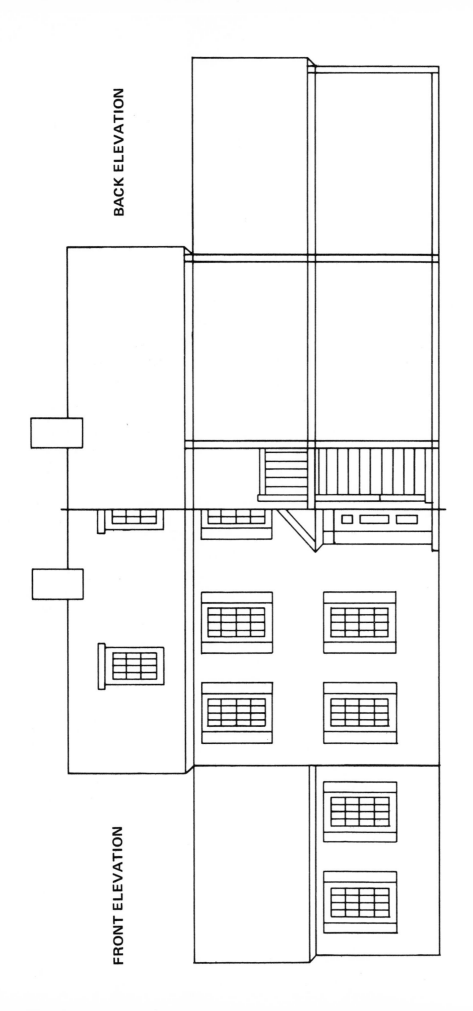

BACK ELEVATION

FRONT ELEVATION

SCALE ▭▭▭▭▭ =3"

PLATE 4B

SIDE ELEVATIONS

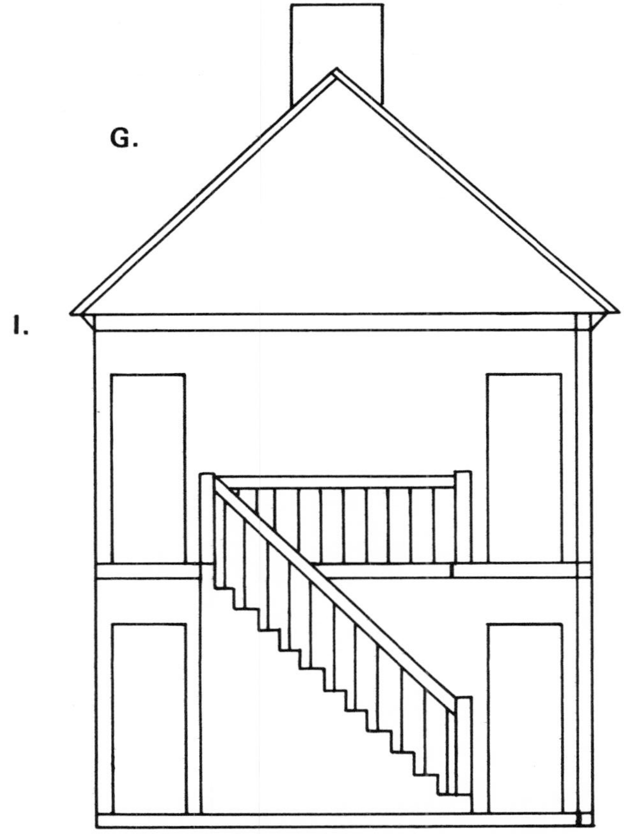

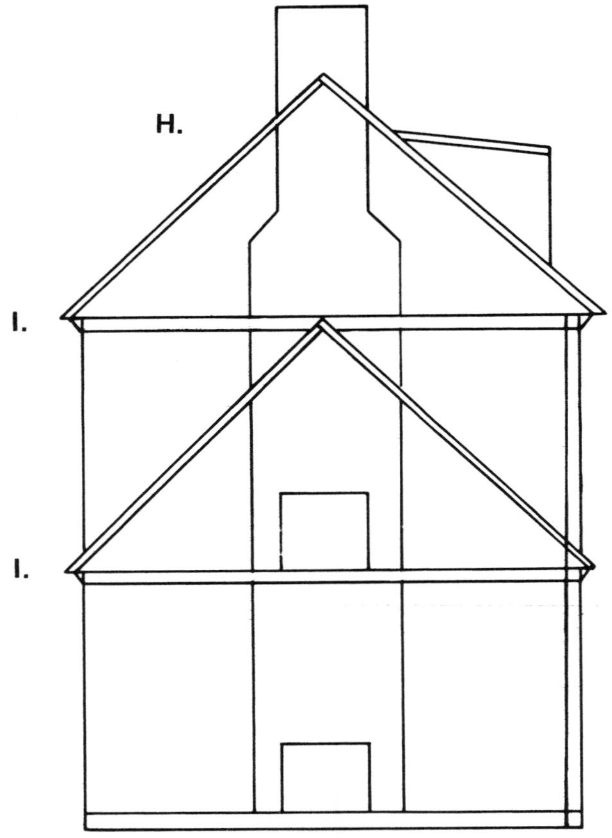

H.

I.

I.

G.

I.

SCALE ▭▭▭=3

G. SIDE ELEVATION SHOWING STAIRCASE, BANNISTERS AND STAIRWELL.

H. SIDE ELEVATION SHOWING MAIN FIREPLACES, ALSO ADDED WING AND DORMER.

I. SIDE ELEVATIONS SHOW EXTENDED PEAKS TO ACCOMMODATE ROOF LINE MOLDINGS.

PLATE 4C

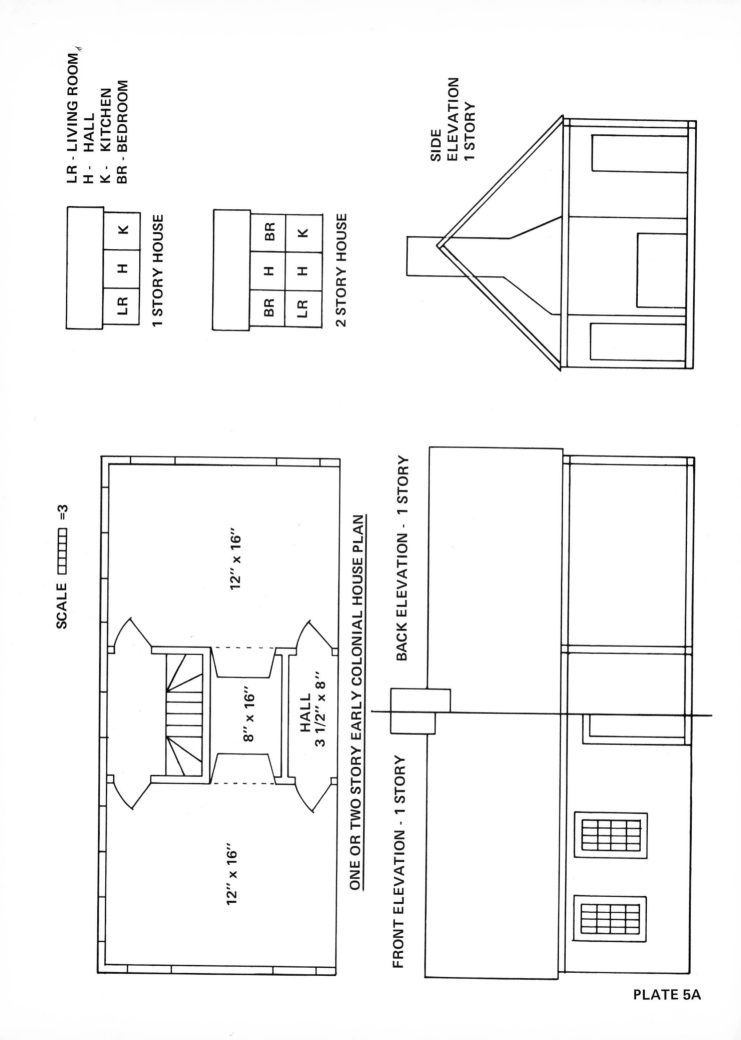

LR - LIVING ROOM
H - HALL
K - KITCHEN
BR - BEDROOM

| LR | H | K |

1 STORY HOUSE

| BR | H | BR |
| LR | H | K |

2 STORY HOUSE

SIDE
ELEVATION
1 STORY

SCALE ▭▭▭▭▭ =3

12″ x 16″

8″ x 16″

HALL
3 1/2″ x 8″

12″ x 16″

ONE OR TWO STORY EARLY COLONIAL HOUSE PLAN

BACK ELEVATION - 1 STORY

FRONT ELEVATION - 1 STORY

PLATE 5A

SIDE
ELEVATION
2 STORY

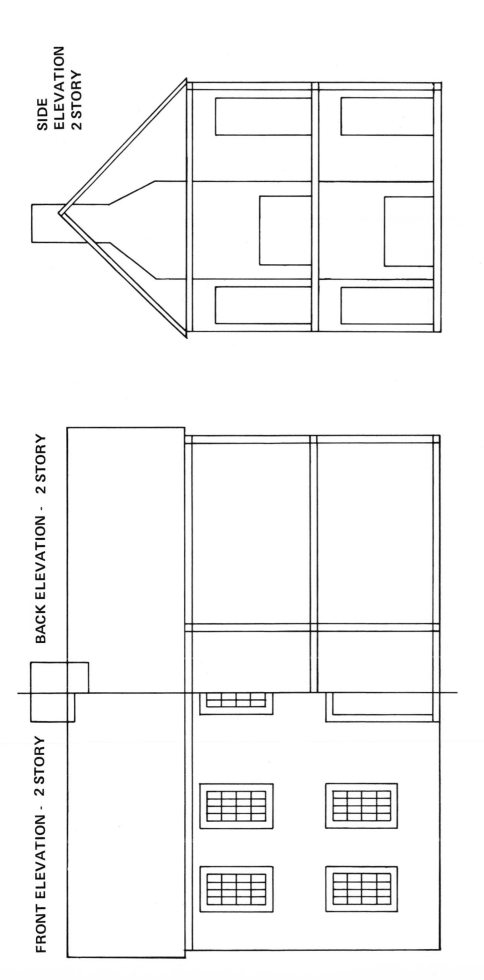

SCALE ▭▭▭▭▭ =3"

BACK ELEVATION - 2 STORY

FRONT ELEVATION - 2 STORY

PLATE 5B

can fit together; you are not limited to this form.

Plates 4 and 5 are floor plans showing houses built of modules. There are two basic modules: one 12″ wide, 16″ deep and 8″ high for the main rooms, and one 8″ wide, 16″ deep, and 8″ high for hallways. If you plan to have the third floor open for viewing, you might want to widen the hallways to 9″ or 10″ to accommodate another staircase on the second floor. Of course, you can use other dimensions, as long as they are consistent throughout your floor plan.

The Georgian house in Plate 4 is the one emphasized in this book because I know it best, but you can see in Plate 5 that the basic modules fit other early Colonial type houses as well. The central fireplace structure, typical of early houses, fits into the 8″ × 16″ × 8″ module. Depending on the number of modules used, how they are arranged, and what interior and exterior details are used, almost any Colonial style house can be built (see Plates 27 through 30).

Most Georgian houses were built two rooms deep. This is not as advantageous for viewing as a house one room deep. For authenticity's sake, let me say that Georgian houses one room deep

were indeed built, though rarely, and the plan in Plate 4 is an adaptation of this. In Plate 5 I have taken the liberty of leaving a space for a hallway, at the back of the house, between the main rooms. To be authentic, the central fireplace structure should extend to the back of the house. I put the hallway in the plans for aesthetic reasons.

A one-story early Colonial house is a good first project. It can be a typical seventeenth-century, one-room-deep house, but it can also be used as a one-room-deep adaptation of a Cape Cod house, since the exterior proportions are similar. The Cape Cod house is primarily an eighteenth-century development, so if you prefer eighteenth-century furniture you might like this idea.

Once you become familiar with modular building, if you study Colonial architectural styles you will see that by varying room sizes, roof styles, exterior details, etc., it is possible to build any house you like. You can build from authentic floor plans. You can also build two-room-deep houses with the front and back walls in place, but hinged to open for viewing the interior. The possibilities are unlimited.

Chapter 3

Building a Module

The basic module is built of five separate units: 1 floor, 1 end wall, 2 side walls, and a ceiling (see Plate 2). In two-story houses, the ceiling of the first story and the floor of the second story are built as a ceiling/floor "sandwich" unit which holds the hidden lighting system. Later in this book, much space will be given to this, but for now we will deal with floors and walls.

When you look at the plans in Plate 6, you will see that $\frac{1}{16}''$ or $\frac{1}{8}''$ has been added to the basic $12'' \times 16''$ or $8'' \times 16''$ room measurements. This is because the walls overlap the floors, the end wall overlaps the side walls, and the ceiling overlaps the walls (see Plate 7). As mentioned before, $\frac{1}{16}''$ does not seem like much overlap but when moldings $\frac{1}{8}''$ thick at the floor and ceiling lines are added to the finished wall, the overlap will be $\frac{3}{16}''$. The final thickness of all the walls (with all moldings), floors, and ceilings will be $\frac{5}{8}''$. When the house is assembled, wood strips $\frac{5}{8}''$ wide $\times \frac{1}{16}''$ thick will cover all the raw edges for a neat appearance.

PLAIN FLOORS

Study Plate 1 again for basic construction. To make plain floors, cut 2 pieces of poster board using the sizes in Plate 6. In cutting, be sure the corners are square. This saves much trouble later. The wood framework (joists) is $\frac{7}{16}'' \times \frac{1}{8}''$ basswood strips. This size is used so that the final floor thickness, with flooring in place, will be $\frac{5}{8}''$. For example:

$$\begin{array}{l} \frac{1}{16}'' \text{ poster board} \\ \frac{7}{16}'' \text{ framework} \\ \frac{1}{16}'' \text{ poster board} \\ \underline{\frac{1}{16}'' \text{ wood floor boards}} \\ \frac{10}{16}'' \text{ or } \frac{5}{8}'' \end{array}$$

$\frac{7}{16}'' \times \frac{1}{8}''$ is not a standard size in basswood so just glue together strips $\frac{1}{4}'' \times \frac{1}{8}''$ and $\frac{3}{16}'' \times \frac{1}{8}''$. Tape the strips together in several places till the glue dries, then remove the tape.

Next, glue framework strips across one piece of poster board as shown in Plate 1, spacing them 3 or 4 inches apart and extending them about $\frac{1}{4}''$ past the poster board on each end. Now, glue short strips of framework, around the edges of the poster board and 3 or 4 inches apart in the center area of the floor for support. Then glue on the second piece of poster board to complete the basic floor "sandwich." Tape the edges at several places and weight the floor with a book

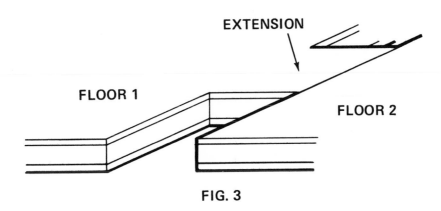

FIG. 3

27

PLANS FOR BASIC HOUSE PARTS

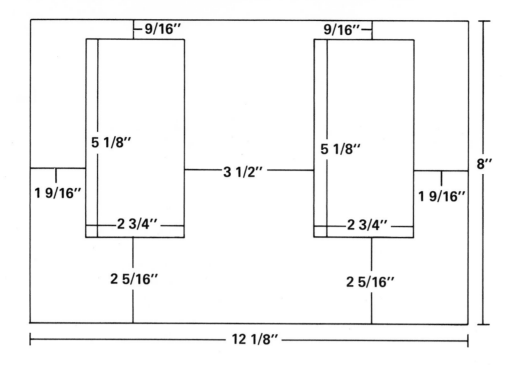

MAIN ROOM END WALL

DOOR, WINDOW AND FIREPLACE OPENINGS MAY BE
MOVED OR SIZES CHANGED AS DESIRED.

SCALE ☐☐☐ =3"

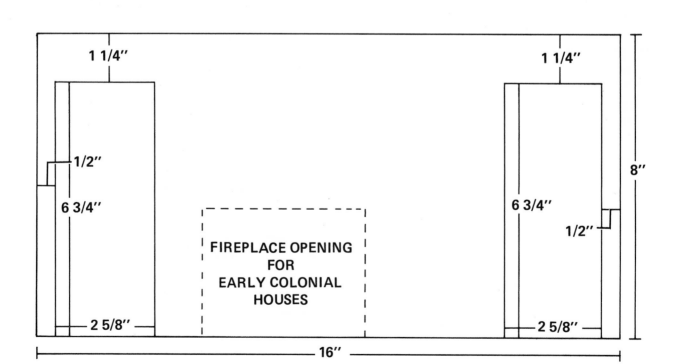

SIDE WALL

PLATE 6A

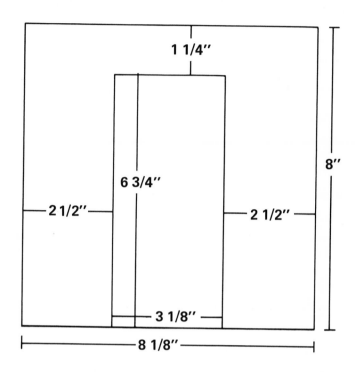

HALL END WALL

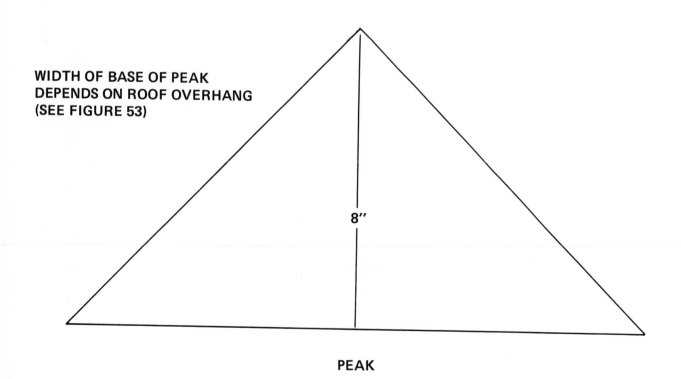

WIDTH OF BASE OF PEAK
DEPENDS ON ROOF OVERHANG
(SEE FIGURE 53)

PEAK

SCALE ⬚⬚⬚ =3″

PLATE 6B

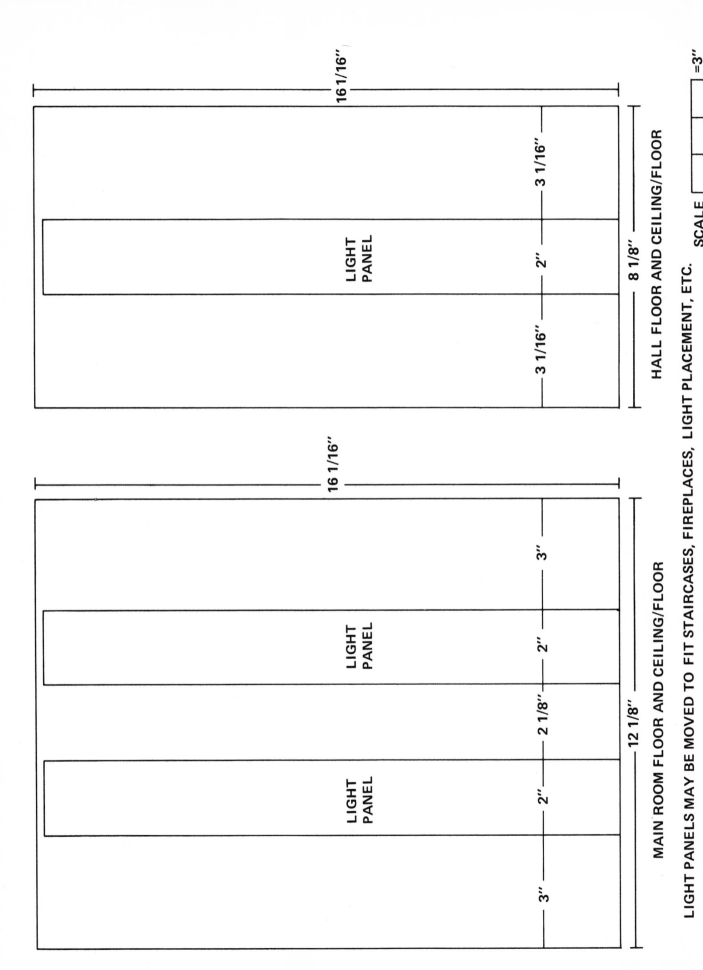

HALL FLOOR AND CEILING/FLOOR

16 1/16"

3 1/16"

2"

3 1/16"

8 1/8"

LIGHT PANEL

MAIN ROOM FLOOR AND CEILING/FLOOR

16 1/16"

3"

2"

2 1/8"

2"

3"

12 1/8"

LIGHT PANEL

LIGHT PANEL

LIGHT PANELS MAY BE MOVED TO FIT STAIRCASES, FIREPLACES, LIGHT PLACEMENT, ETC.

SCALE

=3"

PLATE 6C

ROOM PART OVERLAPS

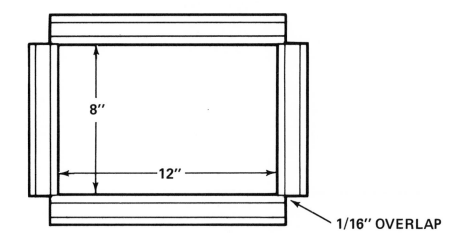

1/16'' OVERLAP

SIDE WALLS OVERLAP FLOOR, CEILING/FLOOR OVERLAPS SIDE WALLS

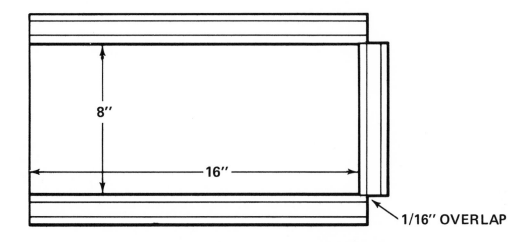

1/16'' OVERLAP

END WALL OVERLAPS FLOOR, CEILING/FLOOR OVERLAPS END WALL

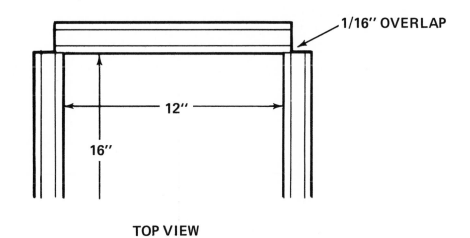

1/16'' OVERLAP

TOP VIEW

END WALL OVERLAPS SIDE WALLS

PLATE 7

on top till the glue dries. The wood flooring will be added later.

When the house is assembled later, where the walls fit, between the floor units, there will be a gap in the floor units at the doorway openings of the walls. This problem can be solved in advance by adding extra wood framework and poster board to one of the floor units (Fig. 3). A ¼″ extension is usual, but do not worry too much about being exact. It can be trimmed down later when the walls are being fitted in place, and wood flooring will cover any mistakes.

Note: if you are planning a fireplace with a marble hearth, see Chapters 7 and 8 before starting your floor.

WALLS

Before you start building the basic wall sandwiches see Plates 8, 9, 10, 11, and 12 for an idea of what the finished wall will be like. The basic wall is made of two pieces of poster board and framework (studs) of ¼″ × ⅛″ wood strips. The basic wall is then ⅜″ thick. With ⅛″ moldings to be added on both sides, the finished thickness is ⅝″.

Cut out the poster board pieces using the sizes given in Plate 6. Be sure to keep the corners square. Cut out door openings and fireplace openings. Before cutting window openings, see Chapter 6. It is generally wise to construct the windows first, then cut the openings to fit them.

Glue the framework studs on one piece of poster board in several places: around the edges, etc., as for floors, and also around door and fireplace openings, using extensions. Glue on the second poster board, tape and weight the wall, as for floors.

There are a few things to keep in mind before beginning construction.

1. Be exact in wall dimensions and keep your corners square.

2. For walls where one side will be an exterior wall (usually window walls), leave the second piece of poster board off for now. Later, when the house is assembled, poster board will be fitted over the entire exterior of the house.

3. For walls with door openings, once the "sandwich" is made the raw edges (Fig. 4A)

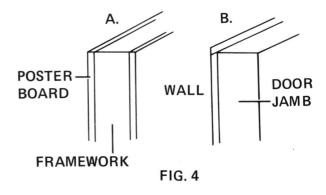

FIG. 4

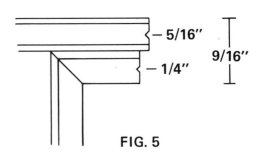

FIG. 5

need to be covered with ¹⁄₁₆″ thick wood to form the doorjambs (Fig. 4B). See Chapter 5 for the construction of doors and installation.

4. For walls with windows, it is best to construct the window first, then fit it to the wall. (See Chapter 6.)

5. For walls with fireplaces, see Chapter 7 for construction and installation.

6. Finished doors, complete with their moldings installed on the walls around the doors, will be very close to 7″ × 3″. You will notice on the floor plans in Plates 4 and 5 that doors often fit between staircases or fireplaces and the edge of the wall. Where this is true, 3½″ has been allowed, so you have ½″ to play with.

7. Finished windows, complete with their moldings installed on the walls around the windows, will be very close to 3⅛″ × 5½″. The molding around the window is ¼″ deep. The suggested molding around the ceiling line is ⁵⁄₁₆″ deep (Fig. 5). This accounts for the ⁹⁄₁₆″ size given at the top of the window openings.

8. Remember that dimensions given in Plate 6 are suggested guides, the ones I used for my own house. You can change them to suit your own needs.

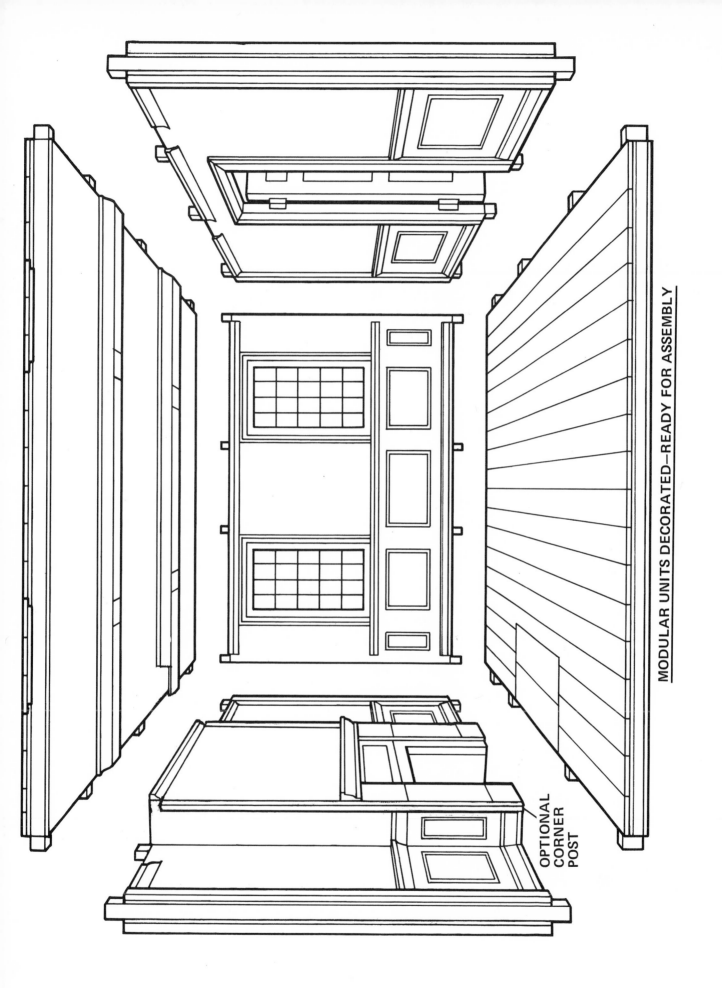

OPTIONAL CORNER POST

MODULAR UNITS DECORATED—READY FOR ASSEMBLY

PLATE 8

THE NEXT STEP

Now you have a floor and 3 walls with door openings and doorjambs, fireplace openings (and, if you have read Chapter 7, some idea of fireplace construction) and possibly windows already set in the walls.

The character of your rooms depends on how the walls, floors, and ceilings are decorated. Chapter 4 on moldings and paneling and Chapter 9 on ceilings and beams will help here, also Plates 8, 10, 11, 12, and the photographs of my miniature house.

The next step in actual construction should be the completion of doors (Chapter 5), windows (Chapter 6), and fireplaces (Chapter 7). But perhaps you would rather build the ceiling/floor units first. Chapters 8, 9, and 10 explain this construction. Whatever you choose to do, read Chapters 4 through 12 before proceeding, to get a picture in your mind of how the various units and parts fit together and interrelate. It is more fun to build than read, but it is better to have some idea where you are going.

Chapter 4

Moldings and Paneling

Moldings can be purchased (see Source List) but are easily made by gluing wood strips together and shaping them (see Plate 9).

Before you do the moldings and paneling you really should construct and install the doors, windows, and fireplaces, first. However, this chapter will give you a better idea of what the finished wall will look like, which should help you in doing the other features. One other word before we start: When actually doing the moldings, mark the position of the ceiling moldings on the wall but do not actually install them until you are ready to do the ceiling and beams because the ceiling moldings on the walls and the beams on the ceiling interlock. Do not worry about this now, just keep it in mind.

As I have said before the emphasis in this book is on the Georgian house but the techniques work just as well for earlier houses. The only difference is that where Georgian moldings and panelings are made of different size wood strips glued together and shaped (see Plates 9 through 12) the earlier moldings are plain, flat, unshaped pieces of wood. For instance, in the Georgian house the molding around the interior door is made as shown in Plate 9. Its finished size is ¼″ wide and ⅛″ at its thickest part. When it is glued on the wall around the door opening the corners are mitered. For earlier houses you would use plain ¼″ × ⅛″ wood strips and leave the corners unmitered. Compare Plates 10 and 11. You can see the idea of molding around the door opening is the same, though the shapes differ.

Before you start construction, I would like to make one recommendation and then discuss the main features of various room styles. The recommendation is this: Use corner framing at both ends of the side walls and any place you can fit it into any corner or jog in the wall. Corner framing is part of the basic framework of real houses. In early houses it is quite prominent. In Georgian houses it is smaller but still visible. How to simulate this will be discussed later but for now, let me just say that using it makes construction of the rooms much easier and stronger. It is especially useful in Georgian houses because it eliminates the need for mitering moldings at the corners. This may not seem like much now, but believe me, it is the best tip I can give you (Fig. 6).

For early Colonial rooms (see Plate 10) it is best to start with a poster board and wood "sandwich" wall and glue moldings and paneling on the board.

In early Colonial rooms at the top edge of the wall there were heavy framework timbers to support the ceiling beams. There were also framework timbers at the corners of the room and timbers visible around the windows and doors. These timbers can be made of ⅛″ thick wood. The heavy timber at the top edge of the wall can be ¾″ to 1″ deep in miniature, the corner framework and baseboards ¼″ to ⅜″, the moldings around the doors and windows ¼″ wide. The ceilings of early houses have one, two, or more heavy beams (perhaps ¾″ × ⅝″) running across the width of the room and numerous smaller cross

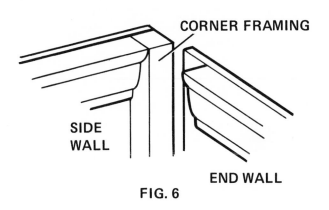

CORNER FRAMING

SIDE WALL

END WALL

FIG. 6

beams (perhaps $\frac{1}{4}'' \times \frac{1}{4}''$ or $\frac{1}{4}'' \times \frac{5}{16}''$) running lengthwise. For a hand-hewn look for these framework timbers and beams, the edges can be carved or sanded into shallow curves, small chunks gouged out and a heavily grained effect can be achieved by rubbing the wood, pressing hard, back and forth over a cheese grater.

In some houses the remaining wall area is rough plastered. For this effect, use Liquitex gel medium, dabbed on with a wadded-up paper towel or stiff-bristled artist's oil painting brush. Gel medium is a white paste-like substance which dries clear. One or more applications will give the desired effect. When the gel medium is dry it can be painted with interior latex house paint or acrylic tube paints.

Some early houses with the same framework timbers had flat or simply shaped, random or uniform width paneling covering the remaining wall area (see Plate 10). This paneling was sometimes painted but was more often a natural wood finish.

As houses developed to the Georgian period, the paneling and moldings became more and more sophisticated in styling and were either natural finished wood or painted. The corner framing became smaller, $\frac{1}{8}'' \times \frac{1}{8}''$ in miniature. The heavy framework timber at the top edge of the wall was replaced by shaped moldings. Beams became smaller and were shaped (see Fig. 30). Baseboards, window, door, and chair rail moldings were shaped (see Plate 9). Wallpaper was often used.

Making Moldings and Paneling

Moldings can be purchased ready-made (see Source List) but it is considerably less expensive to make your own. Plate 9 shows the basic wood sizes and shaping for several useful Georgian moldings. For more complicated moldings, see exterior moldings, Plate 26. To make the moldings, glue the strips together and shape the edges, where needed, with sandpaper. The moldings are best made in long strips, 20″ to 24″ in length. This cuts down on irregularities in shaping. Sometimes you will find your shaping will be easier if you lay the molding strip on a flat surface and, holding an emery board at an angle, sand down to the desired shape. Finish off the molding strip by rubbing with fine steel wool.

You can make yards and yards of molding in an evening while you watch T.V.

Paneling

Plate 9 also shows typical shapes for the edges of vertical paneling. The edges can be shaped with sandpaper or an emery board. Sometimes it is best to carve away some of the wood at the edge of the panel and then sand the finished shape (Fig. 7A). To obtain a nice straight bevel, lay several layers of masking tape where the bevel is to be. Carve away some of the excess wood and finish the bevel with sandpaper or an emery board. The tape prevents you from sanding away too much wood (Fig. 7B).

More complicated paneling can be made by gluing various wood strips on $\frac{1}{16}''$ thick wood base (see Plate 11). For the basic panel, using Weldwood cement, glue on four $\frac{1}{16}''$ thick wood strips in a rectangular shape. If the wood strips are not cut exactly square, there will be tiny gaps at the joints. Fill them in with wood putty or filler and sand smooth, or fill the crack with white glue and while it is not quite dry, sand smooth. The sanded particles get stuck in the glue and act as filler. If you are planning to use an oil base stain as a finish, remember that stain does not "take" the same over filler as it does over wood, so here you have to be careful not to have gaps. (Or perhaps you would prefer, to cover errors, the paint and antiquing finish suggested in Chapter 8 for finishing floors.) Inside this rectangular frame, with white glue, glue wood strips $\frac{1}{32}'' \times \frac{1}{32}''$. These can be mitered if you like but they need not be. For the center panel, cut a piece of $\frac{1}{32}''$ thick wood and bevel the edges as described for vertical paneling, with tape and sandpaper. This works well with the grain.

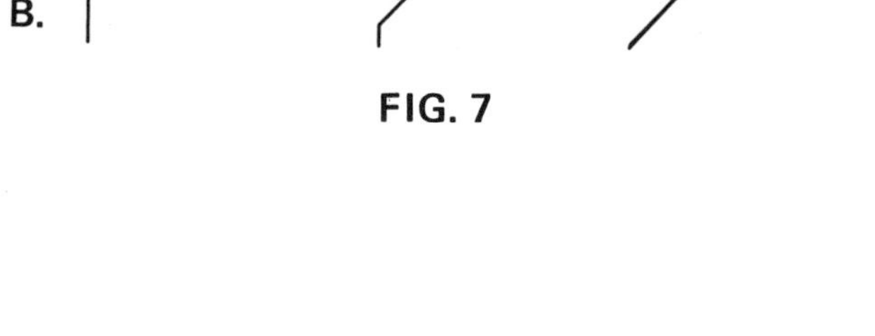

FIG. 7

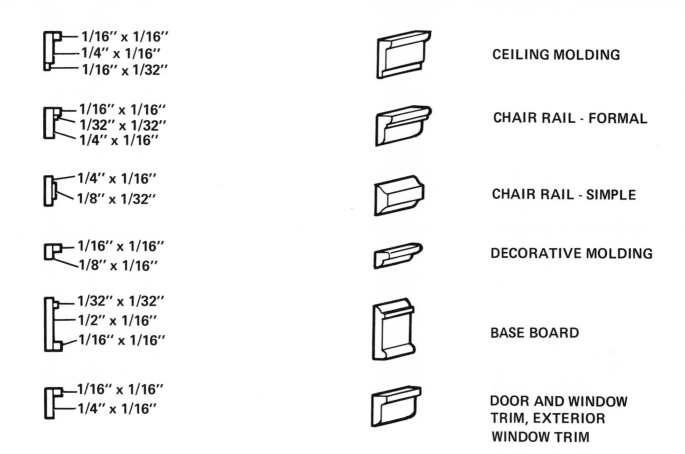

1/16" x 1/16"
1/4" x 1/16"
1/16" x 1/32"
CEILING MOLDING

1/16" x 1/16"
1/32" x 1/32"
1/4" x 1/16"
CHAIR RAIL - FORMAL

1/4" x 1/16"
1/8" x 1/32"
CHAIR RAIL - SIMPLE

1/16" x 1/16"
1/8" x 1/16"
DECORATIVE MOLDING

1/32" x 1/32"
1/2" x 1/16"
1/16" x 1/16"
BASE BOARD

1/16" x 1/16"
1/4" x 1/16"
DOOR AND WINDOW TRIM, EXTERIOR WINDOW TRIM

BEADS FOR VERTICAL PANELS

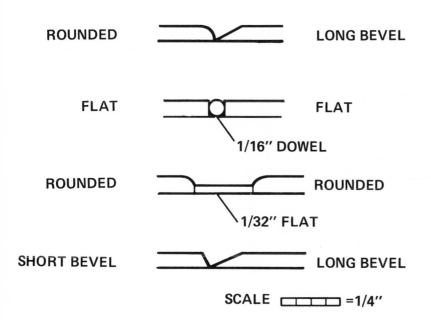

ROUNDED   LONG BEVEL

FLAT   FLAT
1/16" DOWEL

ROUNDED   ROUNDED
1/32" FLAT

SHORT BEVEL   LONG BEVEL

SCALE ▭▭▭ =1/4"

<u>MOLDINGS AND PANELING</u>   PLATE 9

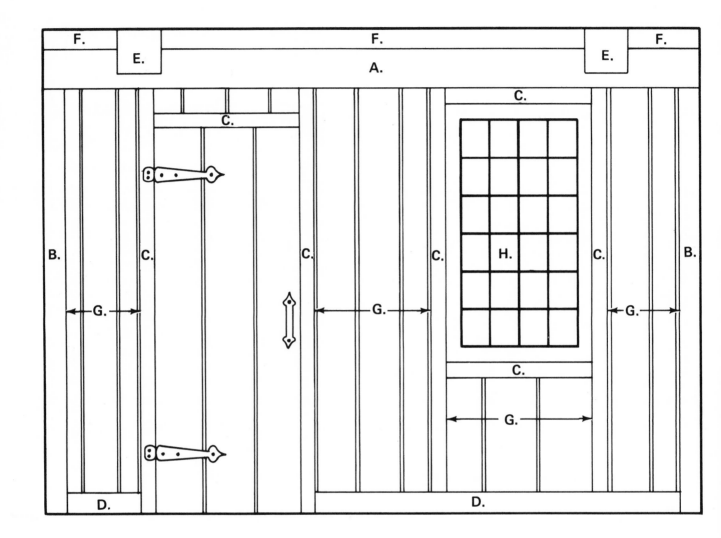

PANELED WALL

A. SUPPORT TIMBER
B. CORNER FRAMEWORK
C. DOOR AND WINDOW FRAMEWORK
D. BASEBOARD
E. SUPPORT BEAMS
F. CROSS BEAMS
G. VERTICAL PANELING
H. FLAT WINDOW

MOLDINGS AND PANELING GLUED ON POSTER BOARD BASE

PLATE 10

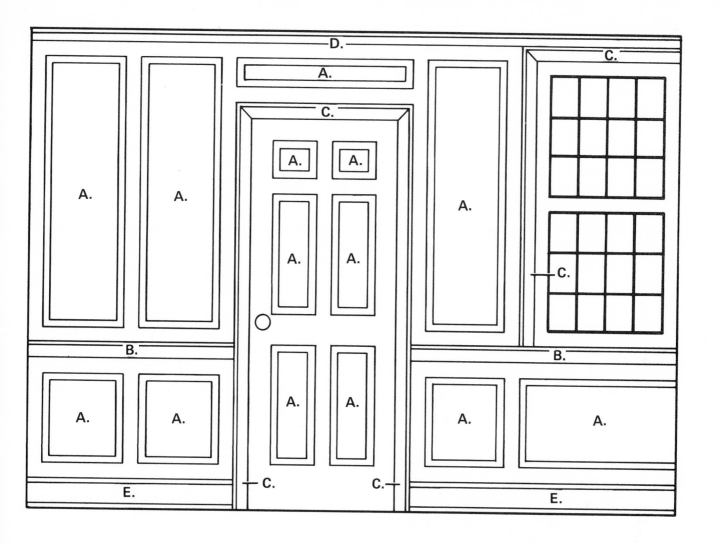

BASIC PANEL AND MOLDINGS USED TO FORM FULLY PANELLED WALL

ALL MOLDINGS GLUED ON 1/16″ THICK WOOD BASE

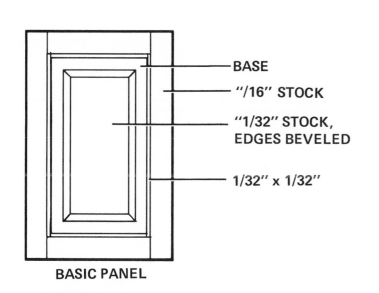

BASE

″/16″ STOCK

″1/32″ STOCK,
EDGES BEVELED

1/32″ x 1/32″

BASIC PANEL

A. BASIC PANEL
B. CHAIR RAIL-FORMAL
C. DOOR & WINDOW TRIM
D. CEILING MOLDING
E. BASEBOARD

PLATE 11

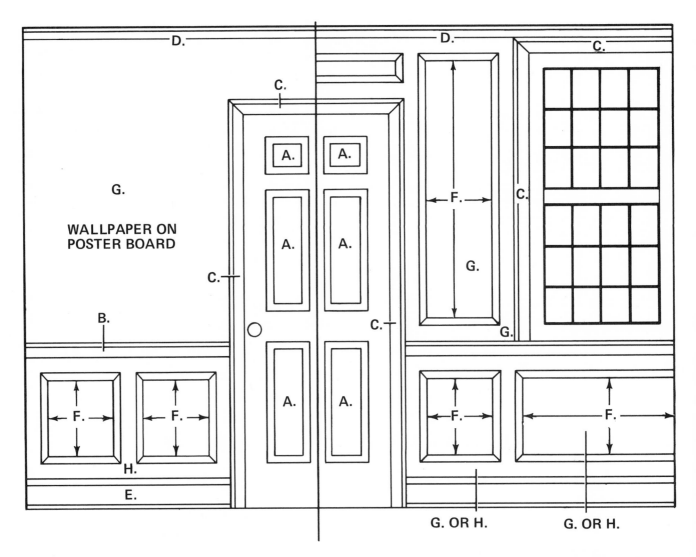

HALF PANELED WALL WITH WALLPAPER

PAINTED WALL WITH MOLDINGS

A. BASIC PANEL
B. CHAIR RAIL-FORMAL
C. DOOR & WINDOW TRIM
D. CEILING MOLDING
E. BASEBOARD
F. DECORATIVE MOLDING
G. POSTER BOARD
H. WOOD

PLATE 12

For across the grain, lay on the tape and sand the bevel against a piece of sandpaper laid on a flat surface (Fig. 8). Glue the beveled piece to the base. Since 1/32″ thick wood curls easily when white glue is used, use Weldwood cement here. This basic panel can be used by itself as a small door, in combination with other basic panels on a large door (Plate 13) or for an entire paneled wall (Plate 11).

For a fully paneled wall, start with 1/16″ thick wood sheets as the wall instead of poster board. Glue paneling and moldings over this. The only problem here is that when planning the basic wall "sandwich," you must plan for "wall studs" to be placed where the wood sheets meet, for support. That is, if the wood sheets are 2″ wide, wall studs must be placed 2″ apart.

For a half-paneled wall, as in Plate 12, with a chair rail and dado, use 1/16″ thick poster board for the upper part of the wall and 1/16″ thick wood sheets for the lower part. For this type of wall it is best to plan a framework stud for support where the wood and poster board meet. For some painted walls a poster board base with decorative moldings added is attractive (Plate 12).

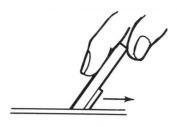

FIG. 8

Chapter 5

Doors

The earliest doors were made of three or four boards held together with horizontal cross braces on one side. To make this, start with a 1/16″ thick wood sheet, cut to size. With Weldwood, glue 1/16″ thick vertical wood strips to both sides of the 1/16″ thick base to form a door 3/16″ thick (see Plate 10). Add wood strips (3/16″ × 1/32″ or 1/4″ × 1/32″) for the cross braces.

In later doors, the vertical panels and bracing disappear in favor of simple paneling shapes such as plain rails around the edges of the door, a narrow center strip and one or two cross strips; all flat unshaped wood strips glued to both sides of the central base. Both these doors are suitable for early Colonial houses and fit into the door frames described in Chapter 4 (see Plate 10).

By the Georgian period, the doors are basically like the one shown in Plate 13 with shaped rails and cross pieces and center panels. As before, it is made of 1/16″ thick and 1/32″ thick wood pieces glued to both sides of the central 1/16″ thick base. The door openings have shaped moldings around them glued on the wall and overlapping the doorjamb almost completely. For the technique of making basic door panels, see Chapter 4 and Plate 11.

Doors can be glued on the doorjambs in a closed position or to the door moldings in an open position if you like, but hinged doors are much nicer. For fixed-position doors it is better to paint or stain the door before installing it. This is almost essential if the door is to be hinged. If you install hinged doors first and then paint them, the doors have to be kept propped open during painting to keep the paint on the door edges from touching the doorjamb and getting smeared or stuck. It is easier to paint first and then touch up the paint if it needs it after the door is installed.

When using a hinged door, it is best for proper fit to make the door to fit the opening. Attach the door to the doorjamb with the hinges, and then trim down the other edge of the door if necessary. Repaint the trimmed edge. This may sound wrong, but if you make the door narrower than the opening to account for the thickness of the hinges you can easily cut the door too short. It will then be loose and not stay closed nicely.

Doors can be hinged in two ways. In the first, the door is attached to the doorjamb with silk needlepoint mesh (40 to the inch). This is strong, flexible, can be painted over, and will not crack as easily as paper or tape hinges will (Fig. 9). Since silk hinges are not truly authentic, it is best to place the hinges on the side of the door and doorjamb where they are least visible. The proper hinges (H and L type or strap hinges—see Plate 14) are then simulated on the door and door frame with metal cut from beer or soft drink cans, TV dinner trays, or from construction paper.

Doors can also be hinged with real metal hinges which can be purchased (see Source List). These hinges must be inset as they are on real doors (Fig. 10). Mark the position of the hinges on the door edge. Make shallow cuts on the lines and carve out the insets. Glue the hinges in place with "super glue" and anchor with lill pins ham-

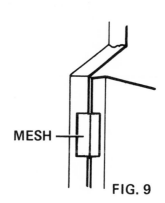

MESH —

FIG. 9

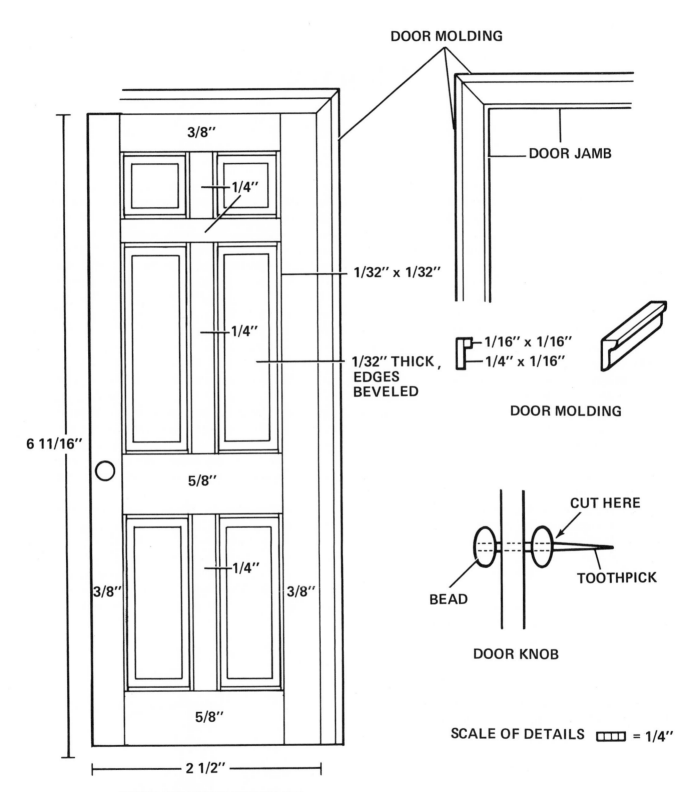

DOOR MOLDING

DOOR JAMB

3/8"

1/4"

1/32" x 1/32"

1/4"

1/32" THICK, EDGES BEVELED

1/16" x 1/16"
1/4" x 1/16"

DOOR MOLDING

6 11/16"

5/8"

3/8"

1/4"

3/8"

5/8"

2 1/2"

SIZES INDICATE WIDTH OF
WOOD STRIPS USED, ALL ARE 1/16"
THICK EXCEPT WHERE MARKED

CUT HERE

TOOTHPICK

BEAD

DOOR KNOB

SCALE OF DETAILS ⬚⬚⬚ = 1/4"

SCALE 1"= 1'

BASIC DOOR

PLATE 13

HL TYPE

STRAP TYPE

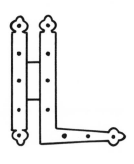

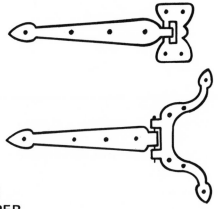

**SIMULATED HINGES
THIN METAL OR PAPER**

DOOR HARDWARE

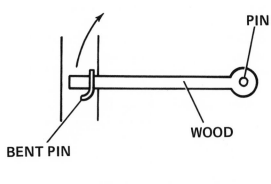

PIN

WOOD

BENT PIN

SIMPLE DOOR LATCH

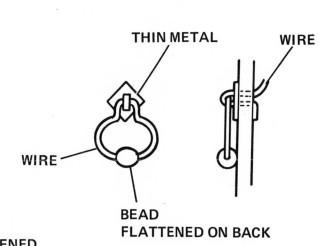

THIN METAL

WIRE

WIRE

BEAD
FLATTENED ON BACK

SIMPLE DOOR KNOCKER

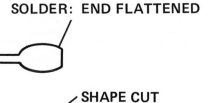

SOLDER: END FLATTENED

SHAPE CUT

SIMPLE DOOR PULL

PLATE 14

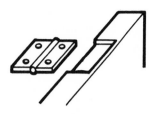

FIG. 10

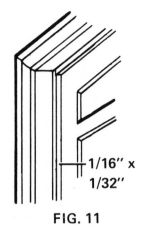

1/16" x
1/32"

FIG. 11

mered through holes in the hinges. Hold the door in position on the doorjamb and mark the hinge positions. Make the insets in the doorjamb. Then glue and pin the door with its hinges to the doorjamb. These hinges can be left as is.

For Georgian doors, close the door, mark its position on the doorjamb and glue $\frac{1}{16}'' \times \frac{1}{32}''$ wood strips on the lines. This forms a doorstop and helps the fit of the door (Fig. 11).

A simple doorknob can be made from two beads and a toothpick as shown in Plate 13. Drill a $\frac{1}{16}''$ hole in the door. The toothpick may have to be trimmed down a bit to fit in the hole. Next, force the beads, with glue, onto the toothpick and trim off the excess. Paint the knobs with metallic brass paint. You might prefer clear beads to simulate glass doorknobs.

Once the door is painted and installed in the doorjamb, the framework for early houses can be glued around the door (see Chapter 4 and Plate 10). For the Georgian house, glue on the door moldings as shown in Plate 13, overlapping the doorjamb. Framework or moldings can be painted now or later.

Door Hardware

Door hardware varies greatly but the most popular are strap hinges or H and L hinges (see Plate 14). For handles, interior doors have simple metal pulls or plain knobs with no back plates. For latches, movable bars were used and later box-like locks. Metal door pulls can be made from solder which is like a soft fat wire. Estimate the length of the finished pull, including the curved and flat parts plus a little extra (see Plate 14). Hammer the ends flat. Simple shapes can be cut on the flat parts with small scissors. Holes can be drilled for pins to hold the pull to the door or it can be glued on with "super glue."

On some doors, the screws which hold the hardware to the door are part of the beauty of the piece. On simulated strap and H and L hinges, the screws can be simulated with a dot of glue.

Chapter 6
Windows

A window is essentially two wood frames with medium-weight acetate for the glass in between; another "sandwich." Plate 15 shows a double hung window which is correct for Georgian houses and some Early Colonial houses. Some early windows, however, were one large flat structure with as many as 30 small panes (5 over 6). Some windows had diamond-shaped panes and were greater in width than length. The early windows fit into the window framework described in Chapter 4. The Georgian windows are set into the window openings and surrounded by mitered moldings much like doors. Once you understand the basic construction of the window, you can adapt the plan in Plate 15 to flat or diamond pane windows.

In making the window, it is best to paint or stain all the wood first with water base paints or stains. This helps to keep the paint off the acetate panes during the final painting. To start: draw, on paper, the pattern of the crosspieces (muntins). Cut the muntins longer than their finished length. Lay the muntins on the pattern, tape them down and mark where they cross, on the bottom set (Fig. 12). Where the muntins cross they will be notched to fit together to make

a strong structure. Untape the muntins from the pattern. To make a notch, cut halfway through the wood with a sharp blade. The wood in the center should just break off with the grain of the wood. If not, carve it out carefully.

Next, retape the muntins on the pattern with the un-notched set of muntins on the bottom (Fig. 13A). Mark the bottom set and make the notches as before (Fig. 13B). The muntins can now be glued together (Fig. 13C). Fill in any gaps in the joints with wood filler or glue and sand smooth as described in Chapter 4.

Next make the window sash. Draw the pattern

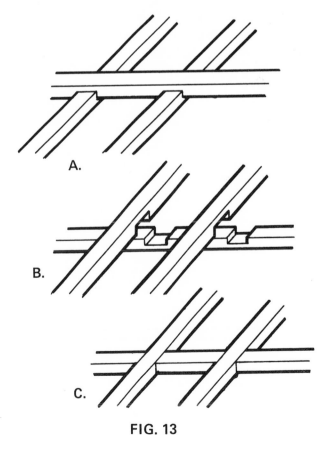

A.

B.

C.

FIG. 13

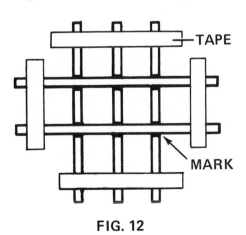

TAPE

MARK

FIG. 12

47

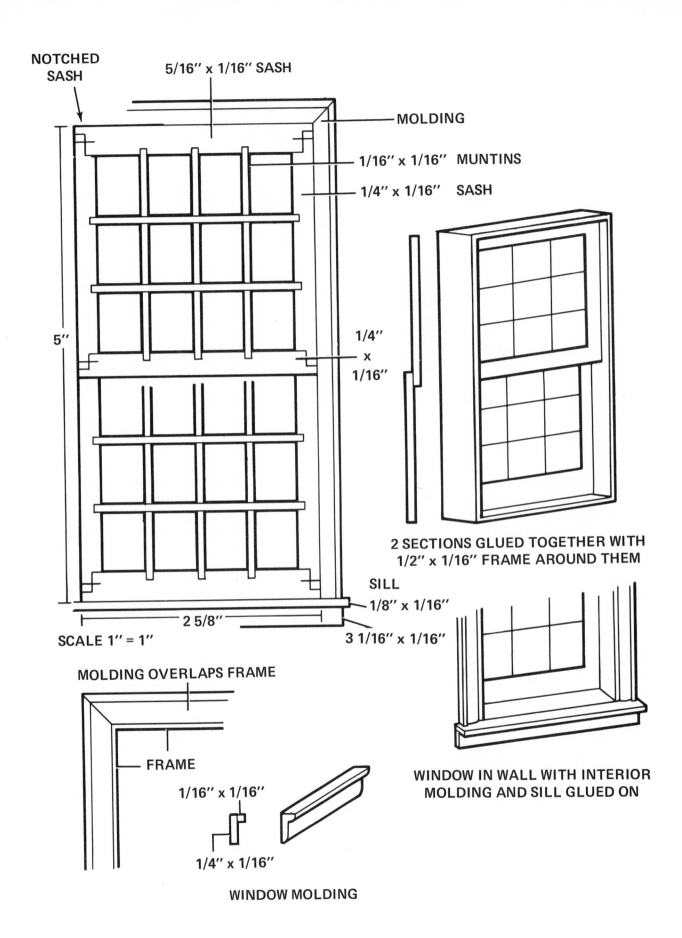

NOTCHED SASH

5/16" x 1/16" SASH

MOLDING

1/16" x 1/16" MUNTINS

1/4" x 1/16" SASH

5"

1/4"
x
1/16"

2 5/8"

SCALE 1" = 1"

SILL
1/8" x 1/16"

3 1/16" x 1/16"

2 SECTIONS GLUED TOGETHER WITH
1/2" x 1/16" FRAME AROUND THEM

MOLDING OVERLAPS FRAME

FRAME

1/16" x 1/16"

1/4" x 1/16"

WINDOW MOLDING

WINDOW IN WALL WITH INTERIOR
MOLDING AND SILL GLUED ON

<u>BASIC WINDOW</u>

PLATE 15

on paper. Lay the sash pieces on the pattern and notch the ends as shown in Plate 15. Glue the sash together. Pins through the notches will strengthen the sash.

Lay the muntins over the sash and mark where the muntins meet the sash (Fig. 14). Notch the sash at the marks. Then cut the muntins to fit into these notches. Glue the sash and muntins together. This makes a good strong window structure. My dog, a collie, has stepped on the windows without any damage to the window (and only slight damage to his rear end). On windows with diamond panes, the sash may be too narrow to stand all the notching. If so, just glue the muntins to the sash.

Fill in any gaps and sand the structure smooth. Retouch the paint or stain and give it its final finish all over, except on the backside (see Chapter 12). Next glue the acetate "glass" on the backside as shown by the dotted line in Fig. 15. Use Weldwood cement for this job. Ordinarily, you would not use Weldwood on acetate, but white glue has a tendency to squish out on the panes when you press the acetate in place. Weldwood will hold the acetate well enough unless you deliberately try to pull it off. Remember, it will also be held in place by another sash, which is made next. One cute trick for acetate, to give it an antique look, is to press it between two pieces of paper towel with a warm iron. The acetate will pick up the texture of the toweling for a kind of uneven bubbly look which is quite pleasing.

Next make another sash as you did the first one, except without notches for the muntins. Paint and finish the sash and glue it to the window structure over the acetate. Now paint and finish some $\frac{1}{32}'' \times \frac{1}{16}''$ wood strips. Cut pieces and glue them to the sash you have just glued on and to each other, but not to the acetate, matching the position of the muntins on the front side of the window structure.

For double hung windows, glue two of these structures together as shown in Plate 15. For all windows, surround the window with $\frac{1}{2}'' \times \frac{1}{16}''$ wood strips to form a frame as shown in Plate 15. The window is now ready to install in the wall.

Lay the window on the wall in the correct position and draw around it. Cut the opening. Glue the window into the wall with the edge of

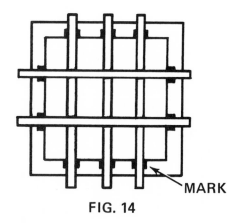

FIG. 14

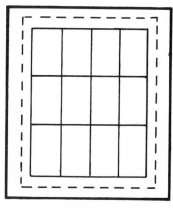

FIG. 15

the frame flush with the inside wall as shown in Fig. 16B. Glue some framework studs around the window on the exterior side of the wall as shown in Fig. 16A. You will notice in Fig. 16B that the window frame extends out past the wall. This is to accommodate the second piece of poster board, on the exterior side of the wall, and the exterior siding.

Once the window is all in place, the interior framework for earlier houses described in Chapter 4 can be glued in place (see Plate 10). For the Georgian houses, window molding is glued on the interior wall around the sides and top of the window, overlapping the frame (see Plate 15). Sometimes, a formal chair rail will act as the window sill (see Plates 9, 11, and 12). Sometimes, you will want a window sill as shown in Plate 15. All framework or moldings and sills can be painted now or later.

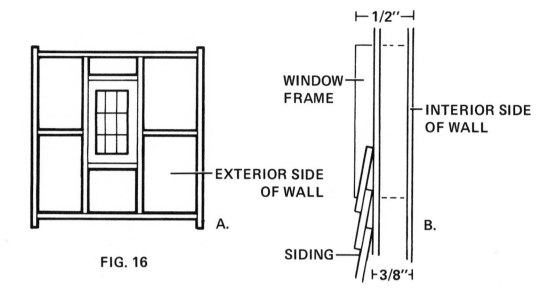

FIG. 16

Odd-Shaped Windows

I have left odd-shaped windows till last. The basic technique remains the same, but the shape takes some extra handling.

On some Georgian houses, you see octagonal-shaped windows. To make the octagonal shape, draw your pattern on a piece of paper. Lay 2 wood strips on the pattern and cut through both pieces at one time to make the mitered angle (Fig. 17). Glue those 2 pieces together. Continue making mitered pieces and gluing them together till the octagon is complete. Notch the muntins and glue them in the octagon. Finish the window as described before.

Lunette windows are shaped with a curve at the top. You can carve the curve if you like (see Fig. 84), or bend wood to make the curve. Unfortunately, wood strips only bend along their narrow edges so you will have to bend four $\frac{1}{16}'' \times \frac{1}{16}''$ strips to make the $\frac{1}{4}''$ wide curve. Soak the 4 wood strips in water till they will bend easily, for several hours or more. Mark the curve on a piece of illustration board. Bend the first strip to fit the curve and hold it in place with pins. Bend the second, third, and fourth strips over the first and hold the whole thing in place with pins till the wood dries and will hold its shape (Fig. 18). Glue the 4 strips together to make the curved piece. Any curved muntins and molding trims are bent the same. Notch the muntins where you

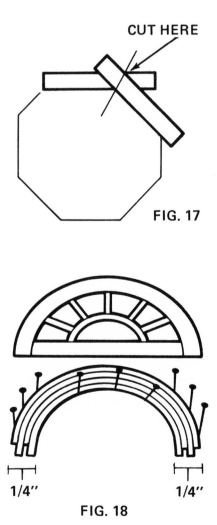

CUT HERE

FIG. 17

FIG. 18

FIG. 19

can, but if the pattern of your window does not allow for notching, just glue them in place. The ½″ × ¹⁄₁₆″ frame can be bent in one piece along its narrow edge.

A Palladian window is a combination of two small side windows and a central window with a curved top (see Plate 30). The curve is made of bent wood like the lunette window and notched and pinned to the straight part of the window for strength (Fig. 19). Since the Palladian window takes extra handling, it is best to partly finish the exterior wall now as well as the interior wall while it is still a separate unit and easy to handle. Glue poster board on the exterior to complete the wall "sandwich." You can also glue on exterior siding before making the exterior moldings or just tape some siding in place temporarily, to allow for space for the siding. For exterior moldings, see Plate 26.

Chapter 7

Fireplaces

For the construction of various fireplaces see Plates 16, 17, and 18. Keep in mind that the hearth, though constructed on the floor, is part of the fireplace (see Chapter 8). The two should be made and painted at the same time.

Early fireplaces were large structures made of brick or stone. The openings were five feet or more in width, four feet or more in height, and two or more feet deep. There was usually a foot or more of brick or stone visible on each side. They had no wood trim except perhaps a very heavy framework beam as a lintel to support the upper brickwork, though an iron bar was more often used as the lintel. Bake ovens were often built into early fireplaces. These were brick-lined holes in the fireplace wall about 2½ bricks wide, 5 bricks high and 2 to 2½ bricks deep. In the seventeenth-century fireplaces, the bake ovens were located in the back fireplace wall. By the eighteenth century, the bake oven was placed to the side of the main fireplace opening.

There are several brick bonds, "common" and "English" being the most used. To lay brick on the fireplace structure and on chimneys, start with wood strips $\frac{3}{16}'' \times \frac{1}{16}''$ cut into about $\frac{5}{8}''$ lengths for the whole bricks and somewhat less than half that for the half bricks. For the hearth, since you see the tops of the bricks, use $\frac{1}{4}'' \times \frac{1}{16}''$ wood strips. Do not worry too much about the exact lengths. Bricks of the time were not machine-made and varied a bit in size. A slight irregularity adds to the charm of the brickwork.

For the mortar, use $\frac{1}{32}'' \times \frac{1}{32}''$ wood strips. To begin: glue a horizontal "mortar" strip on the fireplace structure. Next glue on a "brick," a small vertical strip of "mortar," another "brick," etc., until the first row is complete (Fig. 21). When the row is complete, cut off the excess "mortar." Lay the second row of brick the same way and continue till the entire fireplace structure is covered. At the corners of the structure, for instance, where the front wall and inside wall join (see Plate 16), if the last brick on the front wall was a whole brick, start with a half brick on the inside wall and vice versa. Sand the joint and it will look like one brick.

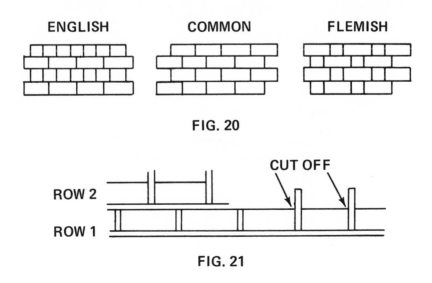

ENGLISH   COMMON   FLEMISH

FIG. 20

ROW 2   ROW 1   CUT OFF

FIG. 21

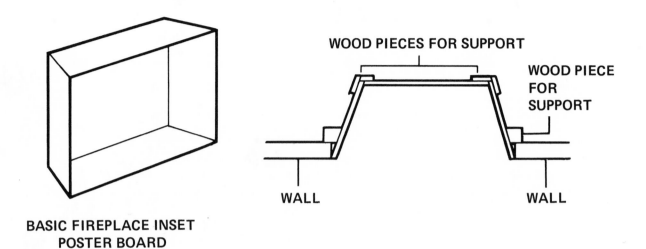

WOOD PIECES FOR SUPPORT

WOOD PIECE
FOR
SUPPORT

WALL

WALL

BASIC FIREPLACE INSET
POSTER BOARD

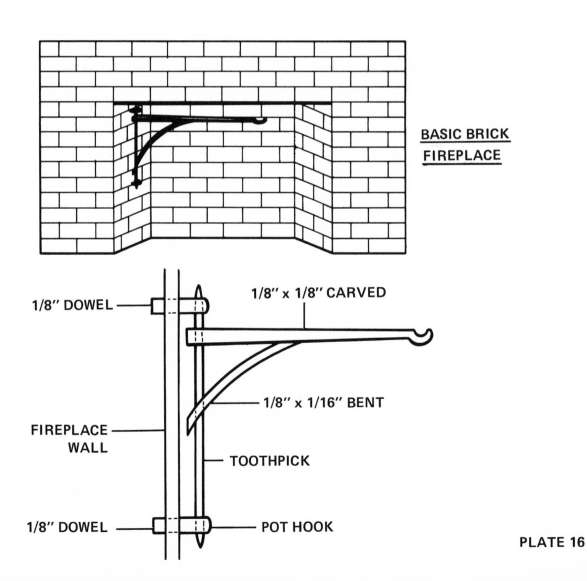

BASIC BRICK
FIREPLACE

1/8" DOWEL

1/8" x 1/8" CARVED

1/8" x 1/16" BENT

FIREPLACE
WALL

TOOTHPICK

1/8" DOWEL

POT HOOK

PLATE 16

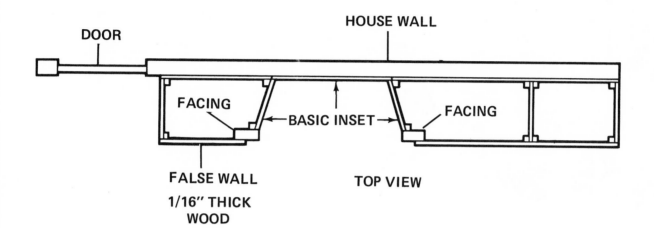

DOOR

HOUSE WALL

FACING

BASIC INSET

FACING

FALSE WALL

1/16″ THICK
WOOD

TOP VIEW

ELEVATION

SCALE [   ] = 3″

EARLY GEORGIAN FIREPLACE WALL

PLATE 17

CEILING, BASEBOARD, AND CHAIR RAIL MOLDINGS ARE MITERED AROUND 3 SIDED STRUCTURE

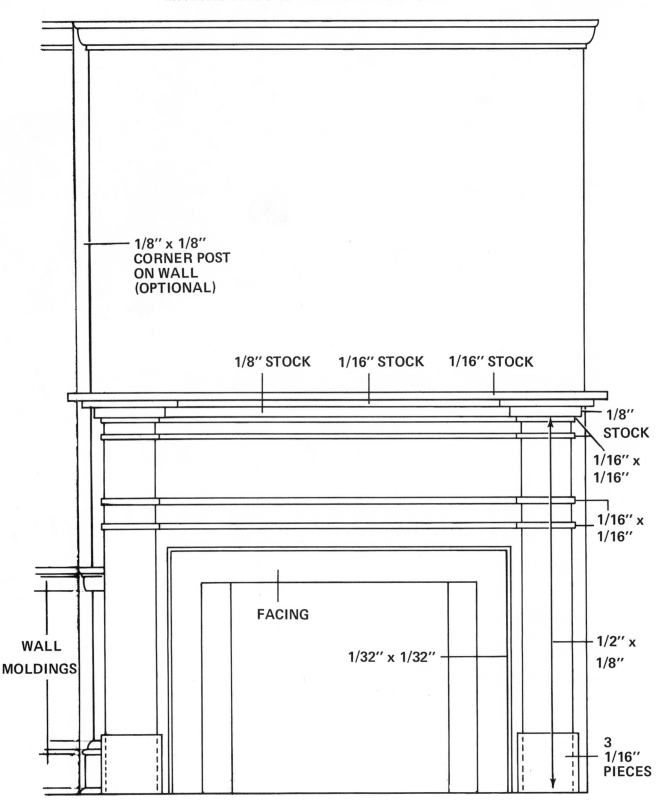

1/8″ x 1/8″ CORNER POST ON WALL (OPTIONAL)

1/8″ STOCK

1/16″ STOCK

1/16″ STOCK

1/8″ STOCK

1/16″ x 1/16″

1/16″ x 1/16″

FACING

1/32″ x 1/32″

1/2″ x 1/8″

WALL MOLDINGS

3 1/16″ PIECES

SCALE 1″ = 1′

LATE GEORGIAN FIREPLACE

PLATE 18A

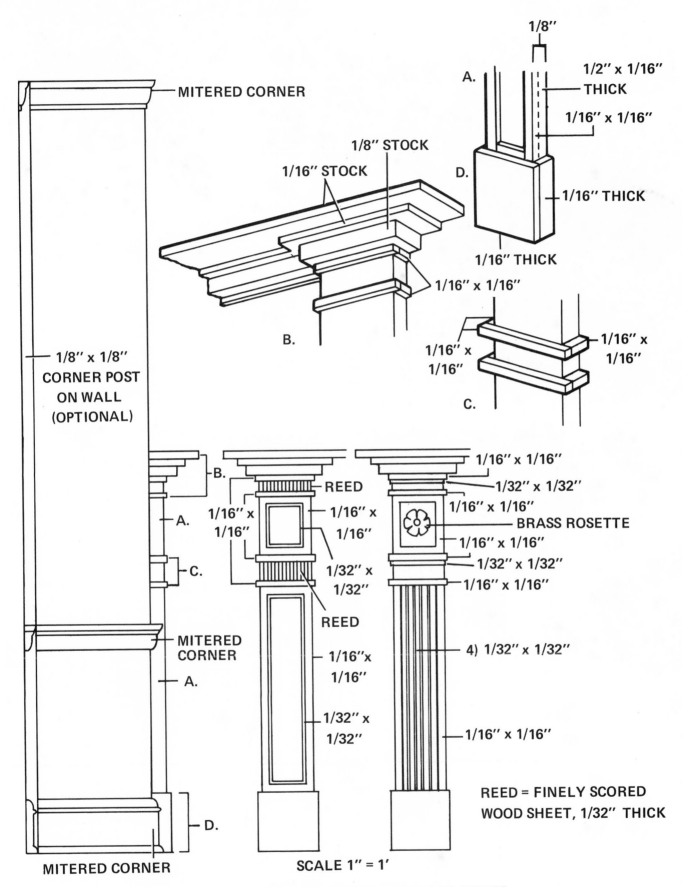

MITERED CORNER

1/16" STOCK

1/8" STOCK

A.

1/8"

1/2" x 1/16"
THICK

1/16" x 1/16"

D.

1/16" THICK

1/16" THICK

B.

1/16" x 1/16"

1/8" x 1/8"
CORNER POST
ON WALL
(OPTIONAL)

1/16" x
1/16"

1/16" x
1/16"

C.

B.

A.

C.

1/16" x 1/16"

REED

1/16" x
1/16"

1/16" x
1/16"

1/32" x 1/32"

1/16" x 1/16"

BRASS ROSETTE

1/16" x 1/16"

MITERED
CORNER

1/32" x
1/32"

1/32" x 1/32"

1/16" x 1/16"

A.

REED

1/16"x
1/16"

4) 1/32" x 1/32"

D.

1/32" x
1/32"

1/16" x 1/16"

MITERED CORNER

SCALE 1" = 1'

REED = FINELY SCORED
WOOD SHEET, 1/32" THICK

PILASTER VARIATIONS ARE 1/16" THICK WOOD PIECES
GLUED ON 1/16" BASE. FINAL THICKNESS: 1/8"

PLATE 18B

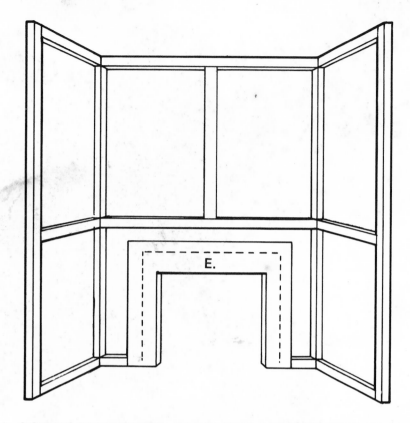

1. 3 SIDED STRUCTURE - BACK VIEW - BRACED WITH FRAME WORK
2. E. INDICATES FACING
3. DOTTED LINE INDICATES OPENING IN
   3 SIDED STRUCTURE

FACING: 3 WOOD PIECES 1/4"
THICK. DOTTED LINE SHOWS WOOD
SUPPORT PIECES ON BACKSIDE. ➝

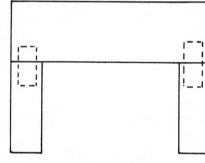

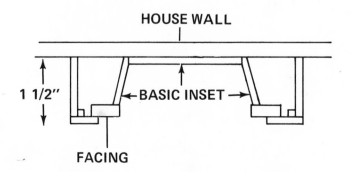

HOUSE WALL

1 1/2" ← BASIC INSET →

FACING

For stone fireplaces, stones can be made from 1/16" thick poster board cut in rectangular or irregular shapes. Coat the face and edges of the "stones" with gel medium dabbed on with a wadded-up paper towel. Two or three coats give a good effect. Glue the stones to the fireplace structure. Add some glue between the stones to act as mortar.

For painting: paint the brick or stone the basic color you want using acrylic tube paints, which dry fast and give a semi-flat finish suitable to brick and stone. When the basic color is dry, apply a whitewash. This is much-thinned acrylic paint. The wash will sink in between the brick or stone to color the mortar and soften the basic color. Next repaint the brick or stone surfaces as desired. Painting brick or stone for a soft effect is difficult to describe; but generally it is better to work with washes and dry brush techniques than to paint a solid color. (For dry brush, dip the brush in paint and wipe the brush almost dry.) You just have to play with the painting. Remember brick and stone vary in lightness and darkness, color, etc., and stone especially has many subtle colors in the basic grey. When you are satisfied with the effect, antiquing ink lightly dry brushed on the face of the brick or stone gives a nice soft finishing touch.

In early Colonial houses, all the room fireplaces were located in the center of the house, sharing a common chimney (see Plate 5). In one-room-deep Georgian houses, fireplaces can be on interior or exterior side walls. Either is valid. The plans in Plate 4 show the fireplaces on the interior walls because I like them better there.

Generally, early Colonial fireplaces had no paneling and were inset into the wall (see Plate 16). By early Georgian times, the fireplaces were smaller, 3 to 3½ feet wide, 2½ to 3 feet high, and 1½ to 2 feet deep. Early Georgian fireplaces were also set into the wall. For this, the plans in Plate 17 show a false wall built with the fireplace inset and glued to the main house wall. You will notice that the false wall takes a jog next to the door. This is so that the basic ⅝" wall thickness can be maintained at the back viewing area of the house. The style of the early Georgian fireplace wall shows a fully paneled wall but very little trim around the fireplace opening itself, just a facing (for construction of a facing, see Plate

18) and simple molding. The other walls of the room can be paneled to match, half paneled, or plain.

By late Georgian times, the fireplaces extended into the room and were surrounded on three sides by walls (Plate 18). These fireplaces were decorated with facades complete with pilasters, moldings, and mantles. If you don't want to miter moldings around the three-sided structure, corner posts can be used at the front edges (Plate 8) and in the corner where the structure meets the house wall (Plate 18). The use of these corner posts depends largely on the style of your room and, to some extent, if the ceiling beams fit right next to the three-sided structure. The styling of the room goes with the fireplace. The simple basic fireplace shown can go in a wallpapered room. The more formal variations can go in a fully paneled room with area above the fireplace paneled to match the room. Or the fireplace wall can be fully paneled and the other room walls half paneled. You can, of course, make your own variations to fit your taste. Designing fireplace facades is an art in itself and fun.

The Georgian fireplace false wall or three-sided structure is best made of wood. The actual front of the fireplace, the part that shows inside the wall or facade, is done as a separate facing piece in brick or marble. See Plates 17 and 18 for how the facing fits inside the wall or three-sided structure. The recessed part of the fireplace (the inset shown in Plate 16) is also constructed as a separate unit and glued to the back of the facing.

For a brick facing, start with 3/16" thick wood and lay brick on the front and inside edge. Also lay brick in the hearth area of the floor (see Chapter 8). For marble facing and hearth, the facing is ¼" thick wood and the hearth 3/16" or ¼" thick and recessed into the floor (see Chapter 8). To paint marble: using acrylic tube paints, give the pieces a coat of black or dark brown. Using marble colors (for instance, gold, brown, tan, a little orange, green, and white) dab on paint with a wadded-up paper towel letting some of the dark base coat show through for the effect of dark graining. To finish the pieces, give them 5 to 6 coats of high gloss oil base varnish. Sand with Wetordry sandpaper, #400 first then #600. A final smoothing with rubbing compound or a pumice and water paste gives an almost glassy shine.

For the inset part of the fireplace, a nice stone block effect can be done. Paint the inside of the inset black or dark grey. Next, split a small piece of poster board and peel off the top layer (Fig. 22). The inside surface has a stone-like texture and is not a bad color as is, but it can also be painted. Cut the poster board layer into block shapes and glue onto the inset, letting a little black space show at the edges.

On all fireplaces, for a used effect, dry brush some black paint on the back and side walls of the inset in places to simulate soot. On the floor of the fireplace you can apply some glue and drop cigarette ashes on it.

One last word on fireplaces. In the seventeenth-century fireplaces used for cooking, the pots hung

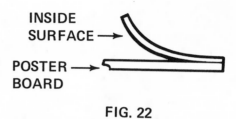

FIG. 22

on chains or long hooks from an iron bar embedded in the side walls of the inset near the top level of the fireplace opening. Cooking fireplaces in the eighteenth century were usually somewhat smaller than those of the seventeenth century and had a movable bracket from which the pots hung on trammels or long hooks. Plate 16 shows the construction of the bracket.

Chapter 8

Flooring

THE HEARTH

Before laying flooring on the plain floors you have already made or the ceiling/floors you will make, remember to plan where the fireplace hearth will go. On the floor, mark the width of the fireplace including any brickwork, molding, pilasters, etc. Set the wall, with the fireplace installed, on the floor and mark the depth of the fireplace. (For early fireplaces set into house walls, of course, there will be no depth to mark.) Next, decide on the depth you want for the hearth. 1½" to 2" is usually sufficient. If your hearth is to be brick or stone 1/16" thick, the flooring can be laid around the hearth area, the hearth laid and painted later. (When painting the hearth, lay masking tape on the floor around the hearth to keep the floor clean.) Marble hearths, since they are thicker, must be inset into the floor. To do this, cut out the marked hearth section. When gluing on the framework joists, glue some around the hearth area to form a space to hold the hearth.

FLOORING

The basic flooring can be done two good ways. First, you can cut your own flooring strips from 2" or 3" wide, 1/16" thick basswood sheets. This is especially good for early houses which had random width flooring (anywhere from 3" to 9" wide or ¼" to ¾" in miniature). To make nice straight cuts, use a good sharp mat knife and a metal straightedge or ruler with a metal edge. By the Georgian period, equal width flooring was preferred, 3" or 6" wide (¼" or ½" in miniature). Wood strips in these sizes are readily available.

The flooring is best glued down with Weldwood cement, though white glue will do as well if applied in dots rather than all over so the wood

will not curl. Avoid getting glue on the surface of the flooring since it will act as a sealer and will leave light spots when you stain the floors. If you do get glue on the flooring, do not worry, there is a way to handle the problem which will be discussed later. The ends of the floorboards should never line up but instead be staggered, as shown in Fig. 23.

If you plan to cut your own flooring from wider sheets, select sheets which have approximately the same lightness or darkness so they will take the stain in an even color. Water base stains are good for floors because of their speed in drying. Oil base stains work beautifully, but do take longer to dry. If you are using wood strips already cut, you may not be able to find enough strips which match in lightness or darkness, especially for a large house. This is a problem because different strips will take the stain differently and give you a spotty, unattractive floor. But there is a solution.

After the floor is laid, using slightly thinned acrylic paints, paint the floor a *light* wood tone color. The paint will sink into the wood somewhat and give an overall even color to the floor. Next, sand the paint with fine sandpaper until the natural wood grain of the wood strips shows through, but do not sand away the even color. Now apply antiquing ink and rub it off. The antiquing will sink into the wood grain to accent it and also act as a stain, giving the flooring a wood color. This technique covers a multitude of

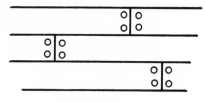

FIG. 23

sins, such as getting glue on the surface of the flooring. It is also a good technique for fully paneled house walls where the wood pieces used are rarely from the same or matching wood sheets.

When the stain (or paint and antiquing) is dry, coat the floor with 3 to 6 coats of latex varnish using a polyfoam brush to minimize brush strokes. Latex varnish is a water base varnish which dries clear and fast so the whole floor can be done in one day. (I do use latex varnish over antiquing ink, which is an oil base. This is not supposed to be done, and I will not really recommend it to you. It is safer to do an oil varnish over antiquing ink. This is beautiful; it just takes longer to dry.) After the first 2 coats of either varnish, sand the floor lightly (and between coats thereafter) with #400 Wetordry sandpaper first and the #600 for the final coats. While sanding a latex varnish, the surface will become cloudy. This is normal. Rub the surface with a barely damp cloth and it becomes clear again. Finish off all varnished floors with .0000 steel wool or rubbing compound and a final coat of paste wax.

FLOOR VARIATIONS

To simulate pegged flooring for early houses, drill $\frac{1}{16}$" holes in the ends of the floorboards (see Fig. 23). Insert toothpicks in the holes, with glue. Break the toothpicks off at floor level and sand smooth while the glue is still damp. Stain and varnish as before.

Parquet floors can be made as simple or elaborate as you like. For a simple checkerboard design (Fig. 24) start with $\frac{1}{8}$" × $\frac{1}{16}$" wood strips. $\frac{1}{16}$" thick wood is used because it is hard to lay this kind of floor without uneven spots. The unevenness can be sanded smooth, without sanding right

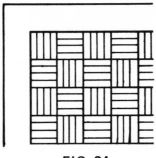

FIG. 24

through the wood (as with $\frac{1}{32}$" thick wood). Glue the wood strips in groups of 4 to a paper backing. When the glue is dry, cut away the excess paper around the edges. The 4 group strips are $\frac{1}{2}$" wide. Next, cut the strips in $\frac{1}{2}$" lengths to make $\frac{1}{2}$" squares. Next, on the floor, starting from the center, mark off a grid in $\frac{1}{2}$" sections and plan for a plain border around the edge. In the parquet area, glue one row of $\frac{1}{2}$" parquet squares, alternating the grain (Fig. 24). There are likely to be some ragged edges. Lay a ruler along the edge and cut away the excess wood. When cutting off the excess, use some care not to cut through the poster board floor.

Weldwood cement can be used for laying parquet. Even though it is a contact cement, it does not get completely hard immediately and the small excess pieces of wood can still be cut away. White glue is also good to use because the parquet squares can be repositioned if you do not get them just right the first time. However, being a water base glue, it does tend to make the parquet squares curl a bit at the edges and increase the unevenness. Each row of squares can be weighted with a book while the glue dries, to minimize the problem, of course, but laying the floor takes longer. You will just have to try both glues and decide which is best for you. Be sure to remove any excess glue from the parquet surface.

Glue on the second row of parquet squares, alternating the grain with the first row. Continue in this manner till the parquet area is done. Lay the plain border of $\frac{1}{16}$" thick wood. It is likely that the floor will be uneven in spots. Sand it as smooth as possible. Stain the floor with an oil or water base stain. The light and dark checkerboard effect will result from the alternating wood grain (If you do want more contrast, brush more stain on alternate squares to darken them.) Then apply as many coats of latex or oil base varnish as needed to cover any remaining unevenness. Many may be needed. Sand and finish the floor as described before with Wetordry sandpaper, steel wool, rubbing compound, and wax.

Stencil designs painted on the floor were popular in the eighteenth century. They can be quite simple or elaborate depending on your taste. Figure 25 shows a simple design which can be done in two colors. Cut the stencils from shirt

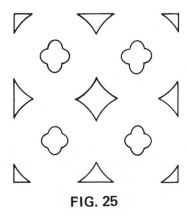

FIG. 25

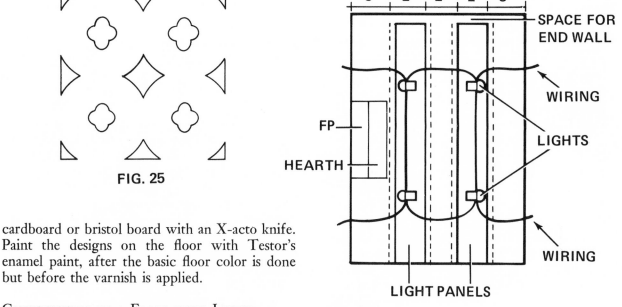

FIG. 26

cardboard or bristol board with an X-acto knife. Paint the designs on the floor with Testor's enamel paint, after the basic floor color is done but before the varnish is applied.

CONSTRUCTION OF A FLOOR WITH LIGHTS

Construction of the floors for the ceiling/floor sections to hold the lights is more complicated. Study Plate 19. Also read Chapters 9 and 10 and see Plate 6.

Figure 26 shows a 12″ wide room with 4 lights. You may want to change the number or placement of lights but the basic instructions apply. In a 12″ wide room the bulbs should be placed 3½″ to 4″ in from the sides of the room for good light coverage. An 8″ wide room needs only one light panel. If there is a fireplace hearth in the room, it is best to plan the space so the small overhang of flooring (indicated by the dotted line in Fig. 26) misses the hearth. A ¼″ overhang is usually enough to prevent light leakage around the light panels. Remember to plan a space ³⁄₁₆″ to ¼″ at the back of the floor to accommodate the end wall and its moldings.

To make the floor, cut out the light panels in the poster board floor (see Plate 6). Make the framework joists ⅜″ × ⅛″ by gluing together ¼″ × ⅛″ and ⅛″ × ⅛″ wood strips. If you figure it out in advance you will see that, when the ceiling and flooring are added, the ceiling/floor panel will be ⁹⁄₁₆″ thick instead of the usual ⅝″. This is planned because sometimes (and only sometimes) the ceiling/floors tend to sag just a tiny bit in the middle at the open back display area where they are unsupported by the end wall

or ceiling beams. The ⅝″ wide facing strip covers this problem if it occurs. However, you can use ⁷⁄₁₆″ × ⅛″ joists as with plain floors if you like.

Mark the joists where they are to be notched, at the edges of the light panels to hold the extra wood strips with magnets attached. It is also necessary to trim down the space between some of the notches to accommodate the wiring (Fig. 27A). Glue the magnet strips to ¼″ × ⅛″ wood strips and trim off any excess magnet strip (Fig. 27B). Glue the joists to the poster board as usual and glue the magnet strips in place (Fig. 27C). Note the ¹⁄₁₆″ space above the magnet strip. This is to accommodate the magnet strip on the light panel (Fig. 28).

Now, to make sure the second magnet strips are not in opposition to the first set, hold the second ones over the first which are already in place. If they do not snap together but seem to be repelled, turn them around. The second set of magnets is then glued to the edges of the light panel and a second piece of poster board is added to fill the space between the magnets (indicated by the dotted line in Fig. 28).

You are now ready to lay the flooring. Do the light panels first, allowing about a ¼″ overhang

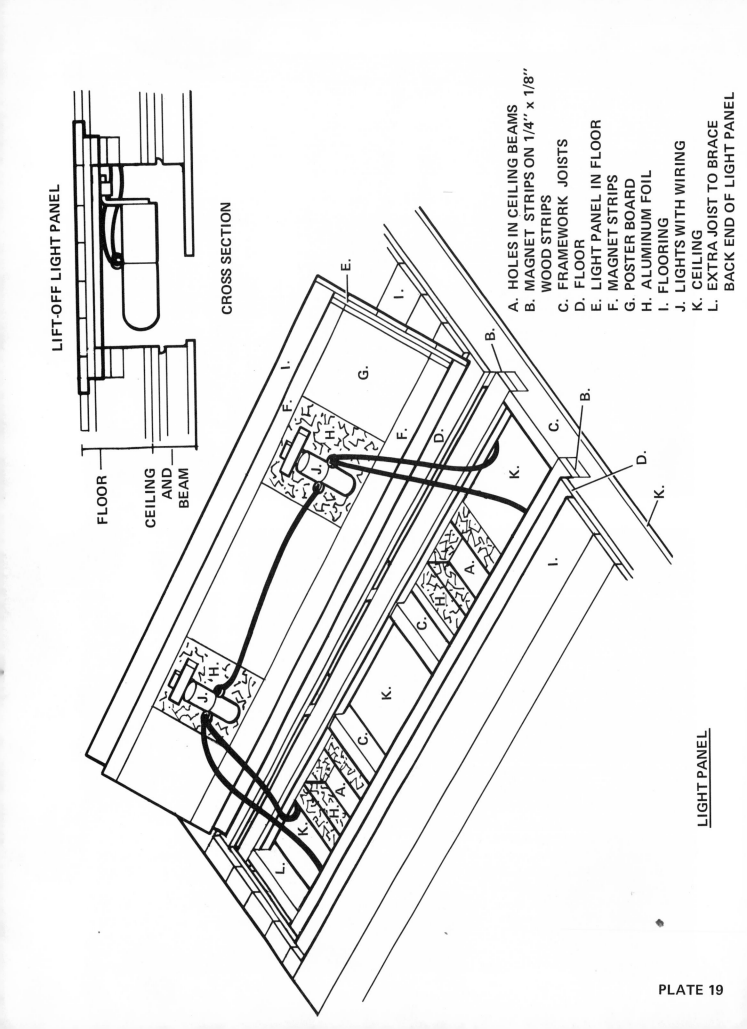

LIFT-OFF LIGHT PANEL

FLOOR

CEILING AND BEAM

CROSS SECTION

A. HOLES IN CEILING BEAMS
B. MAGNET STRIPS ON 1/4" x 1/8" WOOD STRIPS
C. FRAMEWORK JOISTS
D. FLOOR
E. LIGHT PANEL IN FLOOR
F. MAGNET STRIPS
G. POSTER BOARD
H. ALUMINUM FOIL
I. FLOORING
J. LIGHTS WITH WIRING
K. CEILING
L. EXTRA JOIST TO BRACE BACK END OF LIGHT PANEL

LIGHT PANEL

PLATE 19

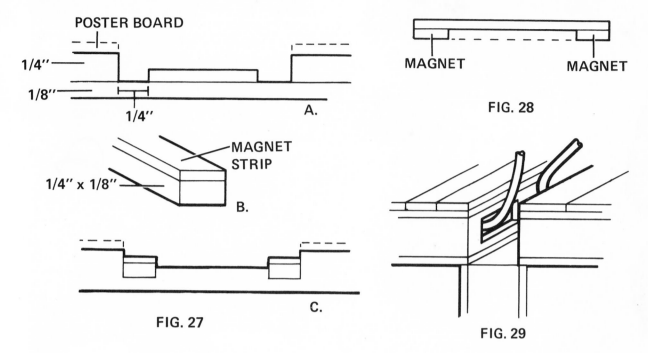

POSTER BOARD

1/4"

1/8"

1/4"

A.

MAGNET STRIP

1/4" x 1/8"

B.

C.

FIG. 27

MAGNET   MAGNET

FIG. 28

FIG. 29

of flooring on both sides of the light panel. When this is done, pop the panels into place in the floor and mark the edges of the flooring on the poster board floor. Remove the panels and lay the flooring on the rest of the floor. Stain and varnish the floor as described, making sure to get color on the edges of the flooring at the light panels, but not varnish.

The floor is now ready to receive the lights, and the ceiling with beams should be made next. Later when the lights are installed, line the area on the light panels with several layers of aluminum foil glued on for safety (those little lights *do* get hot!) and to prevent light leakage. The wiring runs through the framework joists. For

this, drill $\frac{1}{16}$" holes in the joists to hold the wires. $\frac{1}{16}$" holes may be a tiny bit small for the lead-in wire. If so, the holes can be enlarged by "sawing" up and down with the drill bit.

Usually it is best to have the wires enter and exit the floor near the ends where they do not interfere with fireplaces, doors, etc. Here it is best to cut a large hole (Fig. 29). When the house is assembled later and the wiring from each separate ceiling/floor unit is joined together, soldered and taped, this bulky part can be pushed through the hole to the inside of the ceiling/floor unit where it is out of the way and not likely to be damaged.

Chapter 9

Ceilings and Beams

See Plate 19 for the idea of how the beams conceal the lights.

As a general rule, in a 16″ long room, the beams can be placed about 5″ to 5½″ in from the ends of the walls for good light coverage.

Figure 30 shows beams and how they fit into the ceiling line moldings. Notice that the shaping on the Georgian beam (Fig. 30D) matches the shape of the ceiling line molding.

Beams for holding and hiding lights, whether plain or shaped, are basically U-shaped structures with 2 side pieces and a bottom (Fig. 30E and F). In early Colonial houses where heavy support beams and smaller cross beams are used (Fig. 30B), the heavy beams are U-shaped and the cross beams solid.

The beams butt up against the side wall (Fig. 30A) and are held in place by the ceiling moldings (Fig. 30C and D). You will see that the beams are 1/16″ shorter on each side than the width of the ceiling (Fig. 30A). Also, see that the ceiling moldings are notched or cut out to fit the beams. This eliminates the need for mitering.

When you are decorating the walls, it is best to leave the ceiling line moldings till last. That is, you can mark where the moldings will go, do all the other construction and moldings on the wall, and then do the ceiling line moldings and beams at the same time.

When you are ready for the ceiling line moldings and beams, first construct the U-shaped beams. You will notice in Fig. 30F that the shaped beam has an extra 1/16″ × 1/16″ piece on the front edge. This looks odd in the plan but it has a purpose. It acts as a light baffle. That is, when the beams are seen straight on, you really cannot see where light is coming from. There is no 1/16″ × 1/16″ piece on the back of the beam because the light would reflect on it and accentuate where light is coming from. To accommodate this shape,

once the beam position is established, a small piece is added to the ceiling molding (Fig. 31). This light baffle structure is really quite inconspicuous. In the heavy beams, the lights are not as close to the light holes so the problem is not as great, but a small baffle will be hardly noticed, especially if the beams are hand-hewn and weathered (see Chapter 4). While you are making the beams, it is good to put crosspieces in the beams at several places for strength and close to where the light holes will be, to prevent light leakage.

Once the beams are made, they are glued to the ceiling. The beams can be painted before being glued to the ceiling but it is better to wait until the light holes are cut. Using the floor, prepared for lights, as a guide, figure where the beams need to be cut for the light holes to expose the bulbs. These will be ½″ wide (the width of the bottom piece in the U-shape). ¾″ is usually long enough to expose the bulb. Cut the beams and mark through them where the ceiling is to be cut. To do this, poke a pin or awl up through the light hole and pierce the ceiling in several spots. Do not worry too much about the placement of these holes; you cannot poke through the ceiling outside the beams. Begin cutting the ceiling where the guide holes are. Start with a small hole and gradually cut the ceiling out to conform with the inside edges of the beam (Fig. 32). Extend the open space far enough along the length of the beam to receive the light socket and bulb.

Tape the light sockets and bulbs in the prepared floor unit or at least mark the position of the bulbs on the light panels. Tape the lower ceiling and upper floor together and check to see that the position of the light holes matches the position of the bulbs. They may not line up. This is a common problem. To correct it, cut away some wood from one side of the light hole and

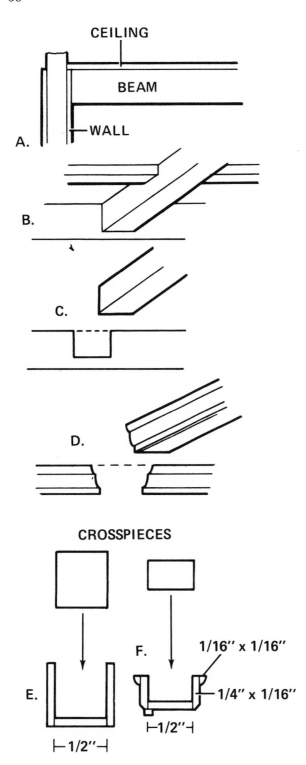

CROSSPIECES

FIG. 30

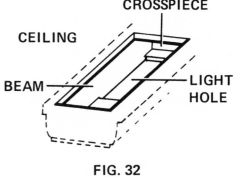

FIG. 31

FIG. 32

add a narrow $\frac{1}{16}''$ thick wood piece to the other side.

When everything is correct, untape the floor and ceiling. The area around the light hole should be lined with several layers of aluminum foil glued on, for safety and to help prevent light leakage. The ceiling and beams can be painted now or later. Paint the ceiling first. Then lay masking tape on the ceiling next to the beams to keep the ceiling clean and paint the beams.

The ceiling and floor are now ready to receive the lights (see Plate 19 and read Chapter 10). Install them in the floor and test to see that they work. Tape the ceiling in place and check for light leakage. Add more aluminum foil if needed. When you are satisfied that everything is correct, glue the ceiling to the floor to complete the ceiling/floor unit.

I have left one thing till last. In the Georgian house, you may want the beams to fit right up next to the three-sided fireplace structure as shown in Fig. 33A. To do this, part of the beam must be cut away to fit around the fireplace structure (Fig. 33B). The molding on the front of the fireplace structure is then cut and glued on to receive the beam (Fig. 33C).

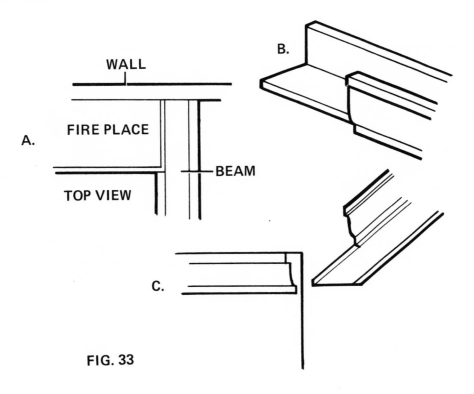

WALL

B.

A.

FIRE PLACE

BEAM

TOP VIEW

C.

FIG. 33

Chapter 10

Lighting

The main advantage of this type of lighting for a whole house, aside from the beauty of hidden lighting, is the easy access to the light fixtures to replace burnt out bulbs. Study Plate 19. It shows the bulbs in their sockets (with wiring attached), secured to the light panel and ready to use. To get to this point, you have to know a few things first. You need to know the voltage and amperage ratings of the bulbs you plan to use. Amperage is the amount of current the bulb needs to make it work. I use General Electric Auto and Industrial bulbs, 57X, which are 14 volt and .24 amps, 2 candle power (the amount of light the bulb gives off) and rated at 500 hours of life. The hours rating means that the bulbs running at full voltage will last 500 hours before burning out. If you run lights on voltage lower than they need, they last even longer. Before we get into actual numbers of volts, amps, etc., you should know the materials needed and a general theory of lighting.

To wire a house, you need bulbs, sockets, and lead-in wire. This is thin wire covered with insulation (diameter a little over $\frac{1}{16}$"). You can buy it at any electronics store. It comes in many colors which is helpful, if you are running more than one circuit, to keep track of which wires go to which circuits. Bulbs come in many shapes and sizes. They will have either a screw base (which screws in) or bayonet base (which snaps in). Sockets are standard items and look like that shown in Fig. 39. They are made in either screw or bayonet style to fit your bulbs. You also need a transformer, regular house wiring, and a plug.

Miniature bulbs run on a transformer and all transformers have a primary circuit, which is house current, and a secondary circuit, which is what the miniature bulbs run on. So the electricity runs like this: house current on the primary circuit to the transformer, from the transformer

on the secondary circuit to the lead-in wires in the miniature house, up through the walls and ceiling/floor sections to the contacts on the sockets and into the bulbs, then back through sockets, wires, and transformer to the main house current to complete the circuit. The theory is that the current flows from a power source, through wires, lighting a given number of bulbs or circuits, and back to the power source (see Fig. 34). Lights can be wired up three ways. The first is in series. This is easy to do, but if one light burns out, they all go out. This is fine for small, one-story houses where you use anywhere from 4 to 10 lights. If one goes out, it is not hard to find the bad one. The circuit looks like Fig. 35.

The second way to wire lights is in parallel. In this, if one bulb burns out, the rest stay on. This is because there is one main circuit and individual lights are connected to it (Fig. 36). This system is good for rooms requiring 1 or 2 lights in a ceiling beam across the center of each room, though 4 lights in a room can be done by running 2 parallel circuits side by side, joining them at the transformer. The parallel circuit can be as long and have as many lights as you desire, depending on the amperage of the transformer. This will be discussed more fully later.

The third way to wire the lights is in series and parallel combination. In this, if one light in a series goes out, the other one in that series goes out, but the rest stay on. This system is good for multi-room houses which require 4 lights to a room. The circuit looks like Fig. 37.

12" × 16" rooms get good light coverage with 4 lights. 8" × 16" rooms get good coverage with only 2. For the early Colonial house plans in this book, you may not want any lights in the little back hall, letting the hall be lit by light coming from the main rooms through open doors.

Which system you use really depends on how

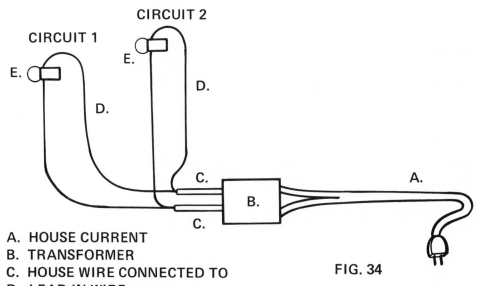

A. HOUSE CURRENT
B. TRANSFORMER
C. HOUSE WIRE CONNECTED TO
D. LEAD-IN WIRE
E. CIRCUITS CONTAINING X
   NUMBERS OF BULBS

FIG. 34

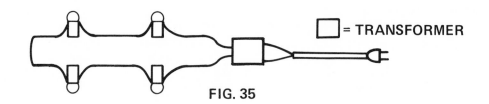

☐ = TRANSFORMER

FIG. 35

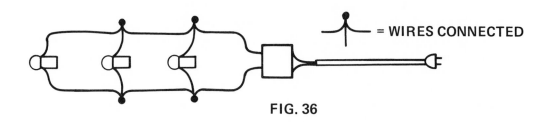

= WIRES CONNECTED

FIG. 36

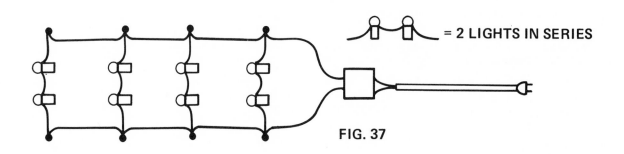

= 2 LIGHTS IN SERIES

FIG. 37

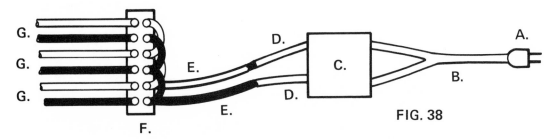

FIG. 38

A. WALL PLUG.   B. HOUSE WIRE.   C. TRANSFORMER.
D. HOUSE WIRE CONNECTED TO E. LEAD-IN WIRE CON-
NECTED TO F. TERMINAL STRIP.   G. LEAD-IN WIRES
TO MINIATURE HOUSE.

much light you want and where you want it. To experiment, make a cardboard box the size of your room. Wire up some lights temporarily. To begin, cut some lead-in wire to the approximate length needed. With scissors, cut gently through the plastic insulation (about ½″ to ¾″ from the end) and pull it off to expose the wire. Then, twist the wires to contacts on the sockets and transformer. Cut holes in the box about ½″ × ¾″. Lay the bulbs over the holes so the light shines into the box but don't allow the bulbs to hang down inside the box. Cover the lights with something to keep the light directed down into the box, a heavy cloth or small cardboard box will do. The light in the room is now very close to the finished effect of lights hidden in the ceiling beams. Experiment with different bulbs, positions in the room, and number of bulbs used till you see what you like. Then build your ceiling/floor panels to fit your system.

Next, you must decide whether to wire the house in one long circuit, or one circuit for each floor. It makes very little difference, since separate circuits join up at the terminal strip or transformer anyway, but for a very large house, separate circuits are probably best. One expert told me that if you run one *very* long circuit (rather than 2 or 3 short ones), the candle power of the bulbs at the end of the circuit is slightly reduced. Determine which walls will carry the wires to the ceiling/floor sections so you can install the wires while making the walls. When assembling the house later, the wall wires and the ceiling/floor wires will be connected. When

installing wires, always leave plenty of excess to work with.

If you run one, or more than one circuit, for neatness' sake, you might want to use a terminal strip. This is a plastic strip with several contact points on it. This is how it works using three circuits (Fig. 38):

The lead-in wires and terminal strip can be held in place on the underside of the base you put your house on (see Chapter 13). The lead-in wires to the house come up through holes in the base directly into the house and the house wire (d) comes through a hole in the side of the base and can be many feet long so the transformer can be kept far away from the house. This way the electrical stuff, which is ugly, is either hidden or far away from the house (Fig. 56).

Now for the numbers, volts and amps. 12-volt bulbs are most common and can be run in series or in parallel on a 12-volt transformer. 13- and 14-volt bulbs will also run on a 12-volt transformer. Since they will not be running at full power, they will last longer, but there may be a slight reduction in brightness. In a series and parallel circuit, 12-volt bulbs run on a 24-volt transformer. To figure the amperage needed for your transformer, you need to know the amperage of each bulb. This is usually listed on the box or the dealer where you buy the bulbs can tell you. You can also call the local distributor. (The people at G.E. know "that dollhouse lady" only too well.) Now take the number of bulbs you plan to use and multiply by the amperage of the bulbs. Two bulbs wired in series in a parallel circuit count as one bulb because the current has to flow through both of them to get back to the power source. As an example, my house is quite large and requires 48 14-volt bulbs. They are wired in a series and parallel circuit so they count as 24. The amperage for each bulb is .24. Therefore, multiply 24 $\times$ .24 which is 5.76. Remembering that two 14-volt bulbs in a series need a 24-volt transformer, the final result is that a 24-volt, 6 amp transformer is needed. If you cannot find a transformer with your exact amp requirements, you can use one with more amperage. Though my lighting system requires about 6 amps, I have a 24-volt, 8 amp transformer (Stancor, model no. P-6379).

All that is left now is how to mount the sockets and how to solder. Sockets look as shown in Fig. 39 and can be the screw-in or snap-in (bayonet) type, to suit the type of bulb you have. To mount the socket on the 2″ wide light panel (see Plate 19) you will have to cut off most of the arm with wire clippers. Next, notch a piece of ⅛″ × ⅛″ wood to hold the remaining part of the arm. This is glued to the light panel and holds the socket in place. A tight fit is desired (Fig. 40). You may, for safety's sake, want to cover these wood holders with aluminum foil.

To solder, you need solder wire, soldering paste, and a soldering iron or a wood burning tool, which works just as well. Strip about ½″ of in-

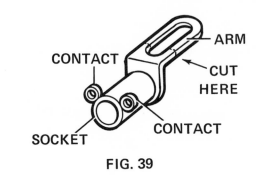

FIG. 39

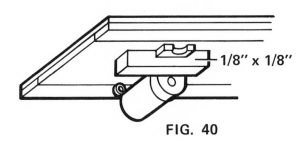

FIG. 40

sulation off the ends of the lead-in wires. Twist these onto the socket contact or to each other, depending on what you are connecting. Dip the solder in the soldering paste and hold it on the connection. Hold the soldering iron on the solder till it melts and runs into the connection. That is all there is to it. Wrap some plastic electrical tape around the connection and you are done.

Chapter 11
Staircases, Bannisters, and Balusters

The house plan in Plate 4 for the Georgian house shows a straight staircase in the center hall. Plans, details, and instructions are given for it, since it is an integral part of the house. The staircase commonly starts from the front of the house. But some houses were built with the staircase starting from the back of the house and you may prefer this so you can see the steps easily at the open back of the house. If you are building an early Colonial house there is also a plan for a front hall staircase. You may want to build an early Colonial house with the front open or hinged to show off this important feature of the house. The style and placement of the staircases is really up to the builder. The methods given for designing will help you build any staircase you like.

The staircase is best built as a separate, free-standing unit, with balusters and bannisters in place, and slipped into place while the house is being assembled. Plates 20 and 21 show how to make a grid to get the basic pattern of the staircase. In the example in Plate 21 we use a staircase of 13 steps to fit a space 9″ long and 8½″ high (the height of the wall, 8″) plus ½″ (the thickness of the floor through which it passes). This size fits into the Georgian house very nicely. The staircase fits into the stairwell cut in the second floor hall as shown in Fig. 41. When the flooring is in place on the second floor, the flooring will cover the top step and act as a tread, so when laying flooring in this area, allow some extra. It can be trimmed later to fit the staircase.

Once you have the sides of the staircase planned, cut them out from poster board or ¹⁄₁₆″ thick wood. Since ¹⁄₁₆″ wood sheets usually do not come in such wide pieces it will be necessary to cut the entire side of the staircase from 3 or 4 wood sheets. Tape the wood sheets together temporarily and mark and cut them as you would

poster board. To join them permanently, remove the tape, and line the sheets up with the edges butted together and glued. Brace the joints with ¼″ × ¹⁄₁₆″ wood strips glued over the joints. This will not show since it will be inside the staircase.

Next, cut pieces to fit between the sides at the back and bottom of the staircase (Plate 21). If the staircase is to be 3″ wide, cut the pieces 3″ minus the thickness of the two sides (⅛″) or 2⅞″. Often staircases had small closets built under them (see Plate 24). If you want this, cut a door opening in the side or back of the staircase. Brace the opening with framework studs and build a doorjamb and door just as in a house wall (Fig. 42).

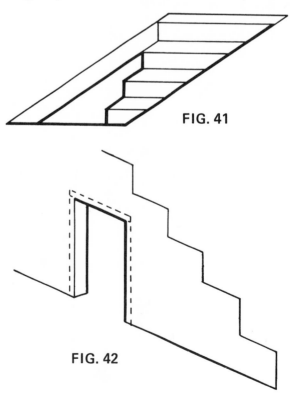

FIG. 41

FIG. 42

DIVIDING A LINE INTO EQUAL PARTS

1. DRAW A LINE AND MARK THE LENGTH OF THE LINE YOU WANT TO DIVIDE. LINE AB. (9")
2. AT A. WITH A TRIANGLE DRAW LINE AC.
3. HOLD THE END OF A RULER AT POINT B. SWING THE RULER ALONG LINE AC TILL THE 13" MARK ON THE RULER CROSSES LINE AC. THIS IS POINT X.
4. MARK POINTS AT 1"INTERVALS ALONG LINE BX.
5. WITH A TRIANGLE DRAW LINES FROM THE POINTS DOWN TO LINE AB.
6. LINE AB IS NOW DIVIDED IN 13 EQUAL PARTS.
7. ANY LENGTH LINE CAN BE DIVIDED IN ANY GIVEN NUMBER OF PARTS. JUST MAKE SURE THE INTERVALS ALONG BX ARE EQUIDISTANT.

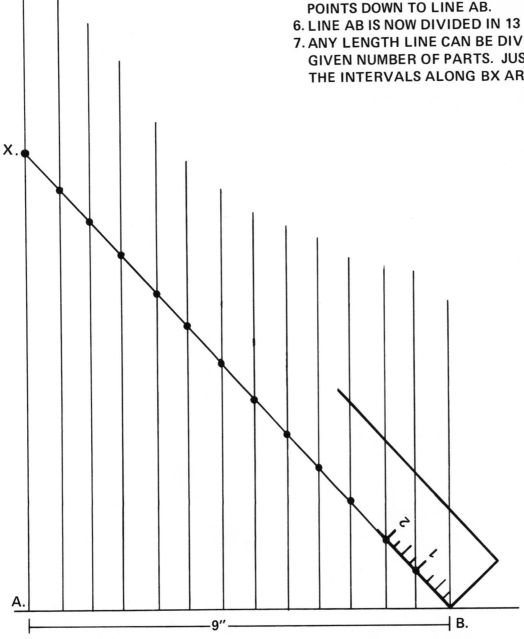

C.

X.

A.

|———————— 9" ————————| B.

PLATE 20

MAKING A GRID FOR STAIRCASE SIDE

1. DIVIDE A LINE THE LENGTH OF STAIRCASE (9''), LINE AB, INTO 13 EQUAL PARTS.

2. DIVIDE A LINE THE HEIGHT OF THE WALL (8'') PLUS THE THICKNESS OF THE FLOOR THRU WHICH THE STAIRCASE PASSES (1/2''), LINE AC, INTO 13 EQUAL PARTS.

3. THE DARK LINE SHOWS THE STAIRCASE SIDE PATTERN.

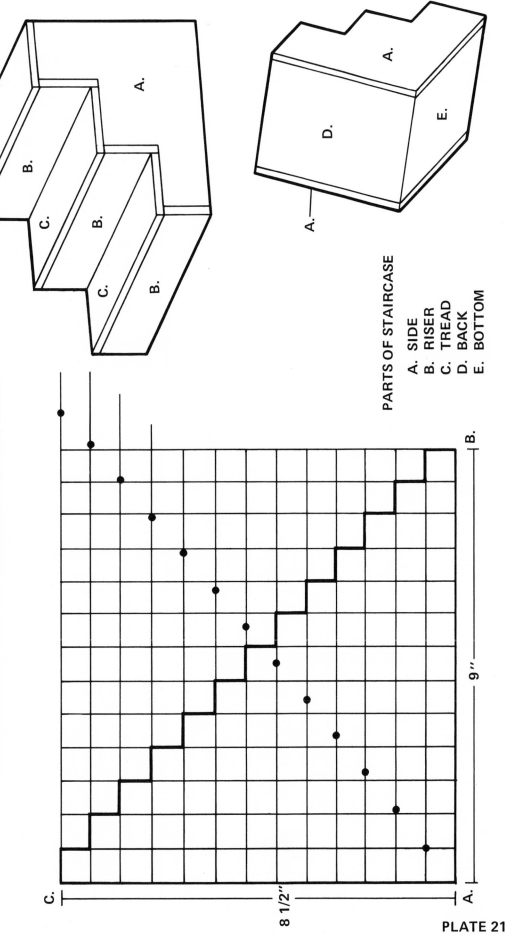

PARTS OF STAIRCASE

A. SIDE
B. RISER
C. TREAD
D. BACK
E. BOTTOM

PLATE 21

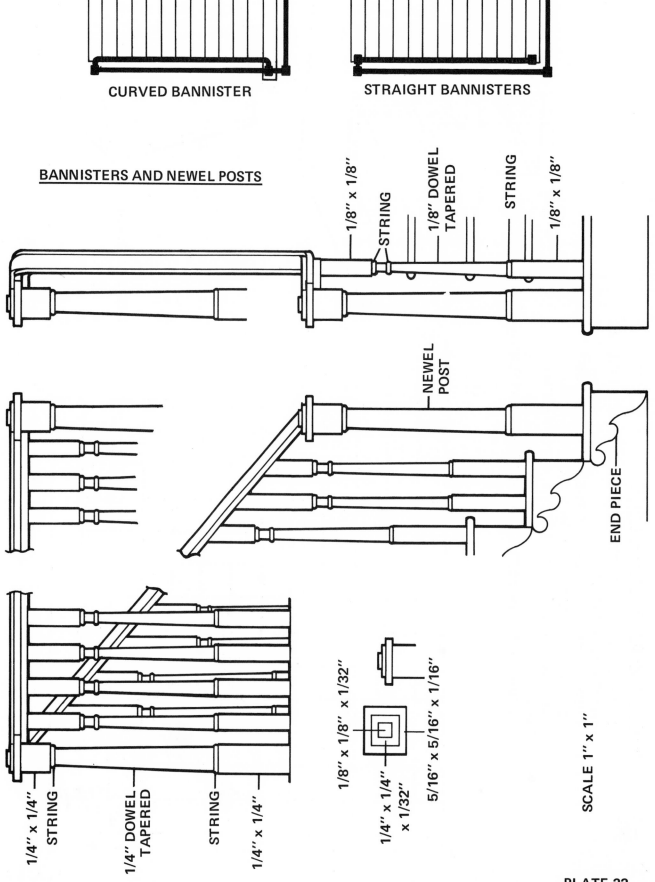

CURVED BANNISTER

STRAIGHT BANNISTERS

BANNISTERS AND NEWEL POSTS

1/8" x 1/8"

STRING

1/8" DOWEL TAPERED

STRING

1/8" x 1/8"

NEWEL POST

END PIECE

1/4" x 1/4"

STRING

1/4" DOWEL TAPERED

STRING

1/4" x 1/4"

1/8" x 1/8" x 1/32"

1/4" x 1/4" x 1/32"

5/16" x 5/16" x 1/16"

SCALE 1" x 1"

PLATE 22

Now cut pieces 3″ wide to fit the height of the risers. Assemble the sides, back, and bottom of the staircase, bracing the corners with ⅛″ × ⅛″ wood strips. Then glue on the risers. Next, cut wood pieces for the treads. The treads should have a slight overhang on the front edge of the step and on the edge away from the stairway wall. The Georgian staircases usually had decorative end pieces at the side of each step as shown in Plate 22. The tread should overhang this also.

If there is to be a wider bottom step as shown in Fig. 43, construct it by adding wood pieces to the staircase side. Cut the riser and tread to fit. If the staircase is to be all one color or natural wood, add the treads now and paint or stain the whole thing now. If the staircase is to have moldings to match the wall, do this now. If the staircase is to be painted and the treads natural wood, paint the staircase and finish the treads separately, then glue them to the staircase.

Bannisters can be made as shown in Fig. 44, from wood strips with the edges rounded and fitted to the balusters. The balusters and newel post are made by a built-up method rather than carved out (see Chapter 15, Fig. 78). Plate 22 shows the basic pieces needed to make the balusters and newel posts.

Once the balusters are made and painted or finished, draw on paper the original pattern of your staircase with the treads added and the height (33″ to 36″ in real size) and slant of the bannister. Place the balusters in position on the

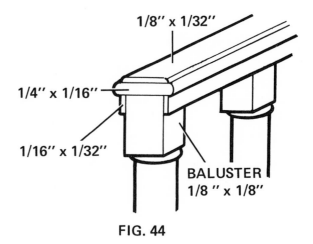

1/8″ x 1/32″

1/4″ x 1/16″

1/16″ x 1/32″

BALUSTER
1/8 ″ x 1/8″

FIG. 44

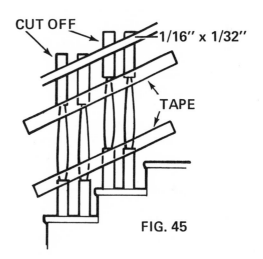

CUT OFF

1/16″ x 1/32″

TAPE

FIG. 45

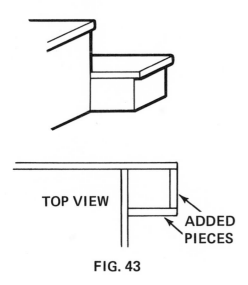

TOP VIEW

ADDED PIECES

FIG. 43

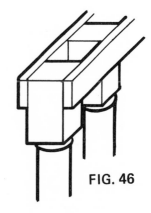

FIG. 46

drawing and hold them down with long strips of tape (Fig. 45). Now glue the ¹⁄₁₆″ × ¹⁄₃₂″ wood strip in position and trim the balusters to fit the slant of the wood strip. Next, leaving the tape on the balusters, take them off the paper and turn them over. Add a strip of tape to this side and glue a $\frac{1}{16}'' \times \frac{1}{32}''$ wood strip on as shown in Fig. 46. Sand the top smooth. The top part of the bannister (Fig. 44) can be glued on now and painted or stained and varnished. The newel post can also be painted or stained and varnished. Leave the tape on the balusters to help maintain their proper position. Glue the balusters (and bannister) and newel post in position on the staircase. When the glue is good and dry, remove the tape.

Sometimes you will want a double curve in the bannister so it can fit into a newel post on a wider bottom step (see Plate 22). To do this soak the $\frac{1}{4}'' \times \frac{1}{16}''$ bannister piece in water till it will bend easily. Draw a pattern of the first curve you want on a piece of illustration board. Bend the wood to fit the curve and hold it in place with pins till the wood dries and holds its shape (Fig. 47A). To this piece (Fig. 47B) at the side, add a wood piece wider than the finished second curve (Fig. 47C). Cut this curve. Add the main $\frac{1}{8}'' \times \frac{1}{32}''$ top piece to the bannister. Since the wood is thin it can be bent with very little soaking. Carve the second curve on it and glue it, and the small side piece, to the $\frac{1}{4}'' \times \frac{1}{16}''$ bannister piece (Fig. 47D). Round the edges (Fig. 44). At the top of the staircase, the curves are done the same, except the curves are reversed.

Add any carpeting you like, leaving some extra at the top to work with in the second floor hall.

The carpeting is glued on, but stair rods can be added for an attractive look or to cover the joint if the carpet needs to be pieced (Fig. 48). The rods are stiff steel wire, held in place with straight pins pushed into the staircase.

VARIATIONS

The seventeenth-century three-spiral staircase shown in Plates 23 and 24 can be varied in the number of steps used. Three or four steps can be used in the spiral. A step can be added to extend into the hall area (Fig. 49X).

You might want a curved staircase. The curves can be equidistant or be narrow at the top step and sweep out to a wide step at the bottom. On a piece of illustration board, mark the curves you desire. Hold thin cardboard strips, on edge, on

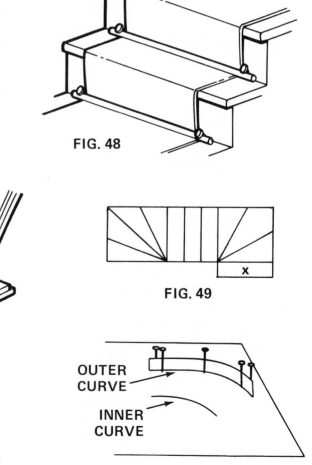

FIG. 48

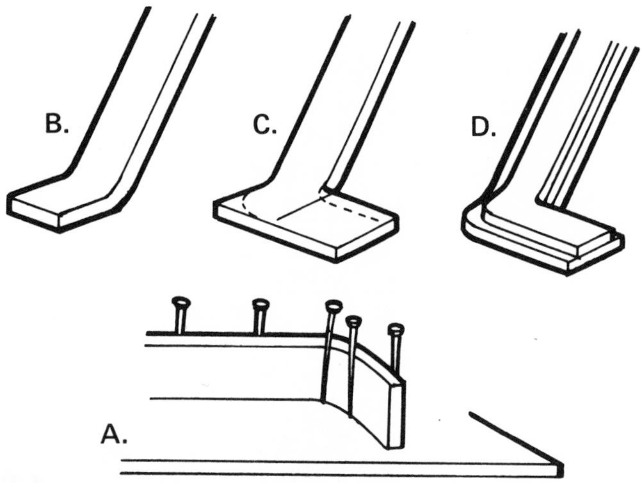

FIG. 47

FIG. 49

OUTER
CURVE

INNER
CURVE

FIG. 50

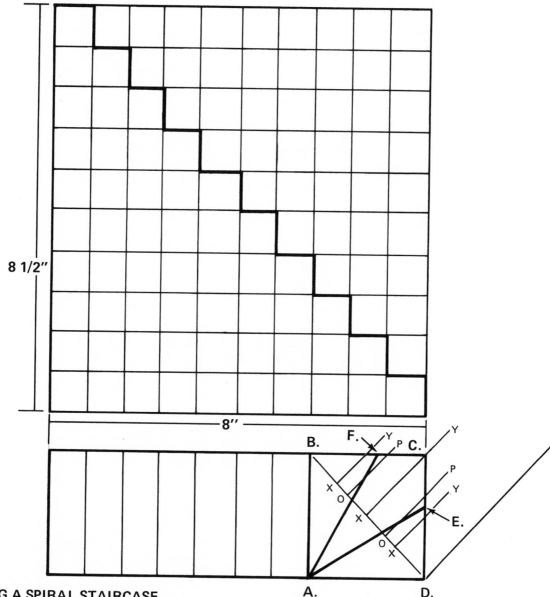

8 1/2"

8"

MAKING A SPIRAL STAIRCASE

1. MAKE STAIRCASE PATTERN GRID.
2. MAKE TOP VIEW.
3. DRAW A. B. C. D., 3 STEP SPIRAL AREA.
4. DIVIDE LINE BD IN 3 PARTS, LINES OP.
5. DIVIDE LINE BD IN 4 PARTS, LINES XY.
6. HALFWAY BETWEEN OP AND XY, MARK POINTS E. AND F.
7. DRAW LINES AE AND AF.
8. MAKE THE 3 STEPS AS SEPARATE OPEN TOPPED BOXES USING PROPER RISER HEIGHT.

9. GLUE THESE BOXES TOGETHER.
10. CUT OUT TREADS.
11. CONSTUCT REMAINING 7 STEPS AS FOR STRAIGHT STAIRCASE.
12. GLUE THE STRAIGHT AND SPIRAL PARTS TOGETHER.

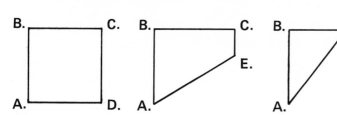

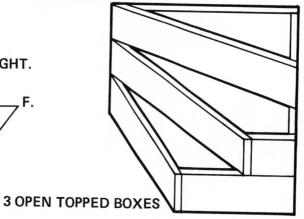

3 OPEN TOPPED BOXES

PLATE 23

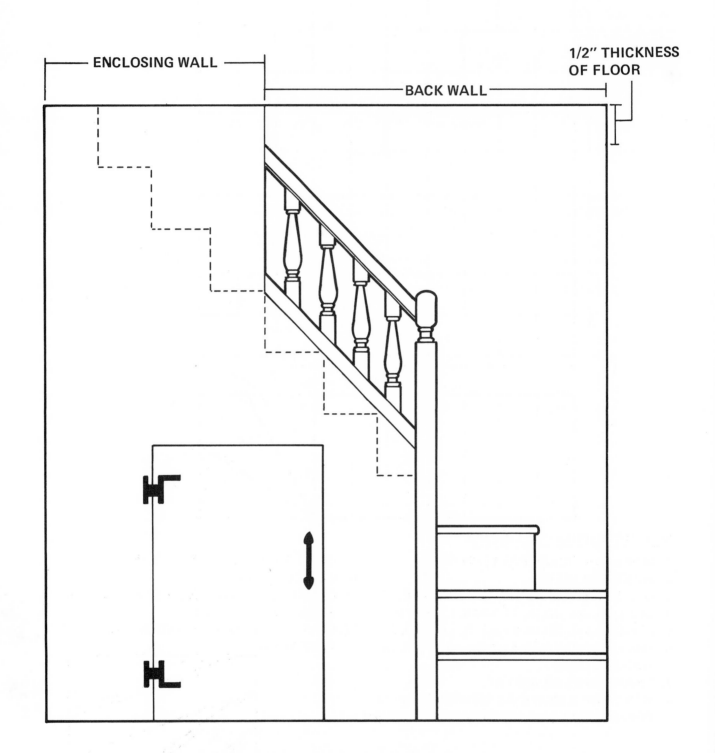

ENCLOSING WALL

1/2" THICKNESS OF FLOOR

BACK WALL

TYPICAL SEVENTEENTH-CENTURY FRONT HALL STAIRCASE
WITH THREE STEP SPIRAL

PLATE 24

the curves (Fig. 50). Mark the length of the curves on the cardboard and make two grid patterns for the staircase sides, one for the shorter inner curve and one for the longer outer curve. The back piece of the staircase is made as usual and the bottom piece will follow the curve. The risers and treads are cut to fit the staircase sides.

THE STAIRWAY WALL

The stairway wall is a problem, but not a large one. As shown in Fig. 51, you can see that when the interior walls are constructed, decorated, and then put together, there will be a gap in the stairway wall between the top of the first floor wall and the bottom of the second floor wall where the ceiling/floor fits in. This problem is similar to the gap in the floor units at the doorways (see Fig. 3). This can be corrected in two ways. First, in construction, you can plan carefully where the stairwell in the second floor ceiling/floor panel will be. To cover the gap in the wall there, add extra poster board on that side of the wall, on one of the two wall sections. When the house is assembled there will be only a small crack to be patched. Or, you can wait until the house is assembled and fill in the gap with a separate piece of poster board glued in place. The extensions in the wall form a backing for the separate piece. This way, I think, is easier in the long run. Either way, the patching is done as the house is assembled (Fig. 61) at a point where there is easy access to the area to be patched.

To patch the cracks in the wall where the gap is filled in, fill the cracks with white glue and sand smooth. It may be necessary to do this 2 or 3 times for a perfect patch.

If the wall is painted, simply repaint that small section of the wall, blending the paint into the already painted first and second floor walls. If there is to be a chair rail and dado running up the stairway wall this can be made now. It is made as a separate unit on a piece of $\frac{1}{32}$" thick wood with chair rail, baseboard, and decorative moldings glued in place. It is painted and glued into place on the stairway wall. Do not forget to take into consideration the thickness of this separate unit when planning the width of the staircase in relation to the width of the stairwell. $\frac{3}{32}$"

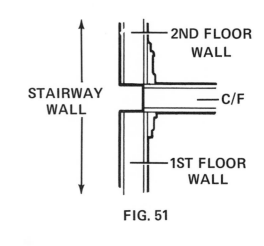

FIG. 51

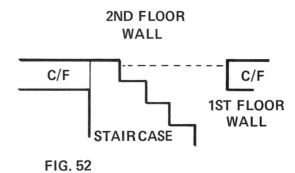

FIG. 52

can make a lot of difference.

If the stairway wall is to have simple vertical paneling, the problem is easier. When paneling the first and second floor walls, prepare painted or stained and finished paneling for the entire stairway wall. Glue the paneling to the first and second floor walls, but leave the gap and stairwell area unpaneled. When the house is assembled, it is a simple matter to cover the gap with the prepared paneling from the second floor ceiling molding down to the first floor baseboards.

A wallpapered wall is harder but not impossible (Fig. 52). Plan to cover the gap with additions on both stairway walls (dotted line) with most of the addition on the first floor stairway wall. When papering the first and second stairway walls, be careful to match the patterns as closely as possible. When the house is assembled, the joint between the two walls can be covered with a molding of the simple chair rail type, glued on to the wall level with the top step of the staircase. With this method, too, both the lower and upper hallways can be papered, one papered and one painted, or painted different colors.

Chapter 12
Painting and Decorating

Whenever possible use water base, acrylic, and latex paints, stains, and varnishes. They are easy to use, easy to clean up with water and above all, they dry fast.

Generally, a miniature room is painted and wallpapered like the real thing. That is, for flat finish walls and ceilings, latex interior house paint can be used. This can be painted directly onto poster board or wood without any primer.

Latex paint is usually purchased, in the smallest amount, in pint cans. This is a lot of paint and obviously you will not want a pint for each color you need. Fortunately, it is a water base paint and can be mixed with any other water base paint, including acrylic tube paints and tube water colors. So, starting with a pint of white latex for the ceilings and acrylic or water color tube paints, you can mix enough paint for an entire house in any colors you like. The biggest advantage of latex paint is the nice, even finish it gives. Matching color woodwork would ordinarily be painted with a semi-gloss enamel interior house paint. However, matching colors is difficult, so instead paint the wall and woodwork with the latex and give the woodwork two or more coats of latex varnish. This gives the woodwork a semi-gloss finish.

Sometimes the color of painted woodwork (especially in wallpapered rooms) needs to be softened or have molding details accented. A *very* light application of antiquing ink thinned with turpentine and rubbed off almost entirely will achieve this effect. When the antiquing is dry, you can finish it off with latex varnish. (You really should not use latex varnish over antiquing ink, although I often do.) You may prefer to use an oil base varnish. A water base antiquing can be made of mixed brown and black acrylic tube paints, greatly thinned down to achieve a similar effect. If you use this, paint the woodwork, give

it a coat or two of latex varnish as a sealer, use the water base antiquing, and finish off with two or three coats of latex varnish.

White woodwork can be done with latex interior house paint or white acrylic tube paint. Lightly sand the larger surfaces with very fine sandpaper (#600 or Wetordry). Two or three coats of latex varnish give a nice semi-gloss finish. If you prefer, you can use a white latex as a sealer coat and white semi-gloss enamel as a finish coat. This is *really* lovely but takes longer.

Natural wood finishes can be done in many ways. The fastest is with water base stain or thinned down wood tone acrylic tube paints. Both are dry and ready to work within an hour or less. These are especially good for small things such as window parts and exposed interior framework in early houses. If you want to antique it for accents, first give the piece two coats of vinyl spray or latex varnish as a sealer. When this is dry, the piece can be antiqued with thinned down acrylic tube paint, brushed on and rubbed off or brushed off with a dry paintbrush. Finish with two more coats of spray or latex varnish for a semi-gloss finish or leave it as is for a flat finish.

An oil base stain can also be used if you like the look of it better, as I do. Then thinned antiquing ink can be applied lightly and left as is for a flat finish or varnished with oil base varnishes (flat, semi- or high-gloss). This takes longer, of course, to dry. Antiquing ink over a painted wood tone base (see Chapter 8) is also excellent for interior framework in early houses, left as is for a flat finish, or varnished with a semi-gloss oil base varnish. For large surfaces such as floors and fully paneled walls where an even wood tone is needed, see the methods described for finishing floors in Chapter 8.

Wallpaper was used extensively in Georgian houses. For wallpaper in miniature houses, real wallpaper is best. Early houses tended to have large-patterned papers. There are many real size wallpapers with tiny prints which look right in small scale. Wallpaper can be purchased through dollhouse catalogs in small amounts or perhaps your local wallpaper dealer will give you old sample books with suitable patterns. More likely you will end up buying a roll of wallpaper. This may seem exorbitant, but building a house is a large achievement and in the end you will be happy to have what you really want. Some papers of the multi-stripe, multi-pattern type can be used by cutting out the stripes you want and hanging them in strips just as for full-size wallpaper, butting the edges together. Sometimes one roll of wallpaper of this type can provide patterns for several rooms. This is good because the colors of the paper will blend and so will the rooms.

When you look at many miniature houses, the color of each room is lovely but when seen all together, there is a red room, a blue room, a yellow room, etc., which gives a spotty effect. You might prefer the blended look of all warm color rooms with cool accents or all cool color rooms with warm accents. This sounds limiting but is really not. With the wide range of warm or cool colors, wallpapers, textures and paneling, each room can be quite different but still blended.

Many early houses have stenciled trim around the doorways, windows, ceilings, and baseboards. If you do not want to do the stenciling yourself, you might find a suitable strip in a multi-pattern paper. If it happens to have a tiny stripe at the edge, just glue the strip in place and paint the rest of the wall up to it. It will take several coats of paint to match the thickness of the paper. If the strip you like has no tiny stripe on the edge, mix a color to match the background color of the strip. Build up the paint to match the thickness of the paper and blend the paint over the edges of the paper. This gives the effect of stenciling done on a solid-color wall.

Any woodwork trim should be painted before the wallpaper is glued on. Also, before applying the wallpaper, it is best to cut it to size, as far as possible. To apply wallpaper to the wall, use wallpaper paste or slightly thinned white glue applied to both the paper and the wall with a paintbrush. The paper may stretch a bit and bubble, just as it does on real walls. Press out any large air bubbles with a cloth. If necessary, prick the small bubbles with a pin and press out the air. Smooth the paper as much as possible with a dry cloth. As the paper dries it will shrink and tighten up so do not worry too much about small imperfections. While applying the paper, trim off any excess with a very sharp blade and clean any glue off the woodwork with a damp cloth.

Chapter 13

Assembling the House

Now you have the major walls, floors, and ceilings made, the staircases ready to be put in place, and the decorating done. Before you put the house together, read Chapter 16 for making curtains and draperies. It is best to do these now while you still have easy access. You may also want to attach wall sconces and pictures now.

When the walls are completely decorated and everything is in place, the house is almost ready to assemble. But first you have to build two more things: the peaks and the base.

PEAKS

The peaks are made in the usual "sandwich" way with extensions on the bottom for stability (Fig. 54X). The size of the peak depends on the height you desire and the size of the overhang to cover moldings or facings (Fig. 53; see Plates 25 and 26). To figure the width of peak in the example you need:

1. Inside dimension of the room—16″
2. Thickness of the front wall—⅜″ or ⁵⁄₁₆″
3. Thickness of back facing which covers raw edges of walls and floors—¹⁄₁₆″
4. Depth of front molding (see Plate 26), ⁵⁄₁₆″, minus the thickness of the roof (¹⁄₁₆″) and the thickness of the roofing (¹⁄₁₆″)—³⁄₁₆″
5. Same for back molding—³⁄₁₆″

The total for the peak at its widest part is then 16¹³⁄₁₆″.

On a piece of poster board, drawn a line 16¹³⁄₁₆″ long (AB). Mark the center (C) and make a perpendicular line at C to the desired height of the peak (D). Draw lines AD and BD. Cut out two of these pieces and construct a peak "sandwich" with framing extensions at the bottom for stability (Fig. 54X).

THE BASE

The base for the house is made of ¾″ plywood. Mark the dimensions of the house and add space for any landscaping you want. Cut the plywood. Attach ½″ × ¾″ wood strips to the base, with glue and screws around the edges and at several places in the center (Fig. 55). This keeps the wood from warping and provides a space for the electrical wiring.

The wires go from the wall plug to the transformer; from the transformer, through a hole drilled in the side of the base to the terminal strip; from the terminal strip, through holes in the base to the house (see Fig. 56 and Chapter 10). When the house is assembled, the wires from the base are led up through holes in the house wall studs and soldered to wiring already installed in the house wall. This way, no wiring is visible anywhere close to the house.

When the house is finished, the base is surrounded with decorative molding. ¾″ quarter round on the bottom part and a ¾″ flat or beaded molding on the top part is simple and attractive. Miter the corners and nail on the molding with finishing nails. Countersink the nail heads and fill in the holes with wood filler. Drill a hole in the molding to match the one in the base for the wire to pass through. After the house is assembled, put tape all around the base of the house and paint or stain and varnish the base. (You can paint the base before assembling the house but then you have to be careful not to drop paint on it, or scratch it, etc., which is sometimes inconvenient when you are working.)

STEPS IN ASSEMBLY

The house is assembled one room at a time. It is glued together and small nails are used wherever possible, around the edges of floors and

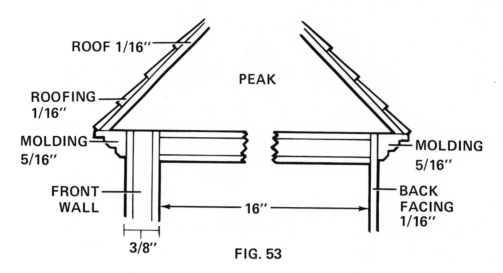

ROOF 1/16″

ROOFING 1/16″

MOLDING 5/16″

FRONT WALL

PEAK

MOLDING 5/16″

BACK FACING 1/16″

3/8″

16″

FIG. 53

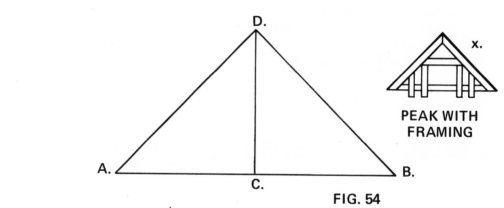

D.

A.

C.

B.

x.

PEAK WITH FRAMING

FIG. 54

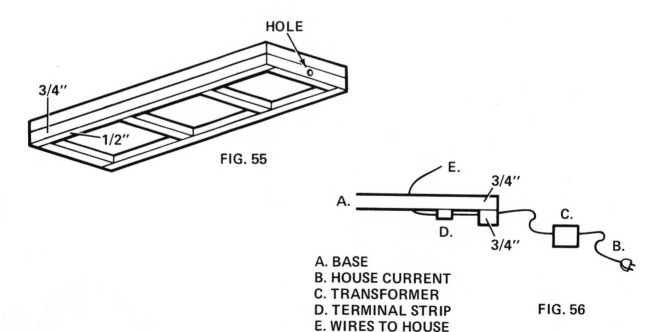

HOLE

3/4″

1/2″

FIG. 55

E.

A.

3/4″

D.

3/4″

C.

B.

A. BASE
B. HOUSE CURRENT
C. TRANSFORMER
D. TERMINAL STRIP
E. WIRES TO HOUSE

FIG. 56

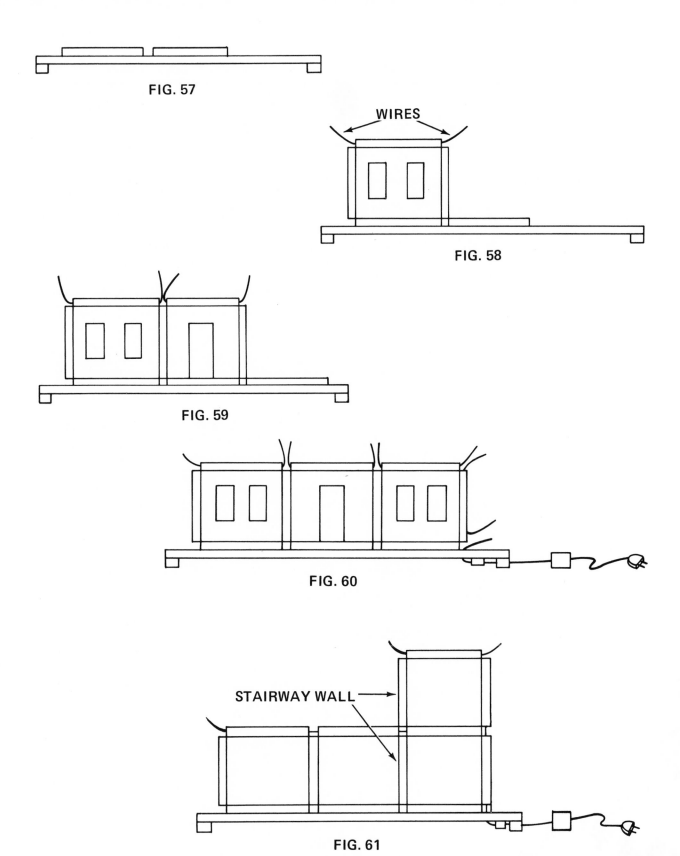

FIG. 57

WIRES

FIG. 58

FIG. 59

FIG. 60

STAIRWAY WALL

FIG. 61

ceilings. The wiring from each ceiling/floor unit can be connected as each room is added. The first twelve steps can now be done. The final steps involve decorating the exterior and are described in Chapter 14. But read through them now for an idea of how to proceed.

1. Construct the base with wiring installed (see Figs. 55 and 56).

2. On the base, glue and nail two plain floor sections (Fig. 57). If you have not done so already, add floor extensions and flooring between the rooms at the doorways.

3. Add three walls and a ceiling/floor section with glue and nails (Fig. 58).

4. Add another plain floor section, two walls, and a ceiling/floor section (Fig. 59). Continue until all first story walls, floors, and ceilings are assembled.

Note: On the early Colonial house plans, install the back hallway wall in the room where it belongs.

5. Solder the wiring connections between the ceiling/floor sections and between the end ceiling/floor section and the side wall. Lead the wires from the base into the side wall and solder the connections inside the wall (Fig. 60).

6. Do the second story in the same way as the first, counting the ceiling/floor sections already in place as plain floors. Start at the side of the house so that when you get to the stairway wall there will be easy access to the wall with no other walls around it (Fig. 61).

7. Patch the stairway wall. Install the staircase. Construct and install the stairwell railing.

8. Continue adding walls and ceiling/floors till the second story is complete. Connect wiring as before.

9. Install the peaks. Tack wood strips lightly across the peaks to hold them in position till you do the roof.

10. At the corners of the house, there will be an open space where the walls meet. Fill these in by gluing $\frac{1}{4}'' \times \frac{1}{8}''$ wood strips into the space. Other spaces, between walls and ceiling/floor sections, etc. need not be filled in.

11. Cut, fit, and glue poster board to the exterior of the house, fitting it around doors and windows.

12. Glue on $\frac{1}{16}''$ thick facing strips to cover the raw edges of the back walls, floors, and ceilings.

13. Construct, finish, and install the roofline moldings. (In the late Georgian house this may involve doing the whole front facade (see Plates 26 and 30)).

14. Glue on the corner posts.

15. Construct, install, and finish the peak moldings.

16. Construct the roof.

17. Construct, finish, and install the chimney, dormers, and roof ridge.

18. Construct, install, and finish the door facades.

19. Glue on the siding, fitting it around door facades, windows, corner posts, roofline, and peak moldings. Paint the siding, corner posts, and facings.

20. Install and finish the roofing material.

21. Construct, install, and finish window moldings or framing. Construct, finish, and install the shutters.

22. Add the decorative trim around the base and finish it.

Chapter 14
Decorating the Exterior

MOLDINGS AND CORNER POSTS

In most houses, there were covering strips or molding of some kind at the front and back of the house, at the roofline, and along the line of the peaks. In the earlier houses these were just plain, flat boards (⅜″ wide × ⅛″ thick). As styles developed, the moldings began to have simple shapes and by the Georgian period were quite elaborate (see Plates 25 and 26). The moldings suggested in this book are all ⅛″ thick at the bottom edge to accommodate the thickness of clapboard siding which was most commonly used. If you plan to use "brick" siding (see Chapter 7), you can adjust the thickness as you desire.

The early moldings are quite easy, just two or three different size wood strips glued together and shaped. The Georgian moldings become more complicated, but are easier to make than they may seem. Figure 62 is the Georgian roofline molding, but the same technique is used for assembling the other Georgian moldings.

First, paint all the wood with one or two thin coats of latex paint and sand lightly. Next, glue the back and top piece together. Then cut many short pieces of ⅛″ × ⅛″ stock. You need not be too exact in cutting; they will be trimmed later. Glue the short pieces to the back and top piece, spacing them ⅛″ apart (Fig. 62B). To do this, glue on one short piece, hold a separate ⅛″ × ⅛″ piece next to it and glue on the next short piece. Pull out the separate piece and the spacing is correct. Continue till all the short pieces are in place. When the glue is good and dry, with a sharp blade, trim the short pieces to match the top piece. Some may come unstuck. Just glue them back. Wrap or glue some sandpaper around a 4 or 5 inch long wood block. Sand the whole front edge smooth and shape the bottoms of the short pieces by rubbing the sanding block back and forth along the entire length of the molding strip. Repaint the sanded edges. Now glue on the ¹⁄₁₆″ × ¹⁄₁₆″ strips at the top of the molding strip, under the short pieces and at the bottom. Finish the molding strip with oil base interior semigloss enamel house paint or with latex interior house paint or acrylic paint and two coats of latex varnish. The moldings suggested are relatively easy to make but have an elaborate, classical look. You can design your own moldings, of course. The basic technique remains the same.

The roofline moldings belong on the front and back of the house and carry around the sides of the house for a short distance, to accommodate the peak line moldings. The corners must be mitered. The side pieces are cut off straight at the ends, and the peak line moldings glued on. Later when the siding is glued on, it is fitted around the molding. In the late Georgian house, the roofline molding can extend across the whole side of the house (see Plate 26).

After the roofline moldings are in place at the front, back, and sides of the house, glue on the peak moldings (Plates 25 and 26). You will note that while the early Georgian houses had rela-

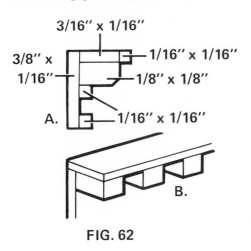

FIG. 62

3/16″ x 1/16″
3/8″ x 1/16″
1/16″ x 1/16″
1/8″ x 1/8″
A.
1/16″ x 1/16″
B.

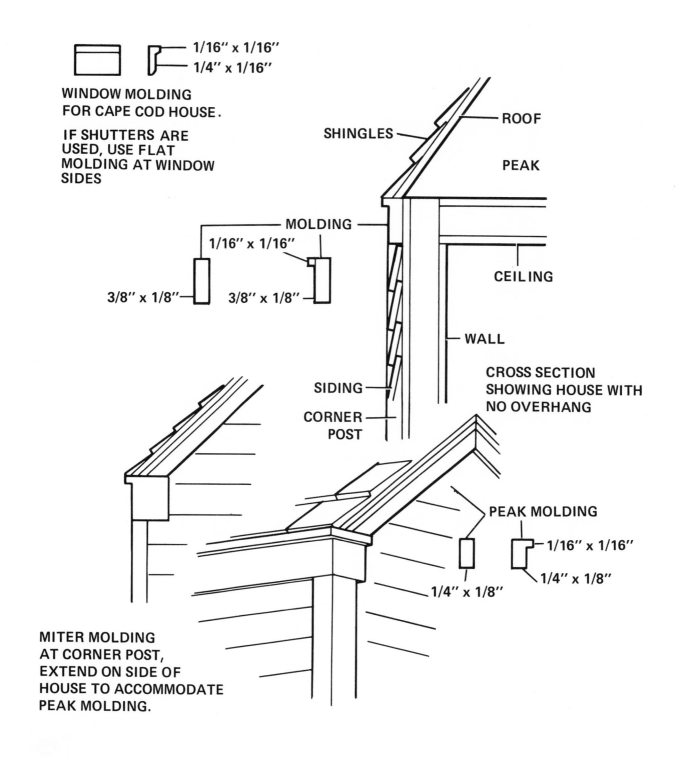

1/16″ x 1/16″
1/4″ x 1/16″

WINDOW MOLDING
FOR CAPE COD HOUSE.

IF SHUTTERS ARE
USED, USE FLAT
MOLDING AT WINDOW
SIDES

MOLDING

1/16″ x 1/16″

3/8″ x 1/8″   3/8″ x 1/8″

SHINGLES

ROOF

PEAK

CEILING

WALL

CROSS SECTION
SHOWING HOUSE WITH
NO OVERHANG

SIDING

CORNER
POST

PEAK MOLDING

1/16″ x 1/16″

1/4″ x 1/8″

1/4″ x 1/8″

MITER MOLDING
AT CORNER POST,
EXTEND ON SIDE OF
HOUSE TO ACCOMMODATE
PEAK MOLDING.

DETAILS FOR EARLY COLONIAL

ONE AND TWO STORY HOUSES

PLATE 25

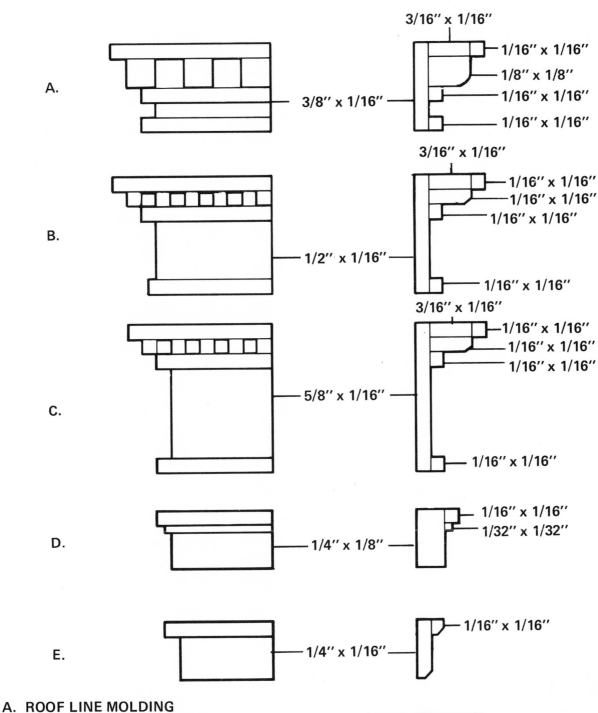

3/16" x 1/16"

A.

1/16" x 1/16"
1/8" x 1/8"
1/16" x 1/16"
1/16" x 1/16"

3/8" x 1/16"

3/16" x 1/16"

B.

1/16" x 1/16"
1/16" x 1/16"
1/16" x 1/16"

1/2" x 1/16"

1/16" x 1/16"

3/16" x 1/16"

C.

1/16" x 1/16"
1/16" x 1/16"
1/16" x 1/16"

5/8" x 1/16"

1/16" x 1/16"

D.

1/16" x 1/16"
1/32" x 1/32"

1/4" x 1/8"

E.

1/16" x 1/16"

1/4" x 1/16"

A. ROOF LINE MOLDING
B. WINDOW CORNICE MOLDING
C. DOOR CORNICE MOLDING
D. PEAK MOLDING
E. WINDOW MOLDING

SCALE [⊔⊔⊔⊔⊔⊔⊔] =1/2"

SUGGESTED GEORGIAN MOLDINGS

PLATE 26A

SHINGLES

ROOF

PEAK

CEILING

WALL

CORNER POST

CROSS SECTION
OF EARLY
GEORGIAN WITH
OVERHANG

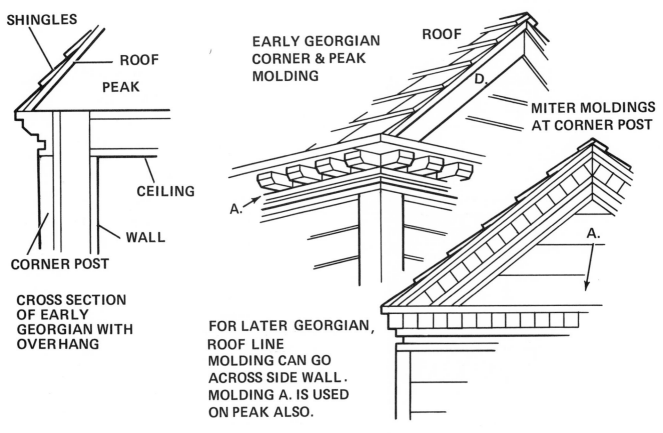

EARLY GEORGIAN
CORNER & PEAK
MOLDING

ROOF

D.

MITER MOLDINGS
AT CORNER POST

A.

A.

FOR LATER GEORGIAN,
ROOF LINE
MOLDING CAN GO
ACROSS SIDE WALL.
MOLDING A. IS USED
ON PEAK ALSO.

FRONT
PEAK EXTENDS
TO FIT PILASTER
AND MOLDING.

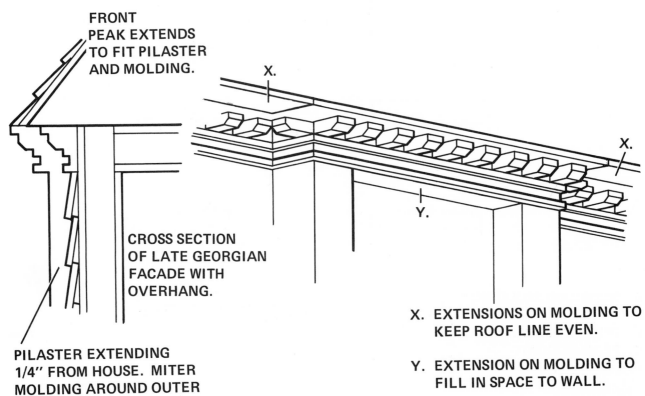

X.

X.

Y.

CROSS SECTION
OF LATE GEORGIAN
FACADE WITH
OVERHANG.

PILASTER EXTENDING
1/4" FROM HOUSE. MITER
MOLDING AROUND OUTER
EDGES.

X. EXTENSIONS ON MOLDING TO
KEEP ROOF LINE EVEN.

Y. EXTENSION ON MOLDING TO
FILL IN SPACE TO WALL.

GEORGIAN DETAILS

PLATE 26 B

tively plain peak moldings; the later Georgians used the heavy moldings for the peak line also.

Most clapboard-sided houses also had corner posts. These give a neat appearance to the corners of the house and are $\frac{1}{8}''$ thick to accommodate the siding. They are glued on as shown in Fig. 63 and run from the base of the house up to the roofline molding. Sand the joint smooth.

Siding

Clapboard siding is made from $\frac{1}{2}'' \times \frac{1}{32}''$ wood strips, glued onto the house and to each other, overlapping the strips slightly. If you use white glue, apply it in small dots so the wood will not curl or warp. This siding can be painted with latex or flat enamel interior house paint.

Shake siding is made the same as for roofing material, and is also applied and finished the same. See "Roofing Materials" in this chapter.

Brick and stone are done the same as for fireplaces. See Chapter 7.

The Roof

Before finishing the roof or the ridge, see "Chimneys" in this chapter. The roof can be any material you desire, but unless you plan to sit on it, $\frac{1}{16}''$ thick poster board is strong enough. Remember it will be strengthened from inside by the peaks and with wood strip "rafters." Poster board is $30'' \times 40''$ so it should be long enough for your roof. If your roof is longer than 40 inches, two pieces of poster board can be butted together and the joint taped all around both sides of the board. Wide paper tape (the kind used for sealing packages) is good.

In the basic house, the front half of the roof is attached to the peaks and the back half lifts off for easy access to the light panels to replace burnt out bulbs. Lay the poster board on the peaks with the bottom resting on the roofline molding. Mark the top edge at the top of the peaks. Also mark the overhang, if any, at the sides of the roof. Cut on the marks. Do the second half of the roof.

The ridge of the roof is made of wood strips glued and pinned together to form an upside down V-shape. It is glued to the back half of the roof and keeps it from sliding off the house (Fig. 64). You can also put small screws through

the roof into the peaks, if you like, for added stability. The screwheads, when painted to match the roofing material, will be inconspicuous. One or two at each end are sufficient. The ridge can be made from $\frac{3}{8}'' \times \frac{1}{8}''$ and $\frac{1}{4}'' \times \frac{1}{8}''$ wood

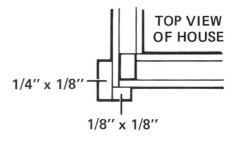

TOP VIEW OF HOUSE

1/4" x 1/8"

1/8" x 1/8"

FIG. 63

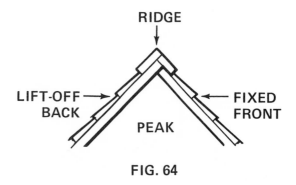

RIDGE

LIFT-OFF BACK

FIXED FRONT

PEAK

FIG. 64

A.

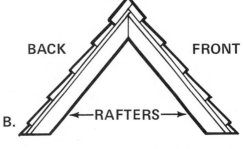

BACK

FRONT

B.

←RAFTERS→

FIG. 65

FIG. 66

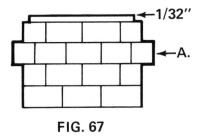

FIG. 67

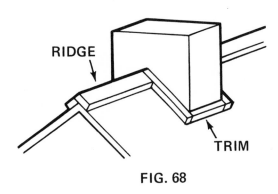

FIG. 68

strips or $\frac{1}{8}'' \times \frac{1}{4}''$ and $\frac{1}{8}'' \times \frac{1}{8}''$ wood strips. The first is stronger; the second more attractive. Even more attractive is $\frac{1}{4}'' \times \frac{1}{16}''$ and $\frac{3}{16}'' \times \frac{1}{16}''$, but this has very little strength and should not be used unless the roof will also be held in place with screws.

For a strong roof, brace it with wood framework rafters between the peaks as shown in Fig. 65A. You will have to shape the rafters where the back and front sets meet at the top of the roof and at the base (Fig. 65B). Best of all is to glue poster board to the inside rafter sections. This way, the entire roof will be a strong "sandwich" except where it rests on the peaks.

Perhaps you would like to have the attic rooms open to view. If so, omit the back half of the roof. The peaks, then, should have no overhang

at the back and their raw edges are covered with $\frac{5}{8}'' \times \frac{1}{16}''$ facing strips as are the other wall, floor, and ceiling edges.

CHIMNEYS

Chimneys are made after the roof has been planned but before the ridge or roofing material is installed. With the poster board halves of the roof tacked lightly in place on the peaks, hold a small piece of poster board at the end of the roof. Mark the upside down V-shape of the roof on the board. Plan which size chimney you desire. Remember that chimneys should not be wider or deeper outside the house on the roof than the fireplace structures are inside the house. That is, if the depth of the fireplace is $1\frac{1}{2}''$ inside, the chimney should be no deeper outside than $1\frac{1}{2}''$ finished with its brick added. The width of the finished chimney should be narrower than the width of the fireplace.

The chimney is basically a four-sided structure of poster board, braced on the inside with wood strips at the corners and covered with "brick" on the outside (see Chapter 7). $\frac{1}{4}'' \times \frac{1}{8}''$ wood strips are glued on around the inside top edge of the chimney to give it the appearance of thickness (Fig. 66). The decorative style of chimney shapes and tops is varied, but Fig. 67 shows a usable shape. At the top is $\frac{1}{32}''$ thick wood glued on and painted to simulate a concrete facing. The added brick trim (A) is simply a second layer of brick glued over the first. $\frac{1}{4}''$ thick wood pieces can be glued inside the chimney to simulate the flues and the inside painted dark grey with black "soot" marks.

Once the chimney is finished, place it on the roof which is still unfinished. Since the back half of the roof lifts off, the chimney must be glued to it and lift off too. Mark all around the chimney. For a neat appearance it is best to glue $\frac{1}{8}'' \times \frac{1}{8}''$ strips around the marks for the chimney on both sides of the roof. This not only helps the appearance and forms a space on the front half of the roof for the chimney to fit into, but it covers any small construction errors at the base of the chimney if it does not fit perfectly. The upside down V of the roof ridge is then glued on to the back roof half at either side of the $\frac{1}{8}'' \times \frac{1}{8}''$ chimney trim (Fig. 68).

DORMERS

Since the dormers for the basic house are not part of any room which will be seen, the insides need not be finished. (If, in your plans, they *are* part of a viewable room, they must be finished inside to match the room and installed in an opening cut in the roof.)

Dormers are made around windows (Fig. 69). Make a window and glue 1/4″ × 1/8″ wood strips all around it to accommodate the exterior molding. See Plate 9 for exterior window molding. The poster board sides of the dormer are cut to fit the slant of the roof. Brace the dormer at the inside corners, around the inside edges and at two or three places across the back with 1/8″ × 1/8″ wood. Hold the dormer in place on the roof and mark around it as you did for the chimney. 1/8″ × 1/8″ wood strips on the outsides and at the bottom of the dormer adds to the neat appearance. Make the dormer, glue it to the roof, and add the 1/8″ × 1/8″ trim. Then add corner posts (1/8″ × 1/8″) similar to those at the corners of the main house, and siding to match the house. Glue on a piece of poster board for the dormer roof and later, add roofing material to match the main roof.

DOOR FACADES

For door facades, see Plates 27 through 30. These will give you a general idea of the proportions and sizes of wood to use. If you are doing your own facade, it is a good idea to work it out on graph paper in 1″ = 1′ scale. In Plates 27 through 30 some things, such as porches, are shown on only one Plate and are the same on other Plates. For moldings used on the facades, see Plates 25 and 26.

Door facades are built up of wood strips of various sizes. As usual, in the earliest houses, the facades were just plain unshaped boards and as the styles developed, they became more and more elaborate until, by the late Georgian times, the facades had side windows, moldings, cornices, and even pilasters which ran from the base of the house to the roofline moldings and Palladian windows (Plate 30). The drawings show the various sizes of wood needed. The facades can be built directly on the front of the house. If you are designing your own facade, just remember to keep the thickness of 1/8″ or more around the edges to accommodate the siding.

Just a few reminders and hints. The Cape Cod facade (Plate 28) overlaps the roofline molding

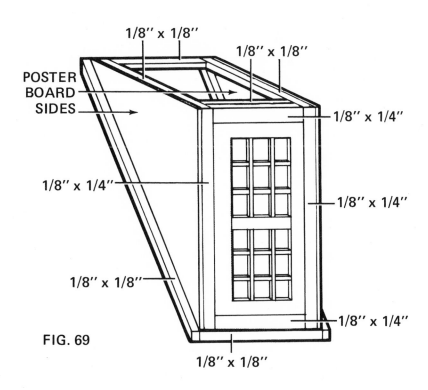

FIG. 69

ALL MOLDING AND TRIM FLAT

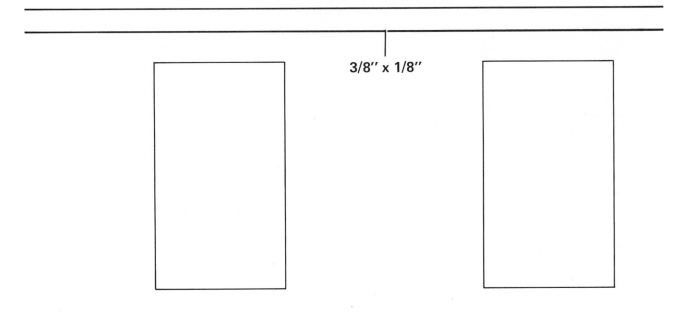

3/8'' x 1/8''

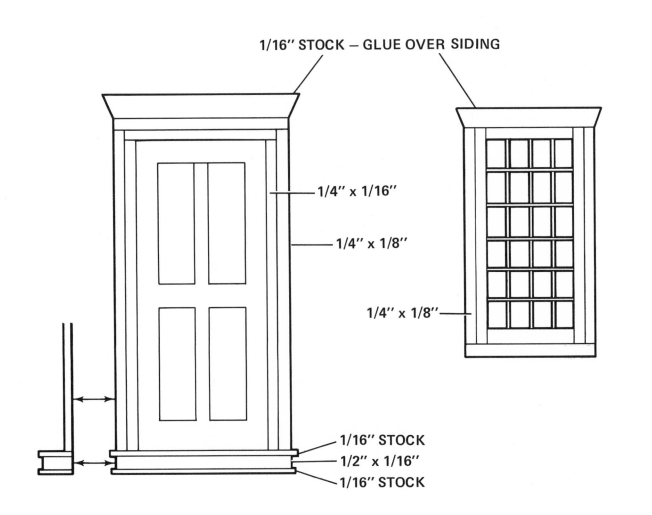

1/16'' STOCK — GLUE OVER SIDING

1/4'' x 1/16''

1/4'' x 1/8''

1/4'' x 1/8''

1/16'' STOCK

1/2'' x 1/16''

1/16'' STOCK

PLATE 27

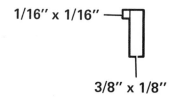

ROOF LINE
MOLDING

1/16" x 1/16" —

3/8" x 1/8"

WINDOW MOLDING

NOTE: 5/8" x 1/16" THICK PIECES AND 1/16" TRIM AT TOP OF
         PILASTERS ARE ADDED TO OVERLAP ROOF LINE MOLDING

5/8" x 1/16"

ROOF LINE MOLDING

1/16" x 1/16"

1/16" STOCK

1/4" x 1/16"

5/8" x 1/8"

SHUTTER

1/8" x 1/16"

3/16" x 1/16"

3 1/16" PIECES

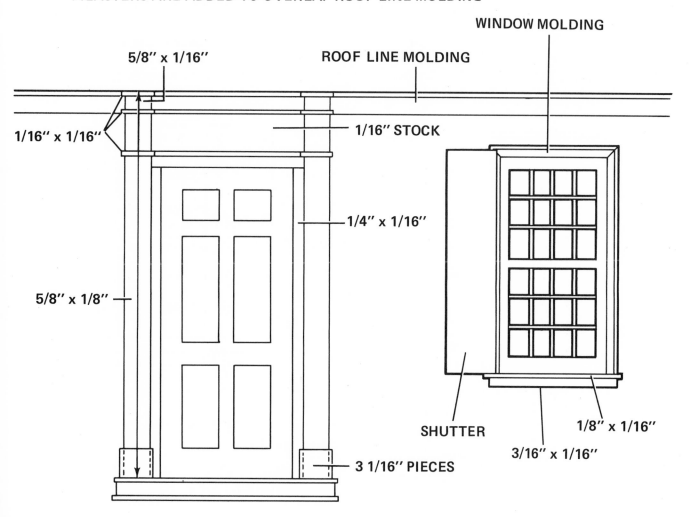

CAPE COD FACADE

PLATE 28

FOR MOLDING, SEE PLATE 26

A.

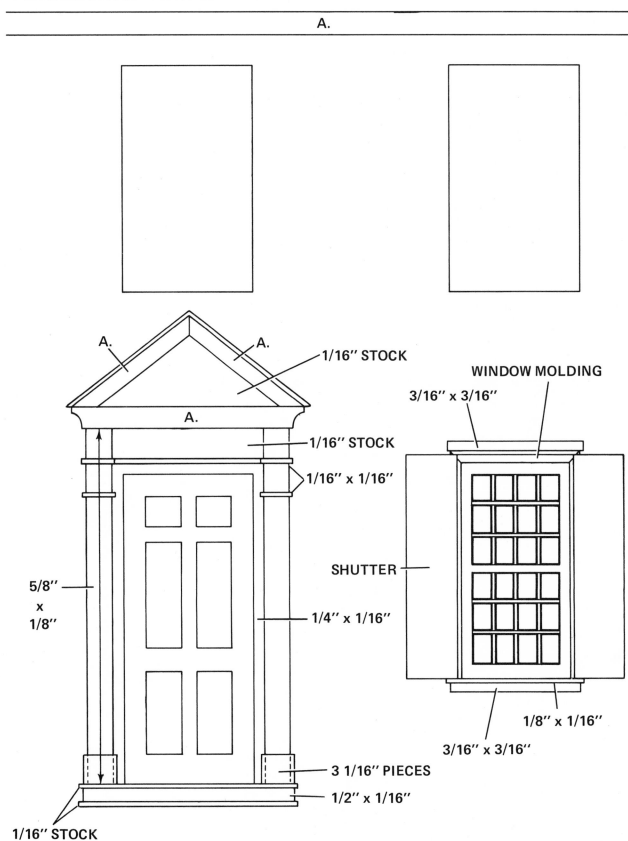

A.

A.

1/16" STOCK

A.

1/16" STOCK

1/16" x 1/16"

WINDOW MOLDING

3/16" x 3/16"

SHUTTER

5/8"
x
1/8"

1/4" x 1/16"

3 1/16" PIECES

1/2" x 1/16"

1/16" STOCK

1/8" x 1/16"

3/16" x 3/16"

PLATE 29

LATE GEORGIAN FACADE

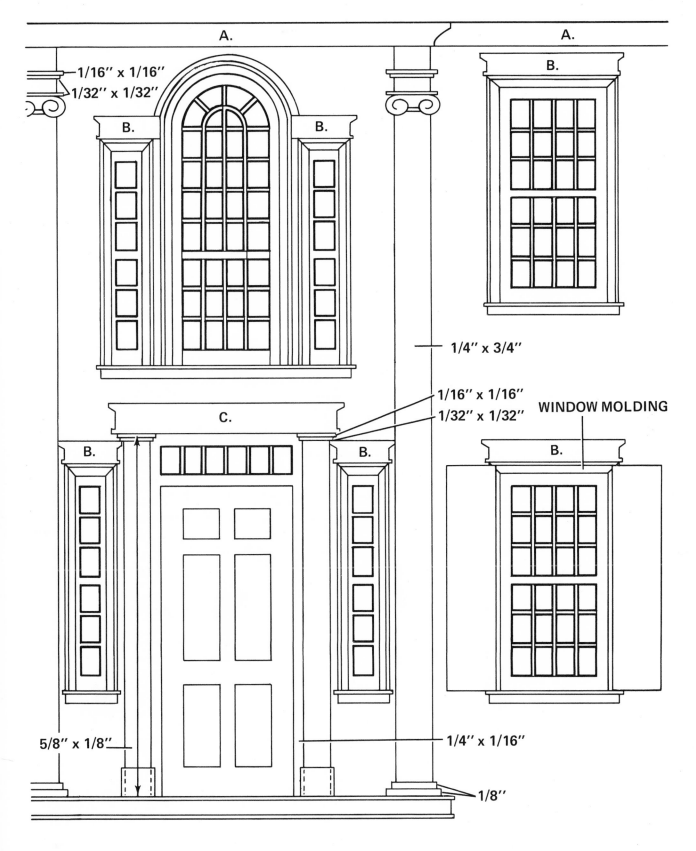

A.

A.

1/16" x 1/16"

1/32" x 1/32"

B.

B.

B.

B.

1/4" x 3/4"

1/16" x 1/16"

1/32" x 1/32"

WINDOW MOLDING

C.

B.

B.

B.

5/8" x 1/8"

1/4" x 1/16"

1/8"

PLATE 30

to $\frac{1}{16}''$ thickness. This can be planned for in an overhang on the peak, but since a house of that type will probably have shake shingles, you can glue a $\frac{1}{32}''$ thick wood strip along the front edge of the roof and allow the shingles to extend a little farther out to cover the $\frac{1}{16}''$ overlap. Irregularities in a shake roof only add to its charm.

In the early Georgian facade (Plate 29), the triangular pediment over the door is made of molding strips glued to the house. After the siding is glued to the house, you might want to put a little roof on the pediment. Use $\frac{1}{16}''$ thick poster board and roofing material to match the house roof.

The late Georgian facade (Plate 30), takes some extra planning. The thickness of the added pilasters and their moldings must be planned for in the overhang of the peaks. The underside of the peaks, not covered by the regular roofline molding is faced with $\frac{1}{16}''$ thick wood to cover the open spaces. This is not a large problem (see Plate 26).

To make the Ionic scrolls shown in Plate 30, start with a block of wood, or two or three pieces of wood glued together. For the scroll shape, carve and sand the wood block to the basic form (Fig. 70). Carve the top of the pilaster to fit the scroll shape (Fig. 70). The scroll itself can be

done two ways. String can be glued around the edge and into the center of the basic shape. Coat the face of the scroll with several coats of white glue to soften and blend the edges of the string (Fig. 70A). Or, the scroll can be carved out with a Dremel tool, if you have one, or burned out with a wood-burning tool with a narrow tip on it. The burnt out area can be further deepened and shaped by pressing and drawing around the scroll with the point of a pencil (Fig. 70B). When the completed scroll shape is glued to the pilaster, the little piece between the scroll halves is added to cover the joint (Fig. 70C). This is just a piece of heavy paper. When doing the heavy moldings around the pilasters, the corners must be mitered and the exposed areas on the underside of the peaks faced with $\frac{1}{16}''$ thick wood.

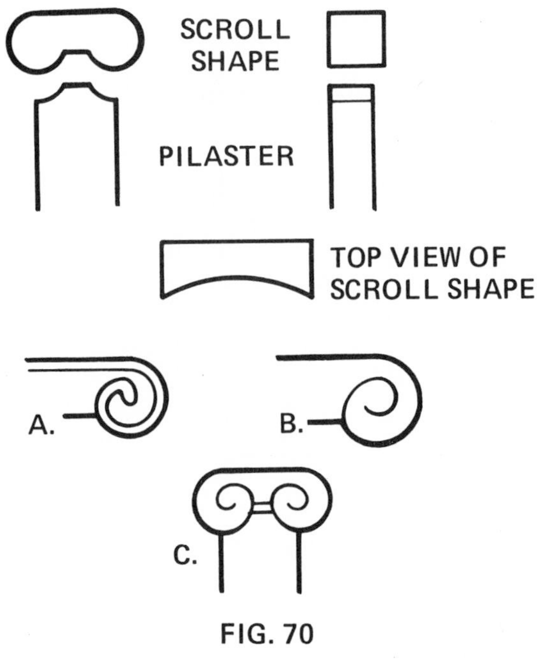

One last word to the imaginative builder. If you prefer Corinthian capitals on the pilasters, they can be done. The Acanthus leaves are simply cut from heavy paper and given several coats of white glue for added stiffness. The leaf is then dampened to soften the glue, curved to shape, and held till the glue dries and hardens again.

ROOFING MATERIALS

Three popular roofing materials are shingles, wood shakes, and slate. Shingles can be made from very fine sandpaper and painted dark, or you can use Wetordry sandpaper which is already dark. The sandpaper can be left as is, or backed with other paper or even thin cardboard for extra thickness if you like. Cut the sandpaper in narrow strips and, with scissors, cut the shingle widths about $\frac{3}{4}$ of the way through the strip (Fig. 71A). Glue the strips on the roof, staggering the cuts and overlapping the rows. Hexagonal shingles can be done also as shown (Fig. 71B).

FIG. 70

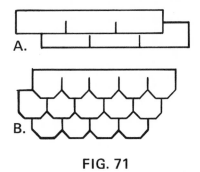

FIG. 71

Shake shingles are fun. They are made from $\frac{1}{32}''$ balsa strips cut across the grain. The cut edges can be left rough for a more rustic look. To make the individual shakes, just snap off pieces of the balsa strip. The random width of the shakes is what gives the roof charm, so in snapping off the shakes do not try to make them even. The shakes are then glued on the roof one by one in rows, overlapping the rows. The shakes are then stained and accented with thinned antiquing ink. They need no other finish.

Slate is made somewhat like shakes and shingles, combined. Making individual slate pieces, from $\frac{1}{32}''$ thick balsa, is authentic but unless you are careful in gluing on the pieces, the effect can be more irregular than you want. Instead, start with a sheet of $\frac{1}{32}''$ balsa, sand the edge across the grain smooth, cut off a narrow strip (as for shingles) and glue it on the roof. With the end of a screwdriver blade, press through the soft balsa, making cuts about $\frac{3}{4}$ of the way up, as for shingles. Make the widths almost, but not quite equal. To get the rough squarish texture of slate, impress the soft balsa with the flat side of the screwdriver blade. The second row of slate strips is glued on to the roof, the rows overlapped and the cuts staggered. This gives a natural, but not too irregular look. In making the vertical cuts for the second and following rows, some care must be taken not to make cuts in the slates of the preceding row. But do not over worry, small mistakes will not show much and large ones can be filled in with wood filler.

To paint the slate, start with a basic cool, blue gray or warm, yellow gray, whichever you like, using water base paints. As in painting bricks for a soft effect, paint individual slates lighter or darker, more or less warm or cool. Some slate roofs even have slates of different colors in them, red gray, green or brown grey. A dark brown acrylic paint wash or antiquing ink accents the slate texture and sinks into the spaces between the slates. Two coats of latex varnish or one coat of semi-gloss oil base varnish give a soft, not too shiny finish.

Window Moldings and Shutters

Again, as usual, the early window trims were plain flat pieces of wood. As the houses devel-

oped, the trim became more elaborate, but not terribly so. The early houses had plain boards on all four sides. Really they were part of the house framework (see Plate 27). There was sometimes a simple sill (a $\frac{1}{16}'' \times \frac{1}{16}''$ wood strip) added at the window level. Sometimes, also, there was a triangular or other shaped decorative trim at the top of the window. All the trim was flat, cut-out pieces, glued on over the siding.

The early Georgian houses had simple moldings at the top and sides of the windows and a sill at the bottom, exactly like the interior moldings (see Plate 9). The Cape Cod house had the same simply shaped window moldings as the Georgian house. Sometimes there was a plain heavier piece of wood ($\frac{3}{32}'' \times \frac{3}{32}''$ or $\frac{1}{8}'' \times \frac{1}{8}''$) added at the top of the Georgian window for accent (see Plate 29).

The window moldings and sill were the same as above for the late Georgian houses, but there was a dentil molding added above the window (see Plates 26 and 30).

In the plans given, the window frames stick out from the front of the house (Fig. 16B) to accommodate the clapboard siding. After the siding is glued on, the exterior window trim is glued onto the frame (overlapping it) and over the siding. It may be necessary to sand the frames down a bit, level with the siding. In the Cape Cod and Georgian houses, the sill is made by adding a $\frac{1}{8}'' \times \frac{1}{16}''$ wood strip to the window frame to form the sill (see Plate 15). The $\frac{3}{16}'' \times \frac{1}{16}''$ piece is added under that, glued on flat against the siding.

If you are using shutters, it is wise to keep the window moldings flat at the sides of the window. Otherwise, the shutters stick out at an angle. Just cut away the $\frac{1}{16}'' \times \frac{1}{16}''$ piece on the window moldings where the shutters will be. To make the shutters, start with $\frac{3}{16}'' \times \frac{1}{32}''$ wood strips. The length depends on how many shutters you want and how wide they are to be. Figure about $1''$ to $1\frac{1}{4}''$ per shutter. Glue the strips to a thin paper backing, overlapping the strips. When the glue is good and dry, cut this big piece into smaller pieces, the width of the center part of the shutter (Fig. 72A). On another paper backing, glue $\frac{1}{16}''$ thick wood strips around the center part to complete the shutter (Fig. 72B). The shutters are painted and glued to the window

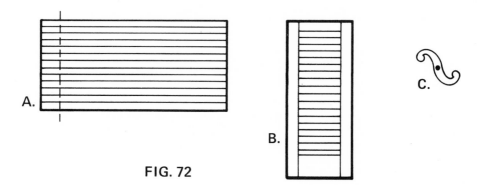

FIG. 72

molding and siding.

The little S-shaped brackets often used to hold the shutters open can be cut from thin aluminum pop cans or heavy paper (Fig. 72C). A hole is made to hold a pin. This simulates the bolt which holds the bracket to the house. A dot of glue will also suggest this. The bracket is painted, and pinned or glued in place.

Chapter 15
Furniture

Many of the furniture designs in this book are made from "built-up" shapes rather than carved out shapes. With this method, furniture shapes ordinarily beyond the beginning or intermediate craftsman, can easily be obtained. Many shapes are built up from various materials: mostly basswood, wood or pearl beads, and string. To cover the various building materials, the finished furniture is painted and antiqued rather than stained. (A water base stain, though, can be used because it is heavy and will cover.)

I am personally fond of this built-up method because it gives the builder a way to make very delicate turnings without using a jeweller's lathe which is often a very expensive tool (Dremel, however, does make one for a reasonable price.) Also, this method requires no unusual skill, but produces skillful-looking results.

I am personally also fond of the paint and antiquing finish, for two reasons. First, it covers a multitude of small mistakes, which for me are inevitable. Second, real wood grain, in miniature, is twelve times too large. To me, the paint and antiquing finish, if well done, looks more like wood in miniature than real wood does (see "Painting Furniture").

Many of the designs in this book do not use the built-up method and can be done in fine woods. Really, all the designs are to learn on. Designing your own furniture is the true goal.

HOLES AND INSERTS

You should always build for a good shape and strong construction. Whenever possible, especially in chairs, pieces should be put together with inserts into holes (Fig. 73). Inserts can be made on round or square pieces. At the end of the chair rung (or any piece) make a mark where the insert is to be and, with a mat knife, make a shallow cut all around the piece (Fig. 73A). A

way to do this on a dowel is to lay the dowel on a flat surface, hold the knife on the mark and, pressing on the knife, roll the dowel under it. Carve away a bit of wood at the mark (Fig. 73B), then carve away the excess wood to form the insert (Fig. 73C). Smooth the insert with an emery board, so it is round.

The hole to receive the insert is then drilled in the chair leg. It can be drilled all the way through the leg. To drill a $\frac{1}{16}''$ hole properly, first mark where the hole is to be. Next, push or hammer a straight pin into the mark. It does not have to go very deep. Remove the pin. Now drill a $\frac{1}{32}''$ hole through the leg in the "pilot hole" made by the pin. Then drill a $\frac{1}{16}''$ hole in the $\frac{1}{32}''$ "pilot hole." This sounds like a lot of

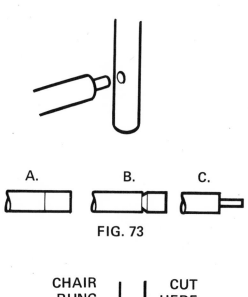

A.   B.   C.

FIG. 73

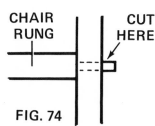

CHAIR RUNG   CUT HERE

FIG. 74

work but drill bits tend to slip somewhat without pilot holes, and in miniature a little slippage can throw things all out of kilter.

The two pieces are then joined together with glue (Fig. 74). If the insert is too long, trim it off and sand the leg smooth. If it is too short, fill in the hole with wood filler and sand smooth. This makes a good strong construction and a painted finish covers where the pieces are joined. This is a lot easier than trying to get the length of the insert and the depth of the hole exact. This hole and insert construction is absolutely essential on the seats of chairs which are to have woven rush seats!

Some pieces are too small for the hole and insert construction. Here the pieces are strengthened with straight pins. For this, the pieces are glued together first. Then a hole is drilled through both pieces and a pin inserted. A hole is drilled to receive the pin because if you try to push the pin in, the wood will probably split. Clip off the head of the pin with a wire clipper (Fig. 75) and push the excess pin in flush with the wood. Regular straight pins in $1/32''$ holes are good for most things but lill pins in a smaller hole may be needed for more delicate things.

Some things such as drawers for chests can be put together with glue alone but wherever possible build for strength.

SIMPLE CARVING ON A DOWEL

Simple carving can be done on a dowel for chair legs and other turnings. Mark the dowel for the major divisions (Fig. 76A). With a mat knife, make shallow cuts all around the dowel. Next, with the knife carve away a small bit of wood at the cuts (Fig. 76B). Refine the shape by carving away more wood where necessary (Fig. 76C). Finish the shaping by sanding with an emery board or sandpaper (Fig. 76D). For a final smooth finish, wrap some fine steel wool around the shape. Hold this in one hand and with the other hand, rotate the carved dowel.

Sometimes you need a tapered dowel, perhaps for a table leg or simple chair back. To taper a dowel, carve the general shape you need (Fig. 77A). Then, holding a piece of sandpaper in the palm of one hand, wrap the dowel in the sandpaper and rotate the dowel with the other hand. This way the dowel is tapered evenly all around.

Finish off with steel wool as described before for a smooth finish (Fig. 77B).

A BUILT-UP SHAPE

The shape in Fig. 78 is the leg of a 1700 joint stool (see Plate 45). It is absolutely the most complicated built-up shape in all the plans in this book. I am using it as an example because it shows, in one piece, almost all the techniques used for built-up shapes. Do not let it scare you. The techniques are easy, taken one step at a time.

The top piece (1) is $3/16'' \times 3/16''$ basswood stock. A $1/16''$ hole is drilled in one end to receive the small insert carved on the $1/16''$ dowel (2). (To make the insert, see Fig. 73.) Once the $1/16''$

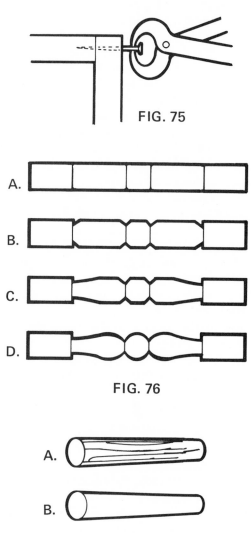

FIG. 75

A.

B.

C.

D.

FIG. 76

A.

B.

FIG. 77

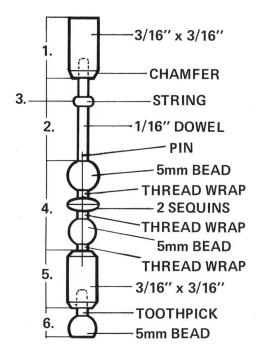

FIG. 78

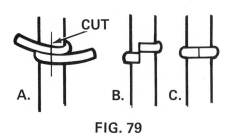

FIG. 79

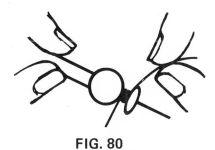

FIG. 80

dowel is glued in place in the ³⁄₁₆″ × ³⁄₁₆″ piece, shape the chamfered (beveled) edge with an emery board held at an angle.

The turning on the dowel (3) is a piece of string. It can be cotton crochet thread or ship rigging cord. Coat the string with glue and wrap

it around the dowel. As the glue dries, cut through both pieces (Fig. 79A) with a very sharp blade and remove the excess (Fig. 79B). Then adjust the ends so they are even (Fig. 79C). A dot of glue at the joint helps to smooth it.

The next section (Fig. 78, 4) called a ball and ring turning is made on a straight pin with the head clipped off. The round ball shapes are 5 millimeter beads, slightly flattened on the ends. The beads used are common simulated pearl beads. Wooden beads are always lovely to use and preferable to pearl, but they are often hard to find. To flatten a bead, put it on a toothpick and with an emery board sand down the bead just a bit.

The center "ring" turning is two sequins glued together. Sequins have a concave shape. To glue them together, load one of the concave sequins with glue and put the second one on top. Let the glue dry. This turning can also be made by sawing a thin slice from a ³⁄₁₆″ dowel. First, drill a hole in the center and then cut the slice with a razor saw. The rounded edges can be sanded later when the leg is assembled.

Next, drill a pin hole in the ¹⁄₁₆″ dowel (Fig. 78, 2) and the lower ³⁄₁₆″ × ³⁄₁₆″ piece (5). Now insert the pin into the dowel with glue. Slip one flattened 5mm bead, with glue, onto the pin. Next slip the two glued-together sequins on the pin. To keep these pieces separated as shown in Fig. 78, coat some sewing thread with glue and wrap the thread evenly around and around the pin (Fig. 80); 10 or 12 times is usually enough. Put the second 5mm bead on the pin and also the lower ³⁄₁₆″ × ³⁄₁₆″ piece. Make "thread wraps" between the 2 sequin turning and the second 5mm bead and also between the second bead and the lower ³⁄₁₆″ × ³⁄₁₆″ piece (5). When the glue dries on the thread wraps, trim off the excess ends with a sharp blade.

All the parts are put together with white glue. This has two purposes. First, it holds everything together. Second, the glue sort of oozes out between the separate parts and blends them together to make a smooth transition between the pieces. You can further smooth the glue with a damp paintbrush.

Now, put on the foot (Fig. 78, 6). This is a flattened and shaped 5mm bead glued on a toothpick, which is then carved down a bit and cut off to form an insert (Fig. 81).

Drill a $\frac{1}{16}''$ hole in the lower $\frac{3}{16}'' \times \frac{3}{16}''$ square piece (Fig. 78, 5), and insert the foot assembly with glue. Bevel the edges of the $\frac{3}{16}'' \times \frac{3}{16}''$ piece as before and the leg is done.

Figure 82 shows another popular turning. Sometimes, as on the bannister chair in Plate 48, there will be several on one leg. The square pieces are first drilled to take pin inserts. The upper square piece is carved to the shape shown in Fig. 82B. It is easier to drill a hole and then carve than drill a hole in the smaller carved area.

Figure 83 shows how to obtain odd size square wood. $\frac{5}{32}'' \times \frac{5}{32}''$ is not a standard size. To make it, glue two pieces of $\frac{1}{32}''$ thick wood to a standard $\frac{1}{8}'' \times \frac{1}{8}''$ wood strip (Fig. 83A). When the glue is dry, cut away the excess, sand the joints smooth and you have the required $\frac{5}{32}'' \times \frac{5}{32}''$ wood strip (Fig. 83B).

You can see that a great variety of shapes can be achieved. Painting and antiquing covers the varied building materials. The biggest advantage of this built-up method is that in making more than one chair or table leg, since you are working with equal size materials, the legs will automatically come out matching in size. Believe me, four matching legs with complex turnings are virtually impossible to carve by hand.

CARVING ON FLAT WOOD

Often flat wood pieces need some carving, such as crest rails on chairs, table legs, mirror frames, etc. For this the grain of the wood must be taken into consideration (Fig. 84A). Do the inside curve first. Cut a little way into the curve on both sides (Fig. 89B). The wood between the cuts will split with the grain of the wood and just fall out or can be carved out. Continue carving into the curve a little at a time until the complete curve is carved. Smooth the curve with sandpaper. The outside curve can then be carved out easily.

Figure 85A shows a table leg with inside and outside curves. Notice that the main part of the leg goes with the grain of the wood. Figure 85B shows the leg with the inside curves cut. The outside curves are then cut to finish the leg (Fig. 85C). This type of leg is usually used as the base of a three-legged table (Fig. 85D). For uniformity, the three legs can be cut to the basic shape,

then held together with a dot or two of white glue and all the edges sanded at one time (Fig. 85E). The legs can then be wet a bit to loosen the glue and be pulled apart. The top edges of

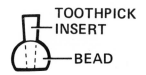

FIG. 81

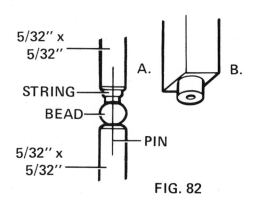

FIG. 82

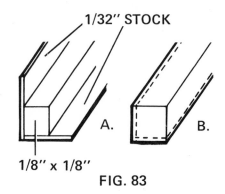

FIG. 83

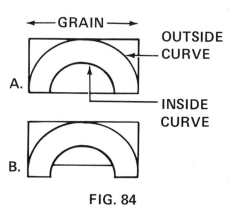

FIG. 84

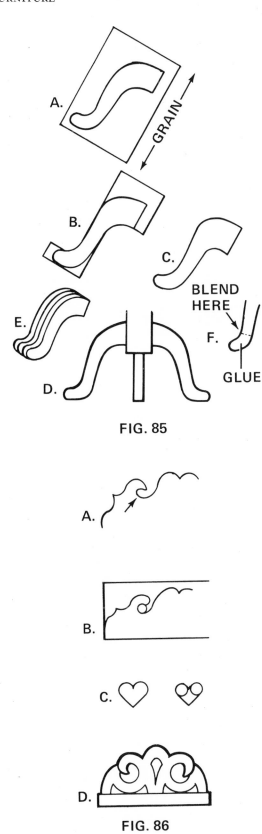

FIG. 85

FIG. 86

the legs are then rounded slightly with an emery board. These legs are basically flat, but perhaps you would like a little added fullness at the feet. For this, dip the foot in white glue (Fig. 85F). As the glue dries, blend the glue into the leg with a damp paintbrush. You may need to dip it several times to get enough fullness. When the leg is painted and finished the "glue fullness" at the foot will look like an integral part of the leg.

Some shapes are more complicated (Fig. 86A). To get that little extreme inside curve (arrow) you can drill out a hole (Fig. 86B) and then carve down to the hole. Tiny Swiss files are very useful here, if you have them. Sometimes when carving complicated curves, it is a good idea to glue the wood to a paper backing. If the wood does split with the grain where you do not want it to, the paper holds it in place till it can be glued back together. When the shape is all carved the paper can be dampened and rubbed off gently.

Heart shapes in Pennsylvania German furniture (Fig. 86C) are done by drilling two holes side by side and carving or filing out the rest of the shape.

The carved crest rail on the bannister back chair in Plate 48 is done in much the same way. The "carving" (Fig. 86D) is made of gold decit paper, glued on a wood base. Decit paper is an embossed paper and comes in many designs and shapes. Cut out the parts of the decit you want to form your desired crest rail design. Glue them onto a piece of wood. The spaces between the decit design are then drilled and carved, or filed out as described before. The finished piece, because of the three-dimensional decit paper, looks like intricate carving. Painting and antiquing accents the effect.

FURNITURE MAKING AND DESIGN

The previous few pages have explained some basic furniture-making techniques. The next pages are given to actual plans to build from. The instructions for the first twelve designs are step-by-step. They contain some techniques already explained and some new ones. After these twelve are a few more designs without step-by-step instructions to practice on. After that you will be ready to design your own furniture.

One word before the fun part starts. In making furniture, make each part, leg, arm, table top,

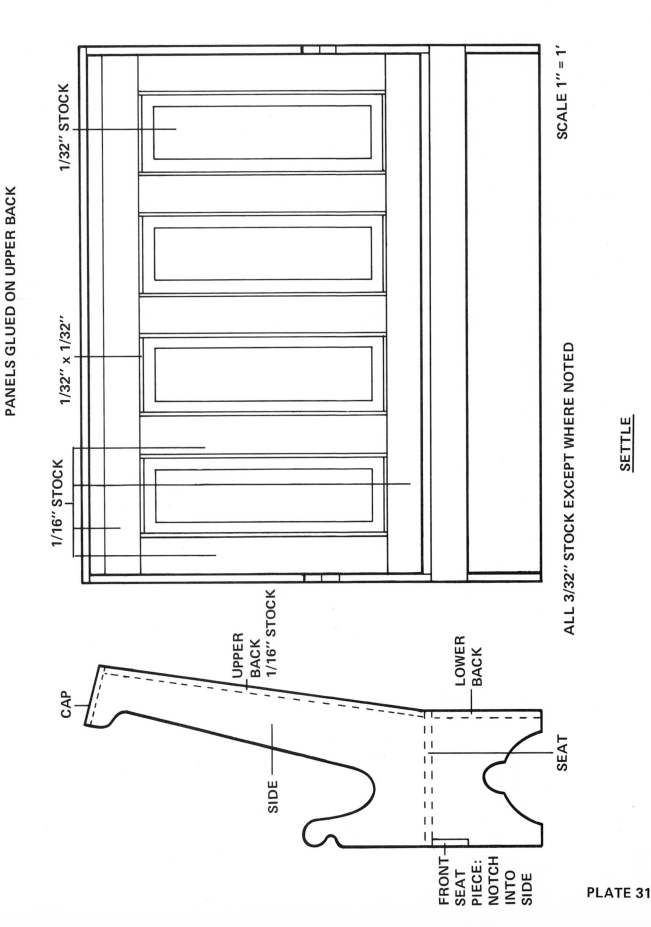

PANELS GLUED ON UPPER BACK

1/32" STOCK

1/32" x 1/32"

1/16" STOCK

SCALE 1" = 1'

ALL 3/32" STOCK EXCEPT WHERE NOTED

SETTLE

UPPER
BACK
1/16" STOCK

LOWER
BACK

CAP

SIDE

SEAT

SEAT

FRONT
SEAT
PIECE:
NOTCH
INTO
SIDE

PLATE 31

etc., as smooth as possible, with #600 Wetordry sandpaper and .0000 steel wool, before assembly. It is difficult to get in corners and tight places after assembly. If you like, you can wait until the piece is assembled before sealing it, but I like to seal the parts with a coat of shellac, thinned with denatured alcohol, before assembly wherever possible. When the shellac is dry, rub the parts with #600 Wetordry or .0000 steel wool.

Some people even paint or stain and varnish each part before assembly. I envy them. I make too many mistakes, which need correction after assembly to be able to do that.

At the end of this chapter is a section on painting furniture to simulate wood and painted pieces. You might look through it now.

The designs following are for both seventeenth- and eighteenth-century pieces to fit into early Colonial and Georgian houses. I hope you enjoy them.

SETTLE

Materials: Mat knife, Elmer's glue, Weldwood cement, sandpaper, emery boards, Swiss pattern files (optional), masking tape, carbon paper.

Note: Sand all wood pieces lightly and smooth them with fine steel wool before final assembly wherever possible. Sand and steel wool the finished piece where needed. Either glue is suitable except where noted.

1. Assembly.
   a. Trace the shape of the sides on paper.
   b. Measure the plans and mark on paper the shapes of the upper back, lower back, seat, front piece, and cap.
   c. Transfer the shapes to the wood with carbon paper. Cut out the pieces. The upper back may have to be done in two pieces. (Glue them together, edges butted together. Tape the joint till the glue dries.) Tape the side pieces together and cut them both out at once. The inside curves can be smoothed with sandpaper wrapped around a small dowel or with a file (Fig. 87).
   d. Cut $\frac{1}{16}$″ thick and $\frac{1}{32}$″ thick wood for the panels on the upper back. Glue on the $\frac{1}{16}$″ thick pieces with Weldwood cement

INSIDE CURVES

FIG. 87

to prevent wood curling. Glue $\frac{1}{32}$″ × $\frac{1}{32}$″ wood strips inside these as shown in the plans, using Elmer's glue. Bevel the edges of the $\frac{1}{32}$″ thick panels. For a clean bevel, lay masking tape on the bevel lines and sand up to the tape. The tape prevents sanding away too much wood. Glue these in place with Weldwood cement.
   e. Glue together the sides, lower back, seat, and front piece.
   f. Glue on the upper back and cap.
2. Finishing.
   Give the settle a coat of shellac, mixed half and half with denatured alcohol to seal the wood. Sand lightly. Paint the settle the desired color or a light wood tone, using acrylic tube paints. Applying antiquing ink. Rub off for a soft, blended effect to accentuate the shapes or brush off with a dry paintbrush for a wood-grained effect. When the antiquing is dry, apply two thin coats of semi-gloss oil base varnish.

LADDER BACK CHAIR

Materials: Mat knife, Elmer's glue, Weldwood cement, razor saw, pin vise with small bit to fit straight pins and $\frac{1}{16}$″ bit, emery boards, sandpaper, carbon paper, wire clippers.

Note: Sand all wood pieces lightly, and smooth them with fine steel wool before final assembly wherever possible. Sand and steel wool the finished piece where needed. Use Elmer's glue except where noted.

1. Chair legs and back.
   Cut $\frac{5}{32}$″ dowels to the proper length. To carve the ball shapes on the dowels, make marks around the dowel for the position of the ball shapes. Make shallow cuts on the marks (Fig. 88A). With a knife, cut away a

CURVE OF SLATS

SHAPE OF ARM
TOP VIEW

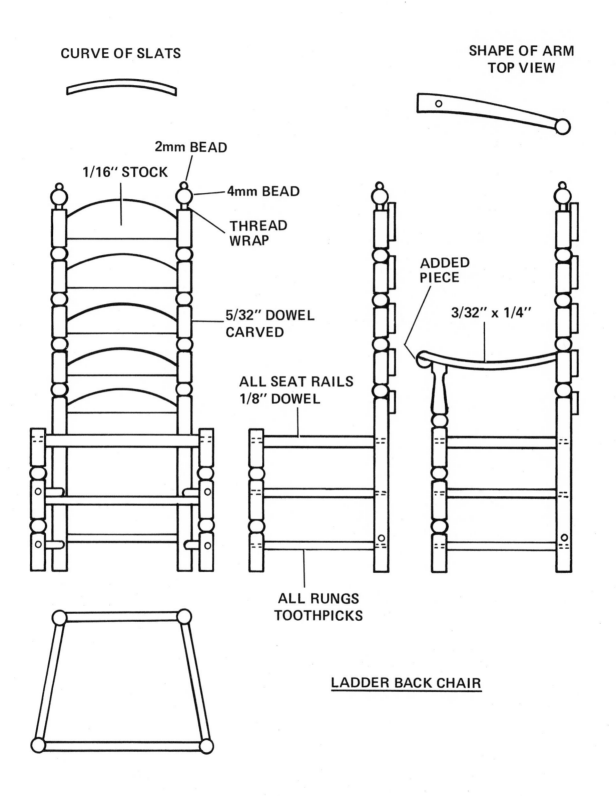

2mm BEAD

1/16'' STOCK

4mm BEAD

THREAD
WRAP

5/32'' DOWEL
CARVED

ADDED
PIECE

3/32'' x 1/4''

ALL SEAT RAILS
1/8'' DOWEL

ALL RUNGS
TOOTHPICKS

LADDER BACK CHAIR

SCALE 1'' = 1'

PLATE 32

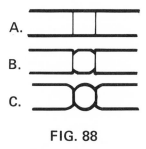

FIG. 88

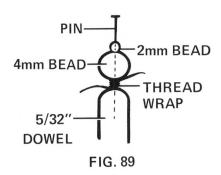

FIG. 89

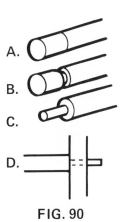

FIG. 90

bit of wood at the marks (Fig. 88B). With an emery board, shape the carving into the ball shape (Fig. 88C). An emery board has a slight curve on the edge which will help in the shaping. Round the remaining edges (Fig. 88C) slightly, with an emery board. Smooth the carving with steel wool, rotating the dowel inside a wad of steel wool.

For the armchair, shape the ball shapes. For the tapered part of the dowel, carve the taper to the general shape. Finish the shaping with an emery board. To make the insert into the arm, see Fig. 90.

2. Finials.

On the pieces for the chair back, drill a pin hole in the top. Place a 2mm and a 4mm bead on a pin, with glue, and insert the pin into the hole. To keep the beads separated from the chair back, place some glue on the pin and wrap thread around the pin, evenly (about 10 or 12 times). Smooth any excess glue with a small, damp paintbrush. When the glue dries, cut away the excess thread ends (Fig. 89). Clip off the excess pin with wire clippers and push the pin in flush with the 2mm bead. Fill in the hole in the bead with a dot of glue.

3. Chair rungs and seat rails.

a. On the chair legs, mark the positions of the front and back rungs and seat rails. Drill $\frac{1}{16}''$ holes, completely through the legs, on the marks.

b. Mark the length of the rungs on toothpicks and the length of the seat rails on $\frac{1}{8}''$ dowel. Mark also for the inserts into and through the holes. Cut the toothpicks and dowels.

c. To carve the insert, make shallow cuts on the marks (Fig. 90A). Carve away a bit of wood at the marks (Fig. 90B). Continue carving away wood to form the insert (Fig.

90C). With an emery board, sand the insert to make it round.

Note: It is best to have the inserts fit loosely in the holes. This permits small adjustments to be made. When the rungs and seat rails are glued into the chair legs, the glue will fill in the extra space. It is helpful to tape the glued pieces to the plans while the glue dries to assure correct position.

d. Glue the front and back rungs and seat rails into the legs. When the glue is dry, cut off the excess insert and sand smooth. Fill in any spaces with glue (Fig. 90D).

e. Repeat the above for the side rungs and seat rails. Notice that they fit into the chair legs at a slight angle. Drill the $\frac{1}{16}''$ holes at that angle.

4. Ladder backs.

Cut $\frac{1}{2}'' \times \frac{1}{16}''$ pieces about $2\frac{1}{2}''$ long. Soak them in water till they will bend easily, overnight or longer. On a piece of heavy scrap wood, bend the ladder back pieces over a $\frac{1}{4}'' \times \frac{1}{8}''$ strip of wood and hold the ends down with $\frac{1}{4}'' \times \frac{1}{8}''$ wood strips nailed into the scrap wood (Fig. 91). Trace the shapes of the ladder back slats on paper. When the wood is dry and will hold its shape, transfer the shapes to the wood with carbon paper. Carve the slats to shape. Glue the slats in place. Weldwood cement gives greater strength. Or drill pin holes through the chair backs and into the slats. Insert pins with glue. Clip off the excess and push the pins in flush with the wood.

5. Arm.

For the armchair, bend a ³/₃₂″ thick wood piece. Glue a small bit of wood on the end for the knuckle. Carve out the shape shown in the plans. Shape the knuckle with an emery board. Round the top edges of the arm slightly. Taper the underside of the arm slightly for a graceful shape. Drill a hole for the insert on the dowel. Glue the arm in place.

6. Finishing.

Give the chair a coat of shellac, mixed half and half with denatured alcohol to seal the wood. Sand lightly. Paint the chair the desired color or a light wood tone, using acrylic tube paints. Apply antiquing ink. Rub off for a soft, blended effect to accentuate the shapes or brush off with a dry paintbrush for a wood grained effect. When the antiquing is dry, apply two thin coats of semi-gloss oil base varnish.

7. Weave the seat.

The string can be given a coat of glue to stiffen it. To do this, put some Elmer's glue on your fingers and pull the string through the glue. Let dry. Figure 92 shows weaving a squared shape. Start by tying the string at the upper left corner. First, however, fill in the space where the chair is wider at the front than at the back. To do this, see Fig. 93. Glue the string part way up on one rail (Fig. 93A). Weave the string over to the opposite rail, cut it off and glue in place (Fig. 93B). You will have to do this several times to fill in the area. When the area to be woven becomes squared off, weave the rest of the seat as in Fig. 92. At the center of the seat there is likely to be a space. To fill this, weave over and under the front and back rails in a figure 8 pattern (Fig. 93C). When the weaving is complete, tie off the string and hide the end in the weaving.

The seat can be painted, antiqued, and varnished to simulate rushing. Paint the string a light or medium yellow. Apply antiquing ink thinned with turpentine. The ink will sink down into the weaving and accentuate it. Follow with a coat of varnish.

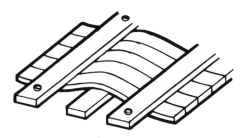

FIG. 91

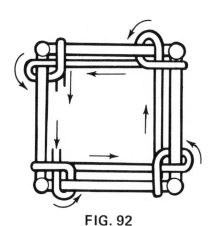

FIG. 92

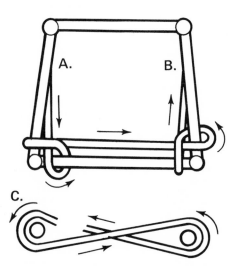

FIG. 93

Tavern Table

Materials: Elmer's glue, mat knife, pin vise with small bit to fit straight pins and $\frac{1}{16}$" bit, emery boards, sandpaper, Swiss pattern files (optional), razor saw, carbon paper, masking tape, wire clippers.

Note: Sand all wood pieces lightly, and smooth with fine steel wool before final assembly wherever possible. Sand and steel wool the finished piece where needed.

1. Legs.
   a. For the round middle section of the legs, cut $\frac{3}{16}$" dowels about $1\frac{1}{2}$" longer than the required length. Mark the major divisions of the section on the dowel and make shallow cuts around the dowel on the marks (Fig. 94A). At the cuts, carve away a small bit of wood (Fig. 94B). At the bottom (arrow), carve away the wood and form a groove with a bit of sandpaper folded over a knife blade or with a file. Taper the main portion of the dowel; carve away wood to the general shape, then smooth with sandpaper or emery board (Fig. 94C). Round off the remaining sharp edges with an emery board. Finish smoothing by rotating the section inside a wad of steel wool (Fig. 94D). With a razor saw, cut away the excess dowel. Drill $\frac{1}{16}$" holes in the ends of the section and insert toothpicks, with glue. Carve down the toothpicks a bit, cut them off, and sand them round to form inserts (Fig. 94E).
   b. To make the foot, place a bead on a toothpick (Fig. 95A). With an emery board, sand the bead to the shape shown in Fig. 95B, first one end then the other. Place the bead on a new toothpick, with glue, break off the tip, and sand flush with the bead. Carve the toothpick down a bit, cut it off, and sand round to form an insert (Fig. 95B).
   c. Cut $\frac{3}{16}$" $\times$ $\frac{3}{16}$" stock to the proper lengths. Drill $\frac{1}{16}$" holes where needed to hold the inserts. Bevel the edges slightly, where needed, with an emery board.
   d. Glue the square and carved sections together. Glue the foot assembly in place.

   e. For the small turning on the dowel section, coat string with glue and wrap around the dowel (Fig. 96A). Cut through both pieces of string with one cut of a sharp knife, while the glue is still damp (Fig. 96B). Adjust the cut ends so they meet (Fig. 96C). A dot of glue helps secure and cover the joint.

2. Framework.
   Trace the shapes of the back, sides, and bottom on paper. Transfer the shapes onto the wood with carbon paper. Cut them out. Glue two legs, one side, and a stretcher together. It is helpful to tape the pieces to the plans while the glue dries to assure proper position. Do the other side. Glue on the back, bottom, and front and back stretchers. After the glue is

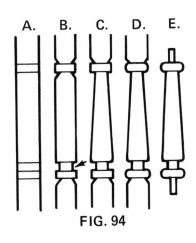

FIG. 94

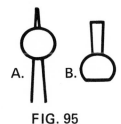

FIG. 95

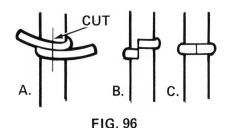

FIG. 96

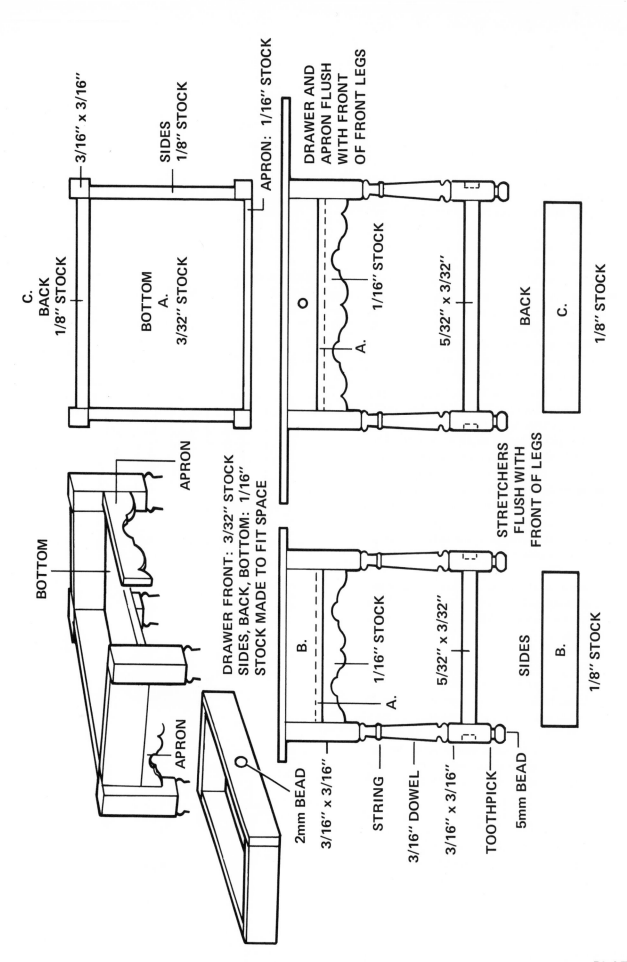

3/16" x 3/16"

SIDES
1/8" STOCK

APRON: 1/16" STOCK

DRAWER AND
APRON FLUSH
WITH FRONT
OF FRONT LEGS

C.
BACK
1/8" STOCK

BOTTOM
A.
3/32" STOCK

O

A.

1/16" STOCK

5/32" x 3/32"

BACK

C.

1/8" STOCK

APRON

BOTTOM

DRAWER FRONT: 3/32" STOCK
SIDES, BACK, BOTTOM: 1/16"
STOCK MADE TO FIT SPACE

APRON

APRON

B.

A.

1/16" STOCK

5/32" x 3/32"

SIDES

B.

1/8" STOCK

STRETCHERS
FLUSH WITH
FRONT OF LEGS

2mm BEAD

3/16" x 3/16"

STRING

3/16" DOWEL

3/16" x 3/16"

TOOTHPICK

5mm BEAD

TAVERN TABLE

PLATE 33

dry, extra strength can be had by drilling pin holes through the legs into the sides, back, and stretchers. Insert straight pins, with glue, clip off the excess pin, and push the end in flush with the wood.

3. Aprons.

Trace the shape of the aprons on paper. Transfer the shapes onto the wood with carbon paper. The scroll shapes go with the grain of the wood for easier carving. Carve the scrolls to the general shape and finish the shaping with an emery board. The inside curves can be smoothed with sandpaper wrapped around a small dowel or with a file (Fig. 97). Glue the side and back aprons in place, flush with the sides and back. The front apron fits flush with the front edge of the front legs.

4. Drawer.

Cut the drawer front to fit the space. Cut the sides, back, and bottom of the drawer to fit the front of the drawer and the depth of the space. Glue the pieces together. Drill a $\frac{1}{16}''$ hole for the drawer knob. After the table is painted and finished, insert a toothpick, with glue, through the hole and glue on a bead (Fig. 98). Cut off the ends of the toothpick and sand flush with the bead and back of the drawer front. Paint and finish to match the drawer.

5. Tabletop.

This may have to be done in two pieces. Glue the pieces together, edges butted together and tape the joint till the glue dries. Glue the

tabletop to the framework. Round the upper edges with sandpaper.

6. Finishing.

Give the table a coat of shellac, mixed half and half with denatured alcohol to seal the wood. Sand lightly. Paint the table the desired color or a light wood tone, using acrylic tube paints. Apply antiquing ink. Rub off for a soft, blended effect to accentuate the shapes or brush off with a dry paintbrush for a wood-grained effect. When the antiquing is dry, apply two thin coats of semi-gloss oil base varnish.

CRADLE

Materials: Elmer's glue, pin vise with $\frac{1}{16}''$ bit, razor saw, emery boards, sandpaper, mat knife, Swiss pattern files (optional), carbon paper.

Note: Sand all wood pieces lightly, and smooth with fine steel wool before final assembly wherever possible. Sand and steel wool the finished piece where needed.

1. Posts.

a. Cut the posts to size. To make the slot to hold the rocker pieces, drill a $\frac{1}{16}''$ hole in the post (Fig. 99A). With a razor saw, make cuts up to the hole (Fig. 99B). The piece for the slot will fall out. Smooth the slot with an emery board or file (Fig. 99C).

b. With a razor saw, cut slices from a $\frac{5}{32}''$ dowel. Glue these to the tops of the posts. When the glue is dry, sand down the dowel slices to the desired thickness. Round the top edges slightly and bevel the top edges of the posts slightly. Drill $\frac{1}{16}''$ holes through the dowel slices into the posts.

c. Flatten the beads for the cradle knobs. To do this, place a bead on a toothpick and, with an emery board, sand the bead to the

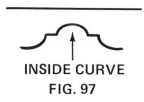

INSIDE CURVE
FIG. 97

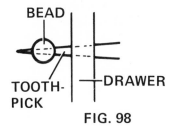

FIG. 98

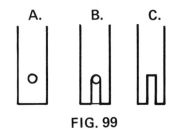

FIG. 99

DETAIL OF KNOB

5mm BEAD

5/32" DOWEL
SLICE

TOOTHPICK

3/16" x 3/16"

BOTTOM
3/32" STOCK

GRAIN OF WOOD

3/16" x 3/16"

3/16" x 3/16"

3/32" STOCK

3/32"
STOCK

1/16" x 1/16"
RAILS GLUED
TO SIDES

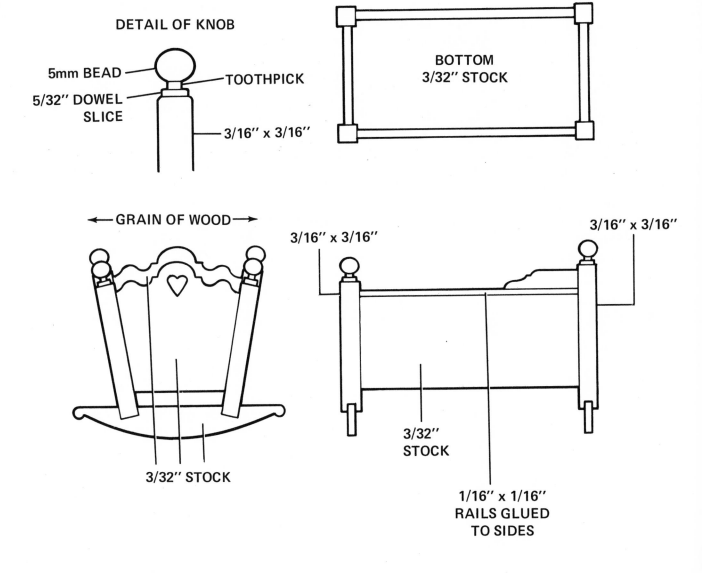

SCALE 1"= 1'

CRADLE

PLATE 34

shape shown, first one side then the other (Fig. 100A). Insert a new toothpick, with glue, break off the tip of the toothpick, and sand flush with the bead. Carve the toothpick down a bit at the bottom and cut it off to form an insert (Fig. 100B).

d. Glue the knobs and inserts into the holes prepared in the posts.

2. Assembly.

a. Trace the shapes of the head- and footboards, sides, and bottom on paper. Transfer onto the wood with carbon paper. Cut out the head- and footboards, sides, and bottom of the cradle. The scroll shapes can be carved with a mat knife, then finished with a small piece of emery board or file. The inside curves can be smoothed with sandpaper wrapped around a small dowel or with a file. For the heart shape, drill two $\frac{1}{16}''$ holes side by side (Fig. 101A). Carve out the heart shape with a sharp knife and smooth with a small piece of emery board or file (Fig. 101B).

b. Glue the headboard and posts and the footboard and posts together.

c. Glue the sides, bottom, headboard and footboard assemblies together, notching the bottom to fit around the posts.

d. Cut out the rockers and glue in place.

e. Glue the $\frac{1}{16}''$ square side rails to the cradle sides.

3. Finishing.

Give the cradle a coat of shellac, mixed half and half with denatured alcohol to seal the wood. Sand lightly. Paint the cradle the desired color or a light wood tone using acrylic tube paints. Apply antiquing ink. Rub off for a soft, blended effect to accentuate the shapes or brush off with a dry paintbrush for a wood-grained effect. When the antiquing is dry, apply two thin coats of semi-gloss oil base varnish.

NORTH SHORE DRESSER

Materials: Mat knife, Elmer's glue, pin vise with $\frac{1}{16}''$ bit, emery boards, sandpaper, Swiss pattern files (optional), masking tape, carbon paper, Weldwood cement.

Note: Sand all wood pieces lightly, and smooth with fine steel wool before final assembly wherever possible. Sand and steel wool the finished piece where needed. Either glue is suitable except where noted.

1. Preparation.

Trace the shapes of the major pieces of the base and the sides of the hutch top on paper. Measure the plans and mark on paper the shapes of all the other major pieces excluding the doors and drawer fronts on the dresser base. Transfer the shapes to the wood with carbon paper. Cut out the pieces as needed. The larger pieces (the hutch top back and base back) may have to be done in two pieces. Glue the pieces together, edges butted together and tape the joint till the glue dries. To shape the sides of the hutch top, tape the two side pieces together and carve both at the same time. Carve the scrolled edges to the general shape and finish the shaping with an emery board and sandpaper. The inside curves (Fig. 102) can be smoothed with sandpaper wrapped around a small dowel or with a file.

2. Base.

a. Glue together the framework of the base as shown in the plans. The front edge is likely to be uneven. To correct this, lay sandpaper on a flat surface and rub the front edge of the base on the sandpaper to even off the edges.

b. Round off the top of the $\frac{1}{4}'' \times \frac{1}{16}''$ piece at the bottom of the base. Glue in place. Trim away any excess when the glue is dry.

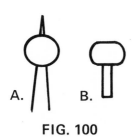

FIG. 100

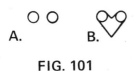

FIG. 101

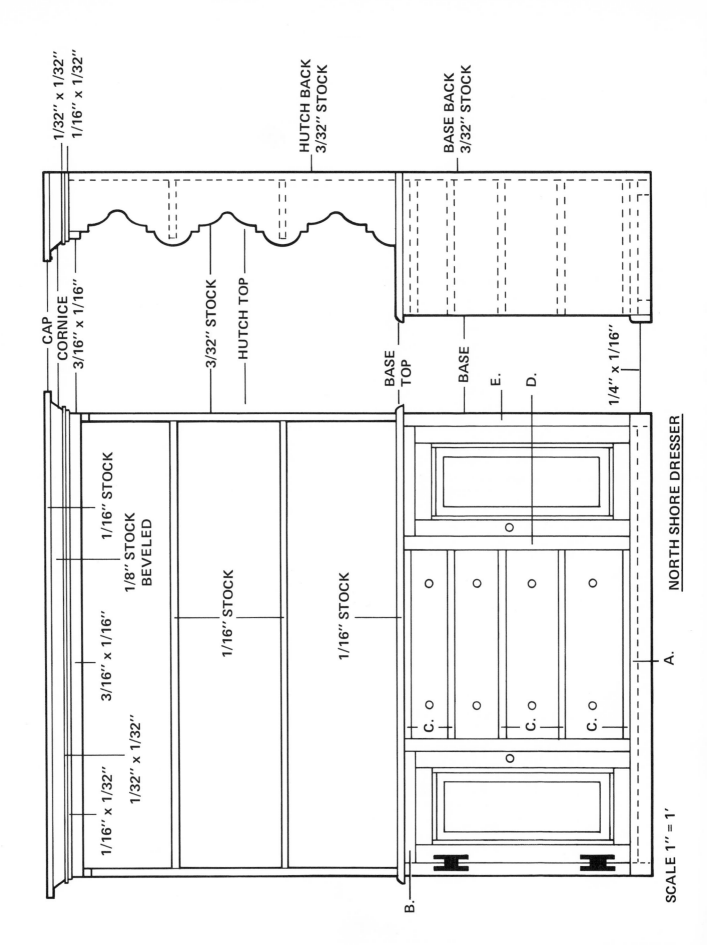

1/32" x 1/32"
1/16" x 1/32"

HUTCH BACK
3/32" STOCK

BASE BACK
3/32" STOCK

CAP

CORNICE
3/16" x 1/16"

3/32" STOCK

HUTCH TOP

BASE
TOP

BASE

E.

D.

1/4" x 1/16"

1/16" STOCK

1/8" STOCK
BEVELED

3/16" x 1/16"

1/32" x 1/32"

1/16" x 1/32"

1/16" STOCK

1/16" STOCK

C.

C.

C.

A.

B.

NORTH SHORE DRESSER

SCALE 1" = 1'

PLATE 35 A

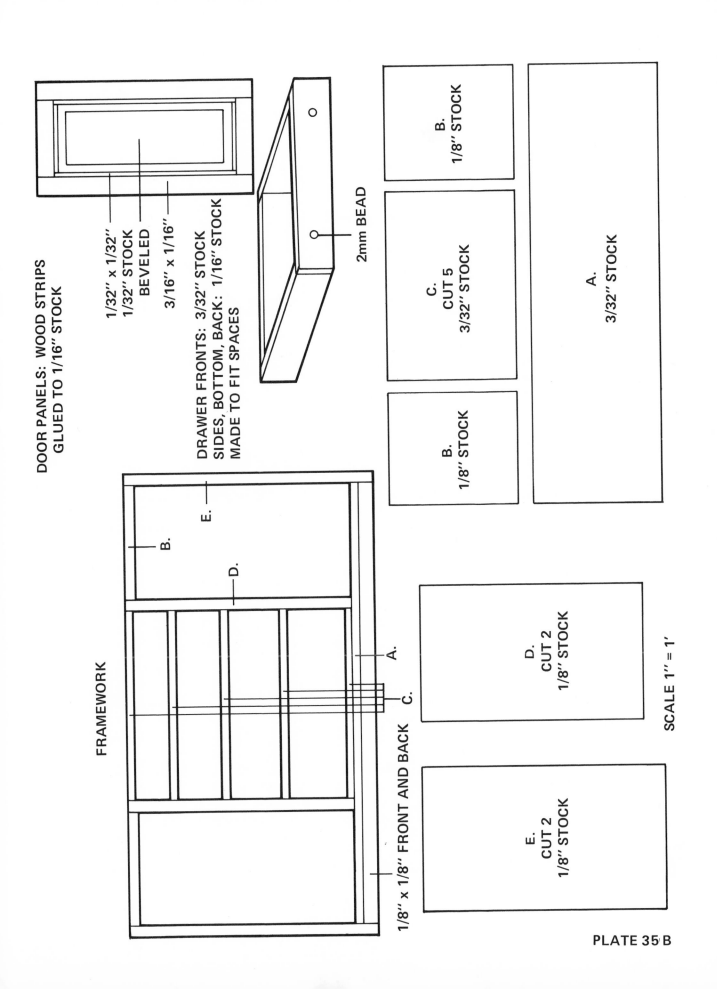

DOOR PANELS: WOOD STRIPS
GLUED TO 1/16" STOCK

1/32" x 1/32"
1/32" STOCK
BEVELED
3/16" x 1/16"

DRAWER FRONTS: 3/32" STOCK
SIDES, BOTTOM, BACK: 1/16" STOCK
MADE TO FIT SPACES

2mm BEAD

FRAMEWORK

B.
E.
D.
A.
C.

1/8" x 1/8" FRONT AND BACK

B.
1/8" STOCK

C.
CUT 5
3/32" STOCK

B.
1/8" STOCK

A.
3/32" STOCK

D.
CUT 2
1/8" STOCK

E.
CUT 2
1/8" STOCK

SCALE 1" = 1'

PLATE 35 B

c. Glue on the $\frac{1}{16}''$ thick base top. Round the edges with sandpaper.

d. Cut the drawer fronts to fit the openings. Fit the sides, bottom, and back of the drawers to fit the drawer front and the depth of the openings.

e. Cut the $\frac{1}{16}''$ thick doors to fit the openings. Glue $\frac{3}{16}'' \times \frac{1}{16}''$ wood strips around the edges. Glue $\frac{1}{32}'' \times \frac{1}{32}''$ wood strips inside these, using Elmer's glue. Cut the $\frac{1}{2}''$ wide, $\frac{1}{32}''$ thick wood strips for the door panels. Bevel the edges. For a clean bevel, lay tape on the bevel line and sand up to the tape. The tape prevents sanding away too much wood. Glue in place with Weldwood cement to prevent wood curling.

f. Hinge the doors as shown in Fig. 103 using Elmer's glue on the mesh hinges. Trim the other side of the door if necessary, for a good fit. Glue small wood bits to the inside of the base as doorstops to keep the doors flush with the front of the base.

3. The Hutch Top.

a. Glue the sides, back, and $\frac{3}{16}'' \times \frac{1}{16}''$ front piece together.

b. Mark the size of the hutch top on the $\frac{1}{8}''$ thick cornice piece. Bevel the edges of the cornice and glue it in place.

c. Glue on the $\frac{1}{16}''$ thick piece for the cap.

d. Glue on the $\frac{1}{16}'' \times \frac{1}{32}''$ and $\frac{1}{32}'' \times \frac{1}{32}''$ wood strips for the trim under the cornice (Fig. 104). Soften the edges with fine steel wool.

e. Do not glue in the shelves yet.

f. Do not glue the hutch top to the base yet.

4. Finishing.

a. Drill $\frac{1}{16}''$ holes for the door and drawer knobs. After the dresser is painted and varnished, glue on the knobs as shown in Fig. 105. Cut off the ends of the toothpicks and sand flush with the bead and backside of the drawer front. Paint and finish the knobs to match the doors and drawers.

b. Give the dresser a coat of shellac, mixed half and half with denatured alcohol to seal the wood. Sand lightly. Paint the dresser the desired color or a light wood tone, using acrylic tube paints. Apply antiquing ink. Rub off for a soft, blended effect to accentuate the shapes or brush off with a

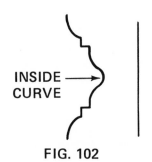

FIG. 102

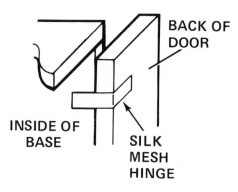

FIG. 103

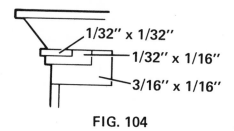

FIG. 104

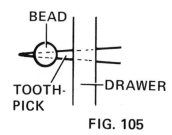

FIG. 105

dry paintbrush for a wood-grained effect. When the antiquing is dry, apply two thin coats of semi-gloss oil base varnish.

c. Glue the shelves in place.

d. Glue the hutch top to the base.

e. Cut black construction paper to simulate hinges. Glue in place. Paint the paper and the visible mesh part of the hinge with black enamel for the look of metal.

TRUNDLE BEDS

Materials: Elmer's glue, Weldwood cement, razor saw, pin vise with small bit to fit straight pins and $\frac{1}{16}''$ bit, mat knife, emery boards, sandpaper, masking tape, wire clippers, carbon paper.

Note: Sand all wood pieces lightly, and smooth with fine steel wool before final assembly wherever possible. Sand and steel wool the finished piece where needed. Either glue is suitable except where noted.

LOWER BED

1. Posts and wheels.

   Cut the posts to the proper length. To make the slot for the wheels drill a $\frac{1}{16}''$ hole in the post (Fig. 106A). With a razor saw, make cuts up to the hole (Fig. 106B). The piece for the slot will fall out. Smooth and widen the slot with an emery board (Fig. 106C). The wheel on its axle turns better if the slot is made generously wide. For the wheels, cut slices off a $\frac{1}{4}''$ dowel with a razor saw. Sand the sides smooth. Drill a pin hole in the center. Drill pin holes in the posts for the axle. Clip off a straight pin with wire clippers and assemble the wheel and post (Fig. 106D). A bit of Weldwood cement under the head of the pin holds the axle in place. Excess pin on the other side of the post can be sanded off flush with the post.

2. Headboard.

   Mark the size of the $\frac{1}{16}''$ thick panels on wood and cut them out. Glue the posts, crosspieces and the large $\frac{1}{16}''$ panel together. On the smaller $\frac{1}{16}''$ panel, bevel the edges. For a clean bevel, lay tape on the bevel line and sand up to the tape. The tape prevents sanding away too much wood. Glue the panel in

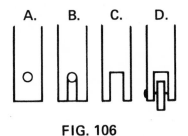

FIG. 106

place with Weldwood cement to prevent wood curling.

3. Assembly.
   a. Drill $\frac{1}{16}''$ holes in all the crosspieces and side pieces.
   b. Glue the end posts and one crosspiece together.
   c. Glue the headboard and footboard assemblies together with the side pieces.
   d. Glue in the extra crosspiece near the headboard.

Note: Extra strength can be had by drilling pin holes at the joints. Insert straight pins with glue, clip off the excess, and push the pin in flush with the wood.

UPPER BED

1. Posts.

   Cut posts to the proper length. With a razor saw, cut slices from a $\frac{1}{8}''$ dowel. Glue these to the posts. When the glue is dry, sand down the slices to the desired thickness. Drill pin holes through the dowel slices into the posts.

   Flatten the bottoms of the beads slightly. To do this, place a bead on a toothpick and sand the bead with an emery board. Place the bead on a pin, with Elmer's glue and glue into the prepared hole in the post. Clip off the excess pin and push it in flush with the bead. Fill in the hole in the bead with a dot of Elmer's glue.

2. Assembly.
   a. Drill $\frac{1}{16}''$ holes in the crosspieces and side pieces.
   b. For the footboard, glue two posts and a crosspiece together, fitting them around the headboard of the lower bed so it will roll easily under the footboard assembly of the upper bed.
   c. Trace the shape of the headboard on paper. Transfer the shape to wood with carbon paper. Cut out the headboard and round off the top edge slightly with sandpaper. Glue the headboard, two posts, and a crosspiece together.
   d. Glue the headboard and footboard assemblies together with the side pieces. For added strength, use pins at the joints as before.

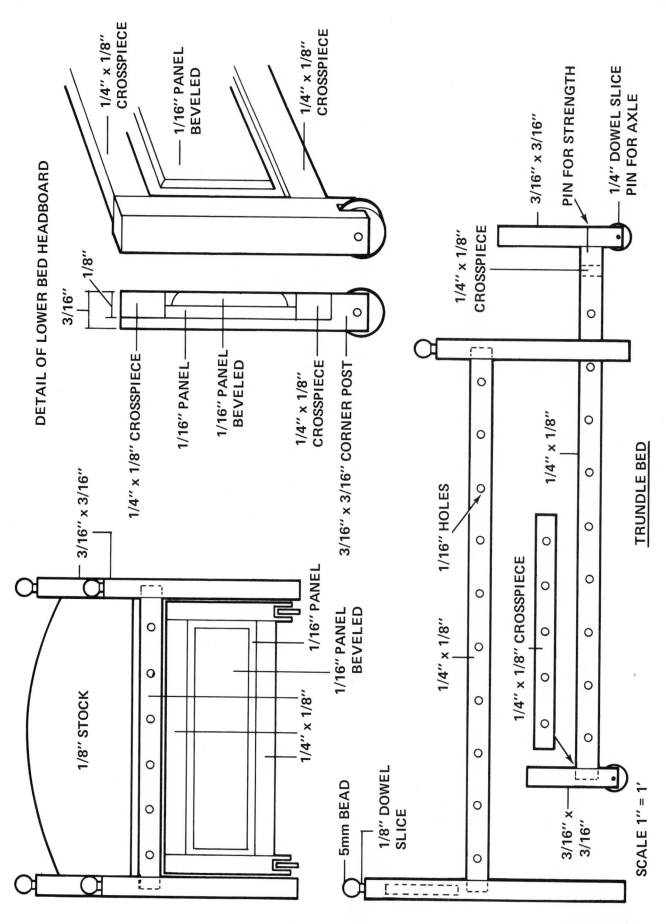

DETAIL OF LOWER BED HEADBOARD

1/4" x 1/8" CROSSPIECE

1/16" PANEL BEVELED

1/4" x 1/8" CROSSPIECE

3/16"

1/8"

1/4" x 1/8" CROSSPIECE

1/16" PANEL

1/16" PANEL BEVELED

1/4" x 1/8" CROSSPIECE

3/16" x 3/16" CORNER POST

3/16" x 3/16"

1/16" PANEL

1/16" PANEL BEVELED

1/4" x 1/8"

1/4" x 1/8"

1/8" STOCK

5mm BEAD

1/8" DOWEL SLICE

3/16" x 3/16"

PIN FOR STRENGTH

1/4" DOWEL SLICE

PIN FOR AXLE

1/4" x 1/8" CROSSPIECE

1/4" x 1/8"

1/16" HOLES

1/4" x 1/8"

1/4" x 1/8" CROSSPIECE

3/16" x 3/16"

TRUNDLE BED

SCALE 1" = 1'

PLATE 36

3. Finishing.

a. Give the beds a coat of shellac, mixed half and half with denatured alcohol to seal the wood. Sand lightly. Paint the beds the desired color or a light wood tone, using acrylic tube paints. Apply antiquing ink. Rub off for a soft, blended effect to accentuate the shapes or brush off with a dry paintbrush for a wood-grained effect. When the antiquing is dry, give the beds two thin coats of semi-gloss oil base varnish.

b. Weave string in and out of the holes in the side pieces and crosspieces in an over and under pattern to form a base for the mattress.

c. To make a mattress, glue three or four layers of art foam together. Dot on the glue rather than cover the entire surface. For a mattress cover, sew two pieces of lightweight cotton together on three sides, right sides together. Clip the seams closely. A bit of glue will prevent raveling. Turn the cover right side out and stuff with the art foam mattress. Turn under the raw edges of the open side and sew closed. Pillows are made the same way, but smaller.

CHIPPENDALE SOFA

Materials: Mat knife, Weldwood cement, masking tape, pin vise with small bit to fit straight pins and $\frac{1}{16}''$ bit, razor saw, sandpaper, emery boards, wire clippers, Elmer's glue, carbon paper.

Note: Sand all wood pieces lightly, and smooth with steel wool before final assembly wherever possible. Sand and steel wool the finished piece. Piece B may have to be cut from two wood pieces glued together, edges butted.

1. Sofa frame.
Trace the shapes of the pieces of the sofa on paper. Transfer the shapes to the wood with carbon paper. Cut them out.

a. Glue pieces A and B together with Weldwood cement to prevent warping of the wood. Round off the top edge slightly with sandpaper. Round off slightly the lower edge of piece A.

b. Glue together two pieces of shape C for the sofa bottom. Glue two for the cushion.

This piece may need to be trimmed later to fit into the sofa.

c. The arms of the sofa are made from four wood pieces glued together (see plans). Use Weldwood to prevent warping. Notice that the curve at the front of the arm (Fig. 107B) is different from the curve at the back of the arm where it fits into the sofa back (Fig. 107A). In both curves, notice that the curves on the inside of the arms go only as far as the $\frac{1}{4}'' \times \frac{1}{8}''$ pieces marked in Fig. 107. Carve these curves carefully, making sure the curve at the back of the arm fits the curve of the sofa back. Sand the arms smooth, blending the front and back curves. The $\frac{1}{4}'' \times \frac{1}{8}''$ and $\frac{1}{4}'' \times \frac{1}{16}''$ outer arm pieces are then rounded off with sandpaper.

d. The arms of the sofa will fit the back of the sofa at an angle (Fig. 108). Therefore, the back of the sofa must be carved to fit this angle. The carving need not be exact on the backside of the sofa back. Any space there can later be filled in. However, the curve on the front side of the sofa back should be kept exact.

e. Tape the back, bottom, and arms of the sofa together. Drill pin holes where the pieces

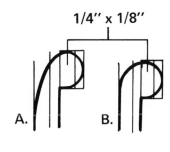

FIG. 107

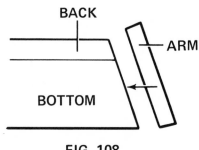

FIG. 108

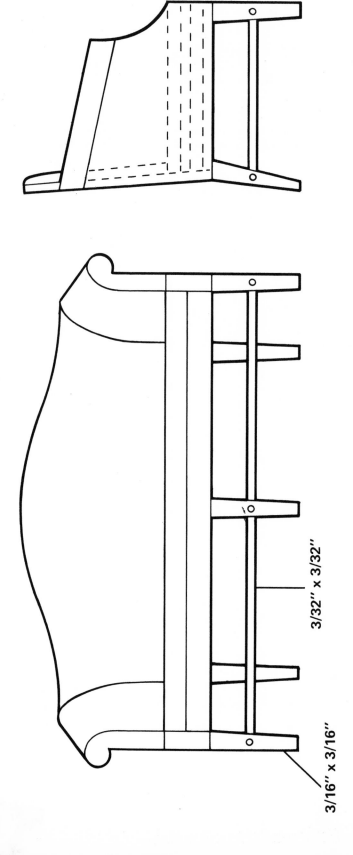

3/32" x 3/32"

3/16" x 3/16"

CHIPPENDALE SOFA

SCALE 1" = 1'

PLATE 37A

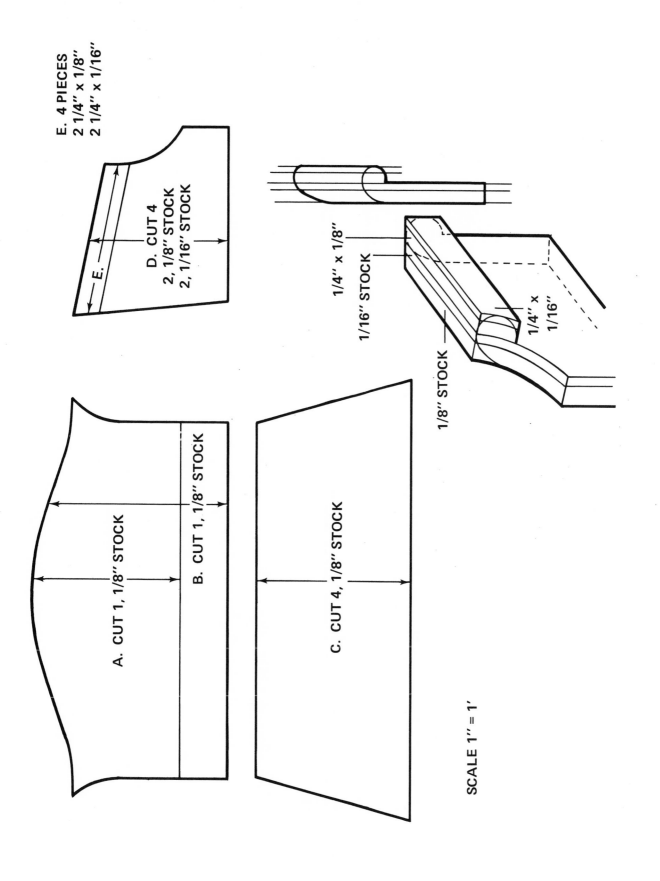

E. 4 PIECES
2 1/4" x 1/8"
2 1/4" x 1/16"

E.

D. CUT 4
2, 1/8" STOCK
2, 1/16" STOCK

1/4" x 1/8"

1/16" STOCK

1/4" x
1/16"

1/8" STOCK

A. CUT 1, 1/8" STOCK

B. CUT 1, 1/8" STOCK

C. CUT 4, 1/8" STOCK

SCALE 1" = 1'

PLATE 37B

meet (3 or 4 are sufficient) and insert pins. Do not glue the pieces together yet. This will be done later, after the sofa is upholstered. Notice that part of the arm pieces extend past the back of the sofa, due to the angle. Carve and sand these off flush with the sofa back.

2. Legs.

  a. Cut the three front legs with a razor saw and taper all four sides slightly with an emery board. Cut the three back legs at an angle (Fig. 109A). Taper the sides of the legs as before. Carve a slight curve on the back and front of the legs (Fig. 109B).

  b. Drill $\frac{1}{16}''$ holes in the tops of the legs and insert toothpicks, with glue. Carve down the toothpicks a bit, cut them off, and sand them round to form inserts (Fig. 109C). Drill $\frac{1}{16}''$ holes in the sofa frame to receive the inserts (straight for the front legs, at an angle for the back legs). The inserts should fit loosely in the holes to allow for adjusting the position of the legs. Later when the legs are glued into place, the glue will fill up the extra space.

  If you like you can use cut off straight pins for the inserts and pin holes in the sofa frame. This is easier to do but the final construction will not be as strong.

  c. The $\frac{3}{32}'' \times \frac{3}{32}''$ crosspieces can be glued to the legs, but for stronger construction, small inserts can be carved and inserted into $\frac{1}{16}''$ holes drilled in the legs. For this, cut the crosspieces long enough to include inserts. Mark the wood for the inserts (Fig. 110A). Carve away a bit of wood at the marks (Fig. 110B). Continue carving away wood to form the insert. Round off with an emery board (Fig. 110C).

  Do not glue the leg framework to the sofa yet.

3. Upholstering.

  Fabric: Medium weight, closely woven fabric is best to use; fabric which will not ravel easily and is dense enough not to allow the glue with which it is applied to soak through to the right side.

  a. Take the sofa apart. Glue art foam to the front side of piece A and the top side of the cushion piece, almost to the edge (Fig.

111A). Dot on the glue rather than cover the entire surface, using Elmer's glue. Cover these pieces with fabric glued only at the edges, also using Elmer's glue. When the glue is dry, trim off the excess fabric.

  b. Glue fabric to the top and front of the sofa bottom piece, covering the entire surface with glue. When the glue is dry, trim off the excess.

  c. Glue fabric to the front edge of the arm. Trim the excess (Fig. 111B).

  d. Glue fabric to the inside of the arm and around the curved part (arrow). Trim the excess (Fig. 111C).

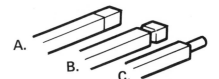

FIG. 109

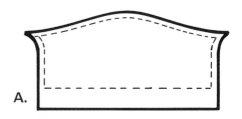

FIG. 110

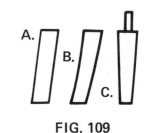

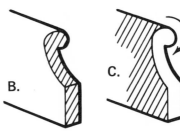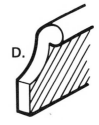

FIG. 111

e. The sofa back, bottom, and arms are now glued and pinned together permanently.

f. Glue fabric to the outside of the arms. Trim the excess (Fig. 111D).

g. If there are gaps in the backside of the sofa, fill these in with wood filler and sand smooth. Glue fabric to the backside of the sofa. Trim the excess.

h. Glue fabric to the underside of the cushion piece. Trim the excess. Glue fabric around all four sides of the cushion piece. Trim the excess.

i. Raw edges where the fabric has been trimmed can be covered with twisted cord to simulate welting. To make a twisted cord, use 2 or 3 threads of a six-thread strand of embroidery floss. Two feet of thread gives a twisted cord of less than one foot.

Tie one end of the threads to a stable object. Hold the other end of the threads in your fingers and twist them until the cord begins to knot up on itself. Hold the cord at the center and bring all the ends together. The cord will then twist tightly on itself. The tighter you have twisted the cord in the beginning, the tighter the final twisted cord will be. Glue the twisted cord carefully over the raw edges of the fabric, applying the glue sparingly with a toothpick. Use a little extra glue where the cord will be cut to prevent raveling.

4. Finishing.
Give the legs a coat of shellac, mixed half and half with denatured alcohol. Sand lightly. Paint legs a wood tone color, using acrylic tube paints. Apply antiquing ink and rub off for a soft, blended effect or brush off with a dry paintbrush for a wood-grained effect. When the antiquing is dry, apply two thin coats of semi-gloss oil base varnish. Glue the leg framework into the sofa framework.

DINING TABLE

Materials: Mat knife, sandpaper, emery boards, razor saw, Swiss pattern files (optional), pin vise with $\frac{1}{16}$" bit, carbon paper, Elmer's glue.

Note: Sand all wood pieces lightly and smooth with fine steel wool before final assembly wherever possible. Sand and steel wool the finished piece where needed.

1. Table legs.
a. With a razor saw, cut $\frac{3}{16}$" dowel to the proper length. To carve the dowel, mark the position of the foot on the dowel. Make shallow cuts around $\frac{3}{4}$ of the dowel and hollow out the shape with a knife and sandpaper wrapped around a small dowel or with a file. Leave the back $\frac{1}{4}$ of the dowel flat (Fig. 112A).

b. Shape the underside of the foot with an emery board (Fig. 112B).

c. Taper the rest of the dowel roughly to fit into the foot. Finish the tapering and smoothing of the leg with sandpaper and steel wool (Fig. 112C).

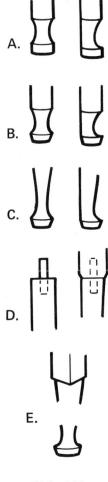

A.

B.

C.

D.

E.

FIG. 112

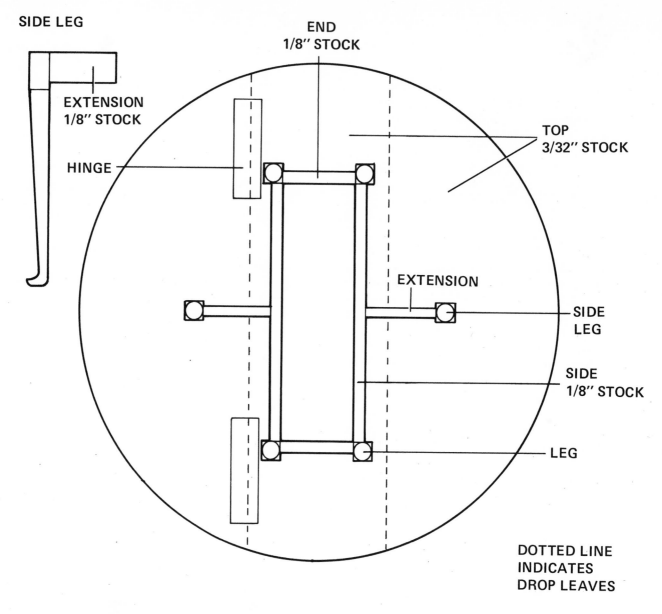

SIDE LEG

EXTENSION
1/8" STOCK

HINGE

END
1/8" STOCK

TOP
3/32" STOCK

EXTENSION

SIDE
LEG

SIDE
1/8" STOCK

LEG

DOTTED LINE
INDICATES
DROP LEAVES

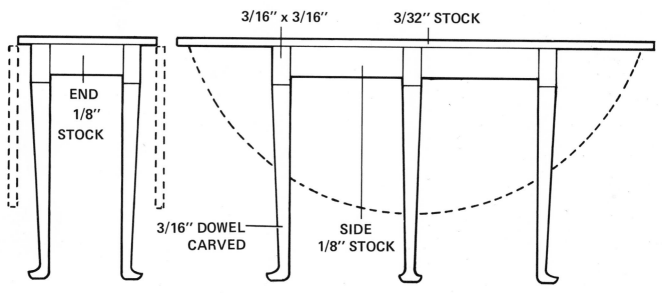

3/16" x 3/16"

3/32" STOCK

END
1/8"
STOCK

3/16" DOWEL
CARVED

SIDE
1/8" STOCK

SCALE 1" = 1'

QUEEN ANNE DINING TABLE

PLATE 38

d. Drill a hole in the top of the leg and insert a toothpick, with glue. Cut the toothpick short, carve it down a bit, and sand it round to form an insert (Fig. 112D). Cut the ³⁄₁₆″ square part of the leg. Drill a hole in this piece. Glue the two pieces of the leg together (Fig. 112D). The round part of the leg is glued into the square part at an angle so that the front of the foot lines up with the corner of the square piece (Fig. 112E). If necessary, trim down the round part to fit the square part.

2. Table framework.

a. Trace the shapes of the side and end pieces on paper. Transfer the shapes onto wood with carbon paper. Cut them out. Make the ends of the table by gluing two legs and an end piece together. It is helpful to tape the glued pieces to the plans while the glue dries, to assure proper position. When the glue is dry, drill ¹⁄₁₆″ holes through the legs and into the end pieces. Insert a carved down toothpick, with glue. Break off the end of the toothpick and sand flush with the legs.

b. Glue the side pieces to the table ends to form the table framework. Drill holes and

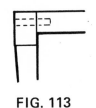

FIG. 113

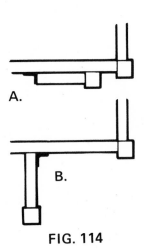

FIG. 114

insert toothpicks as before.

c. Glue the side legs to their extensions (Fig. 113). Add toothpicks for strength. The side legs are attached to the table framework with silk mesh glued on in two stages (Fig. 114A and B). The dark lines in Fig. 114 indicate the hinges.

d. The top of the framework is likely to be uneven. Tape the side legs, in closed position, to the main table framework. Even off the top of the framework with sandpaper.

3. Tabletop.

Trace the shape of the tabletop parts on paper. Transfer the shapes onto wood with carbon paper. Cut out the pieces. Tape them together temporarily. Round the upper edges slightly, with sandpaper. Smooth the tabletop with sandpaper and steel wool. Hinge the pieces together with silk mesh. Do not use mesh where the side legs will swing in and out.

You can paint and finish the framework and top separately and then glue them together or assemble the table and then finish it. If you finish them separately, first tape them together temporarily to see that the side legs and drop-leaf sides work well.

4. Finishing.

Give the table a coat of shellac, mixed half and half with denatured alcohol. Sand lightly. Paint on a wood tone, using acrylic tube paints. Apply antiquing ink. Rub off for a soft, blended effect or brush off with a dry paintbrush for a wood-grained effect. When the antiquing is dry, give the table two thin coats of semi-gloss oil base varnish. Sand the tabletop lightly and apply one or two more coats of varnish. Sand lightly and smooth with extra fine steel wool. Finish off with a coat of paste wax.

CANDLESTAND TABLE OR POLE SCREEN

Materials: Mat knife, carbon paper, Elmer's glue, Weldwood cement, emery boards, sandpaper, pin vise with small bit to fit straight pins, wire clippers.

Note: Sand all wood pieces lightly and smooth with fine steel wool before final assembly wherever possible. Sand and steel wool the finished piece where needed.

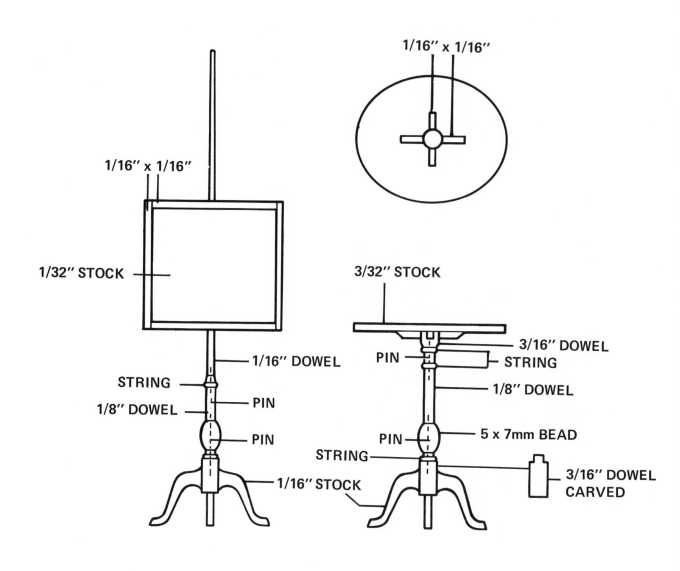

1/16" x 1/16"

1/16" x 1/16"

1/32" STOCK

3/32" STOCK

3/16" DOWEL

1/16" DOWEL

PIN

STRING

STRING

1/8" DOWEL

PIN

1/8" DOWEL

PIN

PIN

5 x 7mm BEAD

STRING

1/16" STOCK

PIN

3/16" DOWEL
CARVED

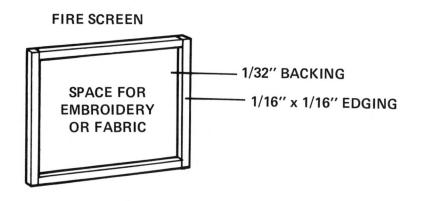

FIRE SCREEN

SPACE FOR
EMBROIDERY
OR FABRIC

1/32" BACKING

1/16" x 1/16" EDGING

SCALE 1" = 1'

CANDLESTAND AND FIRESCREEN

PLATE 39

1. Legs.

    Trace the shape of the leg on paper. Transfer the shape to the wood with carbon paper. The main part of the leg goes with the grain of the wood for easier carving (Fig. 115A). Cut out the legs to the general shape. With Elmer's glue, glue the three wood leg pieces together with two dots of glue. All three legs are then sanded to the finished shape at one time.

    To cut out the legs, carve out the inside curves first. Carve a little way into the curve. The excess wood should fall away with the grain of the wood (Fig. 115B). If not, cut it away. Continue this way until the curve is complete. The outside curves can then be cut. Sand the curves to smooth them. Soak the legs in water for a few minutes till the glue softens and pull the legs apart. When the wood dries, round off the top edges of the legs with an emery board and smooth the legs with steel wool.

    To add a little shaping to the foot, apply two or three coats of Elmer's glue to the foot, blending the glue into the wood with a damp paintbrush.

2. Assembly.

    a. For the carved ¾₆″ dowel piece, on the end of the dowel, mark the carving line (Fig. 116A). Make a shallow cut around the dowel on the mark and carve away a bit of wood (Fig. 116B). Continue carving away wood to finish the shape. Sand smooth with an emery board (Fig. 116C). Cut the dowel to the proper length.

    b. For the string turnings, coat the string with glue and wrap it around the dowel (Fig. 117A). While the glue is still damp, cut through the string with a sharp blade. Remove the string ends (Fig. 117B). Adjust the ends so they meet. Add a dot of glue at the joint (Fig. 117C).

    c. Flatten both ends of the 5 × 7mm bead. To do this, place the bead on a toothpick and sand the ends with an emery board, first one end then the other.

    d. Drill a pin hole in the carved ¾₆″ dowel piece and the ⅛″ dowel piece. Insert a straight pin, with Elmer's glue and add the bead, with glue. Cut off the pin with wire clippers, a little above the bead. Add the

⅛″ dowel, with glue. Smooth any excess glue with a damp paintbrush. After the glue is dry, coat the joints with one or two applications of Elmer's glue to blend the shapes. Smooth with a damp paintbrush.

    e. For the table, drill a pin hole in the end of a piece of ¾₆″ dowel. Round off the end with an emery board and cut it to size. For the pole screen, drill a pin hole in the end of the ¹⁄₁₆″ dowel and cut it to size. To taper the dowel, carve away some wood to the general shape and finish the tapering with sandpaper and steel wool.

    f. For the table, drill a pin hole in the top of the ⅛″ dowel, insert a cut off pin, with glue, and add the piece of ¾₆″ dowel, with glue. For the pole screen, do the same with the ⅛″ dowel and the ¹⁄₁₆″ dowel. Round off the top of the ⅛″ dowel slightly.

    g. Add the remaining string turnings.

    h. Glue the legs on. Use Weldwood cement here. Because it is a contact cement it gives

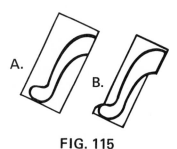

FIG. 115

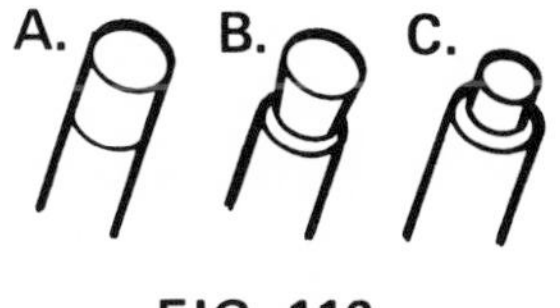

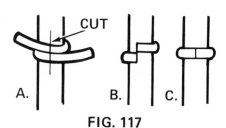

FIG. 116

FIG. 117

instant stability but the legs can be adjusted slightly before the glue sets permanently. Excess glue can be removed with lacquer thinner. Elmer's glue may also be used, but it takes longer to set up.

i. For the table, trace the shape of the tabletop on paper and transfer it to wood with carbon paper. Cut out the shape. Round off the top edges with sandpaper. Smooth the tabletop with steel wool. Glue the tabletop to the table base, making sure it is straight. After the glue dries, glue on the $\frac{1}{16}'' \times \frac{1}{16}''$ pieces for added strength.

j. For the pole screen, glue the $\frac{1}{16}'' \times \frac{1}{16}''$ edge pieces to the $\frac{1}{32}''$ backing piece. Cut away the excess backing. Embroidery or fabric should be mounted on thin cardboard before being glued into place. The firescreen is held in place on the pole with one or two narrow strips of construction paper glued in place.

3. Finishing.

Give the table or pole screen a coat of shellac, mixed half and half with denatured alcohol to seal the wood. Sand lightly. Paint on a light wood tone, using acrylic tube paints. Apply antiquing ink. Rub off for a soft, blended effect to accentuate the shapes or brush off with a dry paintbrush for a wood-grained effect. When the antiquing is dry, give the table or pole screen two thin coats of semi-gloss oil base varnish. For the tabletop, smooth gently with extra fine steel wool and finish off with a coat of paste wax.

BARGELLO PANEL

The bargello design is worked on 40 to the inch silk mesh with one thread of a six-thread strand of embroidery floss. On the mesh, mark the four edges (the size of the firescreen area). Count the mesh holes, in from the edges, to establish the center of the piece. Mount the mesh on a piece of cardboard with the work area cut out, like a frame. Figure out how many whole motifs are needed to reach from the center to (or almost to) the edges. Leaving all thread ends loose and allowing extra thread to work at the edges, work one row of whole motifs from the center to the edges (Fig. 118).

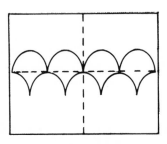

FIG. 118

To work bargello, lead thread to the front of the work through hole 1, over the required number of meshes and to the back of the work through hole 2; to the front through hole 3, over the meshes and to the back through hole 4, etc. (Fig. 119).

Next, fill out to the edges following the established pattern. Weave in the loose thread ends on the backside of the work. Fill in the remaining marked area, following the pattern. To mount the bargello panel, cut a piece of thin cardboard to fit the firescreen area. Cut out the bargello panel, leaving $\frac{1}{4}''$ or more extra mesh around the design. Fold the extra mesh over the back of the cardboard and glue in place. Glue the mounted panel in place on the firescreen.

BASIC CABRIOLE LEG

Materials: Mat knife, Elmer's glue, emery boards, sandpaper, steel wool, razor saw, Swiss pattern files (optional), pin vise with $\frac{1}{16}''$ bit.

Cabriole legs can be made in several ways. The following method looks complicated but is relatively easy and gives strong, more uniform legs in the long run.

1. Basic shape.

The basic pieces for the first step are $\frac{1}{16}''$ thick wood strips glued together (Fig. 120A). Draw the shape of the leg on the glued together pieces and cut out this shape (Fig. 120B). For making two or more matching legs, tape the cut out shapes together tightly (around the middle where they need little shaping) and sandpaper all the legs at one time for the final shaping of this step (Fig. 120C). Hard to get at places can be shaped with sandpaper wrapped around a small dowel or with a file.

WHOLE MOTIF AND REPEATS

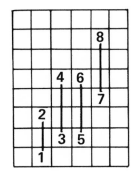

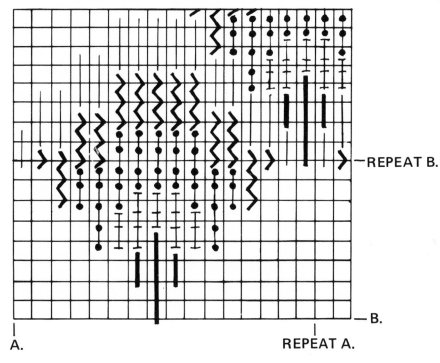

— REPEAT B.

A.
REPEAT A.

— B.

FIG. 119

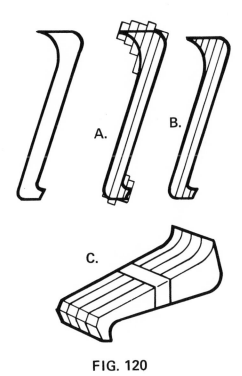

FIG. 120

2. Knee and foot.

The next step is to add thickness at the side of the square basic shape (Fig. 121A). On one side of the leg, glue wood pieces at the top (knee) and bottom (foot) of the basic shape (Fig. 121B). Tape these pieces in place till the glue dries. When the glue is dry, carve the added pieces to fit the basic shape (Fig. 121C). Follow this procedure on both sides of the basic shape (Fig. 121D).

3. Position.

When you look at the top of this built-up shape, you will see a square shape of various layers (Fig. 122A). The leg fits into the furniture framework at an angle. The dotted line in Fig. 122B shows the framework. The dark line shows the shaping of the leg from the squared shape to the angled shape.

4. Carving and finishing.

Figure 123A shows the leg before carving. Figure 123B shows the leg after carving. With this built-up method you will notice that there are visible lines where the pieces have been

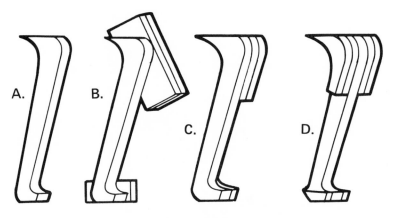

FIG. 121

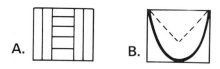

FIG. 122

glued together. These are useful in keeping your carving even.

Generally, right above the foot, it is best to carve just a tiny bit into the basic shape for a more graceful leg. The top part of the leg is then carved and sanded with an emery board almost to a V-shape. The dotted line in Fig. 123B indicates the point of the V. The foot is sanded to a round shape. In Fig. 123C the

point of the V is rounded off and the under-side of the foot angled as shown. Smooth the leg with fine steel wool.

To complete the leg (Fig. 123D) drill a hole in the top of the leg and insert a tooth-pick, with glue. Carve the toothpick down a bit, cut it off, and sand it round to form an insert. For the foot, with a razor saw, cut a thin slice of $1/8''$ dowel and glue it to the bottom of the foot. When the glue is dry, sand this down to the thickness desired.

After the leg is glued into the furniture framework, the top edge of the knee is blended, with an emery board, into the frame-work.

Note: If you have not been able to get the leg as smooth as you desire (especially around the

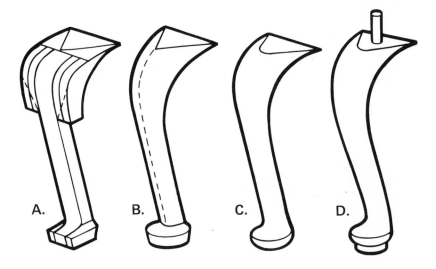

FIG. 123

foot) the entire leg can be given two or three coats of Elmer's glue. Apply the glue (full thickness) with a small paintbrush and smooth and thin it with a small, damp paintbrush. The glue coating will soften rough spots and fill in and blend carving errors. Since the final furniture piece will be painted and antiqued rather than stained, the glue coating will not detract from its appearance.

QUEEN ANNE ARMCHAIR OR SIDE CHAIR

Materials: Mat knife, Elmer's glue, Weldwood cement, carbon paper, emery boards, sandpaper, Swiss pattern files (optional), pin vise with $\frac{1}{16}''$ bit, razor saw.

Note: Sand all wood pieces lightly and smooth with fine steel wool before final assembly wherever possible. Sand and steel wool the finished piece where needed.

1. Cabriole leg.
   Study the instructions for the basic cabriole leg. For the cabriole leg for the chair, the pieces for the basic shape are $\frac{1}{8}'' \times \frac{1}{16}''$ wood strips (see plans: detail of leg). The side pieces are two $\frac{1}{16}''$ thick pieces on each side of the knee and one $\frac{1}{32}''$ thick piece on each side of the foot.

2. Back splat.
   Cut $\frac{1}{4}'' \times \frac{1}{16}''$ wood strips about $1\frac{1}{2}''$ longer than necessary. Tape the ends together. Trace the shape of half the splat on paper and transfer the shape to wood with carbon paper. Carve both pieces at one time to the general shape and finish the shaping with emery boards or with a file. With this method, both sides of the splat will be uniform (Fig. 124).

3. Side rails.
   a. The side rails are made from four $\frac{1}{8}'' \times \frac{1}{16}''$ wood strips, two for each rail. They are bent, glued together, and tapered to the proper shape. To bend the side rails, cut the wood about $1\frac{1}{2}''$ longer than the finished length. Soak the wood in water, overnight or longer, till it will bend easily. Soak also the carved back splat pieces. Trace the curve of the chair back on paper. On a heavy piece of scrap board, using the curve as a guide, mark the largest part of the

curve of the upper back (Fig. 125A) and the largest part of the curve of the lower legs (Fig. 125B). Nail $\frac{1}{4}'' \times \frac{1}{8}''$ wood pieces here. Bend the side rails and splat

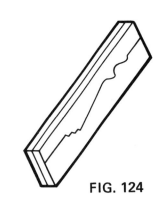

FIG. 124

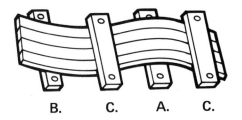

B.   C.   A.   C.

FIG. 125

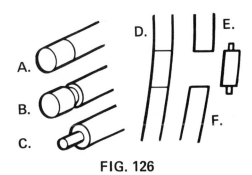

A.

B.

C.

D.

E.

F.

FIG. 126

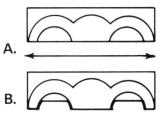

A.

B.

FIG. 127

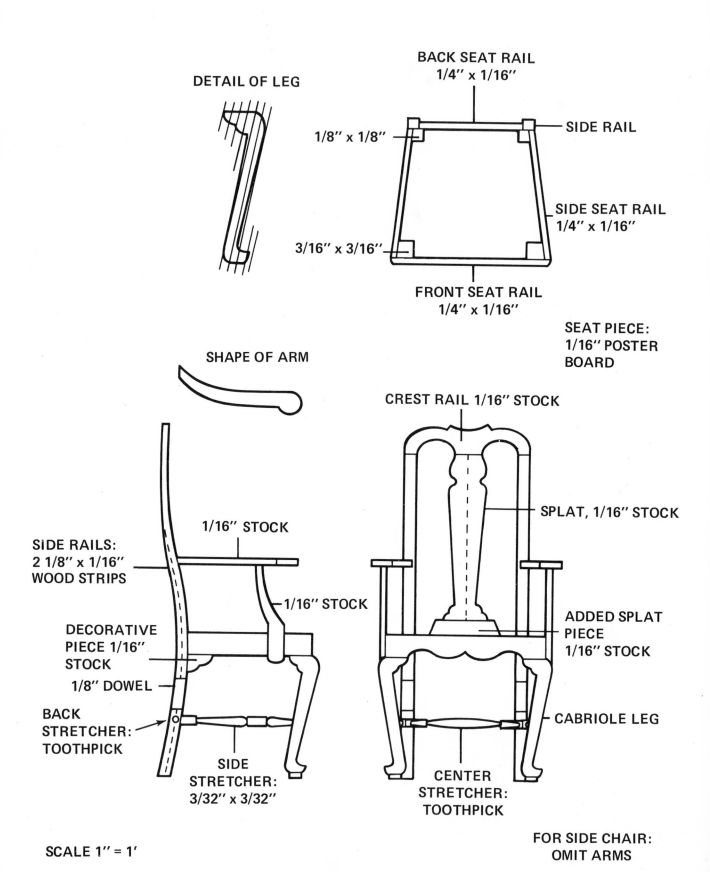

DETAIL OF LEG

BACK SEAT RAIL
1/4" x 1/16"

SIDE RAIL

1/8" x 1/8"

SIDE SEAT RAIL
1/4" x 1/16"

3/16" x 3/16"

FRONT SEAT RAIL
1/4" x 1/16"

SEAT PIECE:
1/16" POSTER
BOARD

SHAPE OF ARM

CREST RAIL 1/16" STOCK

1/16" STOCK

SPLAT, 1/16" STOCK

SIDE RAILS:
2 1/8" x 1/16"
WOOD STRIPS

1/16" STOCK

DECORATIVE
PIECE 1/16"
STOCK

ADDED SPLAT
PIECE
1/16" STOCK

1/8" DOWEL

BACK
STRETCHER:
TOOTHPICK

CABRIOLE LEG

SIDE
STRETCHER:
3/32" x 3/32"

CENTER
STRETCHER:
TOOTHPICK

SCALE 1" = 1'

FOR SIDE CHAIR:
OMIT ARMS

QUEEN ANNE CHAIR

PLATE 40

pieces over these pieces and hold them down with two more wood strips nailed to the board (Fig. 125C).

b. When the wood is dry and will hold its shape, glue two strips together for each side rail, using Elmer's glue. This makes $\frac{1}{8}''$ square side rails. For the round sections on the side rails, carve down a $\frac{1}{8}''$ dowel slightly. Sand it smooth and round. Cut the sections to size, plus some extra for inserts. To make the inserts, mark the inserts on the dowel (Fig. 126A). Make a shallow cut on the mark. Carve away a small bit of wood at the cut (Fig. 126B). Continue carving away wood to form the insert. Sand round with an emery board (Fig. 126C). It is best, during the entire chair construction, to have all inserts fit loosely in their holes to allow for slight adjustments. Glue will fill in the extra space.

Lay the side rails on the plans and mark where the round sections go (Fig. 126D). With a razor saw, cut the side rails (Figs. 126E and F). Drill $\frac{1}{16}''$ holes in the bottom of e. and the top of f. Glue the round section, with inserts into the holes, into the square sections. Use Elmer's glue. Though this formation is rather typical of chairs of this type, this step may be omitted, if desired.

Cut the side rails to the proper length. Taper the side rails to $\frac{1}{16}''$ thickness at the top by carving and sanding. Sand the side rails and smooth with steel wool.

c. Glue the two sections of the back splat together, using Weldwood cement. Excess glue can be removed with lacquer thinner. Sand lightly and smooth with steel wool.

4. Crest rail.

Trace the shape of the crest rail on paper and transfer the shape to the wood with carbon paper. The shape goes with the grain of the wood for easier carving (Fig. 127A). For the inside curves, (Fig. 127B) carve a little way into the curve. The excess wood should fall out with the grain of the wood. If not, cut it away. Continue this way till the curve is complete. The outside curves can then be cut and smoothed with an emery board or a file.

5. Assembly of the chair back.

a. Cut the remaining pieces for the chair back: the added piece at the bottom of the splat, the back seat rail, and the back stretcher. Cut the splat to its proper length.

b. Mark the position of the back stretcher on the side rails. Drill $\frac{1}{16}''$ holes at the marks, through the rails. To make the back stretcher, cut a toothpick long enough to include inserts through the side rails. Mark the major divisions on the toothpick and make shallow cuts at the marks (Fig. 128A). Cut away a bit of wood at the cuts (Fig. 128B). Carve away more wood to form a gentle curve (Fig. 5C). Smooth the stretcher by rotating inside a wad of steel wool. Carve the inserts (Fig. 5D). Keep the fit loose.

c. Glue all the back pieces together. Glue the crest rail, splat, side rails, added piece on the splat, and the back seat rail with Weldwood for added strength. The back seat rail fits flush with the front side of the side rails. Glue the stretcher in place with Elmer's glue. It is helpful to tape the glued pieces to the plans while the glue dries to assure proper position. After the glue is dry, cut off the excess insert on the stretcher and sand flush with the side rails. Fill in any space with Elmer's glue. Smooth the entire back with steel wool. Blend in the curves around the crest rail, splat, and side rails where they join with sandpaper wrapped around a small dowel or with a file.

6. Assembly of the chair front.

Cut out and carve the front seat rail in the same way as the crest rail. Glue $\frac{3}{16}'' \times \frac{3}{16}''$ wood blocks at the ends of the front seat rail, $\frac{1}{16}''$ in from the ends to accommodate the side seat rails (Fig. 129A) and $\frac{1}{16}''$ (or a

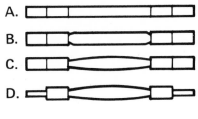

FIG. 128

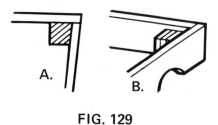

FIG. 129

FIG. 130

little bit more) down from the top, to accommodate the seat piece and its fabric covering (Fig. 129B).

Drill ⅟₁₆″ holes in the blocks for the cabriole leg inserts. Glue the legs into the wood blocks. Check their position carefully. When the glue is dry, trim the wood blocks to fit the legs (from square to triangular).

7. Assembly of the chair.
   a. For the side stretcher, carve the side stretchers from ³⁄₃₂″ × ³⁄₃₂″ wood much the same as for the back stretcher, except the round sections (Fig. 130A) must be carved from square to round. After shaping, smooth with an emery board. Carve inserts on the ends. Drill ⅟₁₆″ holes for the center stretcher (Fig. 130B).
   b. The center stretcher is made the same as the back stretcher, but longer.
   c. Cut out the side seat rails.
   d. Mark the position of the side stretchers on the side rails and on the cabriole legs. Drill ⅟₁₆″ holes in the side rails and legs for the inserts on the side stretchers. The stretchers fit in at an angle, so the holes should be drilled at the same angle.
   e. Glue the chair back assembly and the chair front assembly together with the side seat rails, side stretchers, and the center stretcher, using Elmer's glue. The outsides of the side seat rails fit flush with the outsides of the side rails. Adjust the position of the legs, stretchers, etc., while the glue is still wet.

f. Glue ⅛″ × ⅛″ wood blocks at the back corners for extra strength, ⅟₁₆″ down from the top to accommodate the seat piece. Round slightly the front corners of the seat rails.
g. Cut out the added decorative pieces and glue in place flush with the outside of the side seat rail and the side rails.
h. Cut the seat piece from ⅟₁₆″ thick poster board.
i. For the arms, trace the shapes of the arm pieces, transfer to wood and cut out. Glue in place with Weldwood for extra strength.

8. Finishing.
   a. Give the chair a coat of shellac, mixed half and half with denatured alcohol to seal the wood. Sand lightly. Paint the chair a light wood tone, using acrylic tube paints. Apply antiquing ink. Rub off for a soft, blended effect to accentuate the shapes or brush off with a dry paintbrush for a wood-grained effect. When the antiquing is dry, give the chair two thin coats of semi-gloss oil base varnish.
   b. To cover the seat, glue a layer of art foam on the seat piece. Dot on the glue rather than cover the entire surface. Cut fabric about ½″ larger than the seat piece all around. Cover the seat, gluing the excess fabric on the underside of the seat. Glue paper, cut to shape, on the underside of the seat piece for a neat appearance. The seat piece can be slipped in place, rather than glued. This way the fabric can be changed easily.

QUEEN ANNE HIGHBOY

Materials: Elmer's glue, Weldwood cement, mat knife, carbon paper, masking tape, Swiss pattern files (optional), needle-nose pliers, pin vise with small bit to fit straight pins and ⅟₁₆″ bit.

Note: Sand all wood pieces lightly and smooth with steel wool before final assembly wherever possible. Sand and steel wool the finished piece. Upper framework back may have to be cut from two wood pieces, glued together, edges butted.

1. Cabriole leg.
   Study the instructions for the basic cabriole leg. In the leg for the highboy, the pieces for

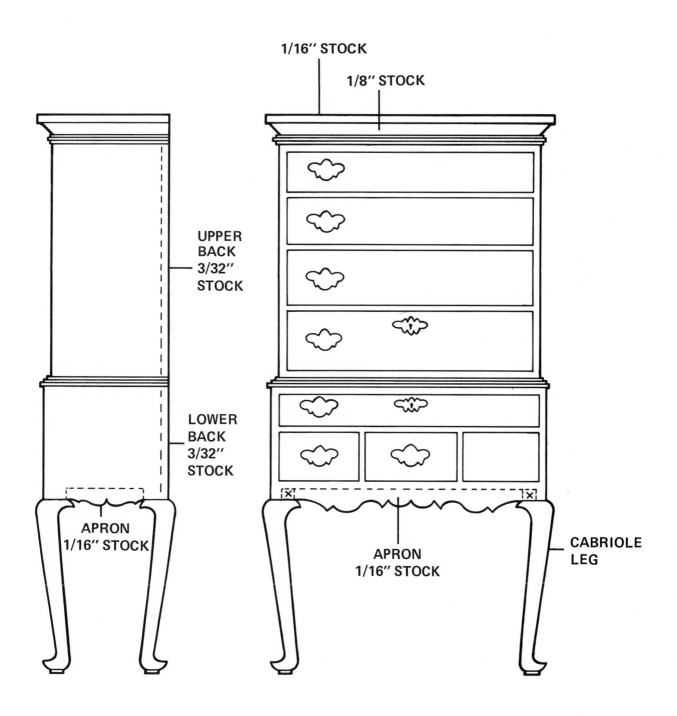

1/16" STOCK

1/8" STOCK

UPPER
BACK
3/32"
STOCK

LOWER
BACK
3/32"
STOCK

APRON
1/16" STOCK

APRON
1/16" STOCK

CABRIOLE
LEG

SCALE 1" = 1'

X: ADDED 1/8" x 1/8" PIECES TO MAKE
CORNER 1/4" x 1/4"

QUEEN ANNE HIGHBOY

PLATE 41A

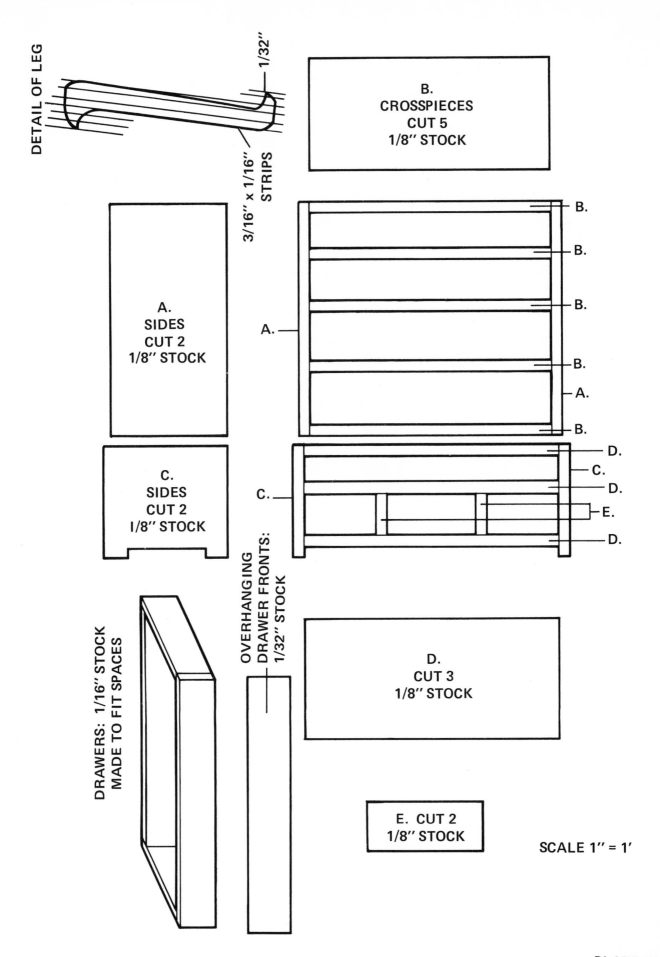

DETAIL OF LEG

1/32"

3/16" x 1/16" STRIPS

B.
CROSSPIECES
CUT 5
1/8" STOCK

A.
SIDES
CUT 2
1/8" STOCK

A.

B.
B.
B.
B.
A.
B.

C.
SIDES
CUT 2
1/8" STOCK

C.

D.
C.
D.
E.
D.

DRAWERS: 1/16" STOCK
MADE TO FIT SPACES

OVERHANGING
DRAWER FRONTS:
1/32" STOCK

D.
CUT 3
1/8" STOCK

E. CUT 2
1/8" STOCK

SCALE 1" = 1'

PLATE 41B

the basic shape are $\frac{3}{16}'' \times \frac{1}{16}''$ wood strips, plus a $\frac{1}{32}''$ bit at the toe of the foot (see plans: detail of leg). The side pieces are one $\frac{1}{16}''$ and one $\frac{1}{32}''$ thick piece on each side of the knee and one $\frac{1}{32}''$ thick piece on each side of the foot. Because of the thickness of the leg, it is necessary, for a graceful leg, to carve into the basic shape a bit more, around the foot, than instructed for the basic cabriole leg.

2. Framework.
   a. Trace the shape of the major framework pieces on paper. Transfer to the wood with carbon paper. Measure the plans and mark on paper the shapes of the upper and lower framework back pieces. Transfer to wood with carbon paper. Cut out the pieces and glue together the upper framework and the lower framework, but not to each other. The front edges of the frameworks are likely to be uneven. To correct this, lay sandpaper on a flat surface and rub the frameworks on the sandpaper to even off the edges. Glue added pieces in the corners.
   b. Cut a piece of $\frac{1}{16}''$ stock to fit the top of the lower framework. Glue in place with Weldwood cement, to prevent the wood from curling. Cut a piece of $\frac{1}{32}''$ stock to fit the bottom of the upper framework. Glue in place with Weldwood. Glue the upper and lower frameworks together (Fig. 131A). With Elmer's glue, glue on $\frac{1}{32}'' \times \frac{1}{32}''$ strips for the trim (Fig. 131B). Soften the edges of the trim with steel wool.

3. Legs.
   Drill $\frac{1}{16}''$ holes in the framework for the leg inserts. It is best to have the inserts fit loosely in the holes to allow for small adjustments of the position of the legs. The glue will fill in the extra space. Glue the legs in place with Elmer's glue.

4. Aprons.
   Trace the shapes of the aprons on paper and transfer to wood with carbon paper. The scrollwork goes with the grain of the wood for easier carving. Cut out the shapes and carve the scrolls to the general shape. Finish the shaping with emery boards or files. The hard to get at places (the inside curves) can be shaped with sandpaper wrapped around a small dowel or with a file. Glue the aprons

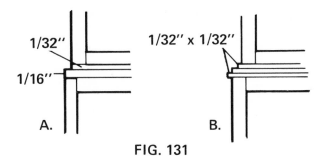

FIG. 131

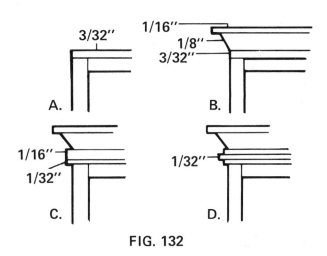

FIG. 132

in place, flush with the front and sides of the highboy. A $\frac{1}{8}'' \times \frac{1}{16}''$ wood strip will do for the back apron.

5. Cornice, cap, and trim.
   Cut a piece of $\frac{3}{32}''$ stock to fit the top of the upper framework. Glue in place with Weldwood (Fig. 132A). Cut a piece of $\frac{1}{8}''$ stock to size, bevel the edges to fit the upper framework, and glue in place. For a clean bevel, lay tape on the bevel line. Carve and sand away wood up to the tape. The tape prevents sanding away too much wood (Fig. 132B). Cut a piece of $\frac{1}{16}''$ stock to overhang the cornice and glue in place (Fig. 132B). Over the added $\frac{3}{32}''$ piece, with Elmer's glue, glue on a $\frac{3}{32}'' \times \frac{1}{32}''$ piece or one $\frac{1}{32}'' \times \frac{1}{16}''$ and one $\frac{1}{32}'' \times \frac{1}{32}''$ piece to cover the edges (Fig. 132C). Over these, in the center, glue a $\frac{1}{32}'' \times \frac{1}{32}''$ strip to complete the trim (Fig. 132D). Soften the edges of the trim with steel wool.

6. Drawers.
   Cut the drawer fronts to fit the openings. Cut the sides, bottom, and back of the drawers to

fit the drawer fronts and the depth of the openings. Glue the pieces together. For the overhanging drawer fronts, cut $\frac{1}{32}''$ stock to size and glue in place with Weldwood. Bevel the edges, as described, using tape as a guide.

7. Finishing.

Give the highboy a coat of shellac, mixed half and half with denatured alcohol to seal the wood. Sand lightly. Paint on a light wood tone, using acrylic tube paints. Apply antiquing ink. Rub off for a soft, blended effect to accentuate the shapes or brush off with a dry paintbrush for a wood-grained effect. When the antiquing is dry, apply one thin coat of semigloss oil base varnish. Glue on gold foil hardware (but not drawer pulls). Apply one more thin coat of varnish, let dry. Add drawer pulls.

8. Hardware.

For the backplates, I used Patricia Nimocks Victorian gold braid #306025. From the gold foil pieces (Fig. 133A), cut the shapes as shown in Fig. 133B. Clip out the shaded area and cut along the indicated lines. Glue the two pieces together on the drawer front (Fig. 133C). When the glue is dry, drill pin holes in the foil pieces and through the drawer front as indicated by the dots in Fig. 133C. For the drawer pulls, bend wire with needle-nose pliers and insert through the pin holes. Crimp the excess wire over on the back of the drawer fronts. Hold a bit of a matchbook cover over the drawer front to prevent making marks on the drawer with the pliers. Paint the wire brass. For the brass color, mix brass Treasure Jewels, a little varnish and a bit of yellow Testor's enamel paint.

For the locks, cut the foil pieces (Fig. 134A) as shown in Fig. 134B on the indicated lines. Glue the two pieces together on the drawer front as shown in Fig. 134C. Drill a pin hole in the center for the keyhole (Fig. 134D).

QUEEN ANNE BED

Materials: Mat knife, emery board, pin vise with $\frac{1}{32}''$ bit and $\frac{1}{16}''$ bit, carbon paper, Elmer's glue, wire clippers, sandpaper.

Note: Sand all wood pieces lightly and smooth with fine steel wool before final assembly wher-

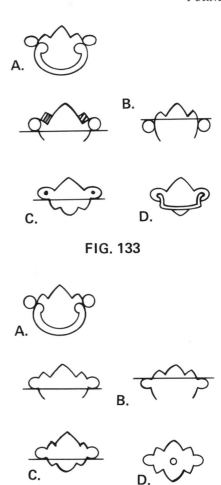

FIG. 133

FIG. 134

ever possible. Sand and steel wool the final piece where needed.

1. Cabriole leg.

Study the instructions for the basic cabriole leg. For the leg for the bed, the pieces for the basic shape are $\frac{1}{8}'' \times \frac{1}{16}''$ wood strips (see plans: detail of leg). The side pieces are one $\frac{1}{16}''$ and one $\frac{1}{32}''$ thick piece on each side of the knee and one $\frac{1}{32}''$ piece on each side of the foot.

2. Bedposts.

a. Cut the $\frac{3}{16}'' \times \frac{3}{16}''$ pieces to size. Drill $\frac{1}{16}''$ holes in both ends.

b. Cut the $\frac{5}{32}''$ dowels long enough to include an insert at the bottom. To make the insert, mark a line around the dowel (Fig. 135A). Make a shallow cut on the mark. Cut away

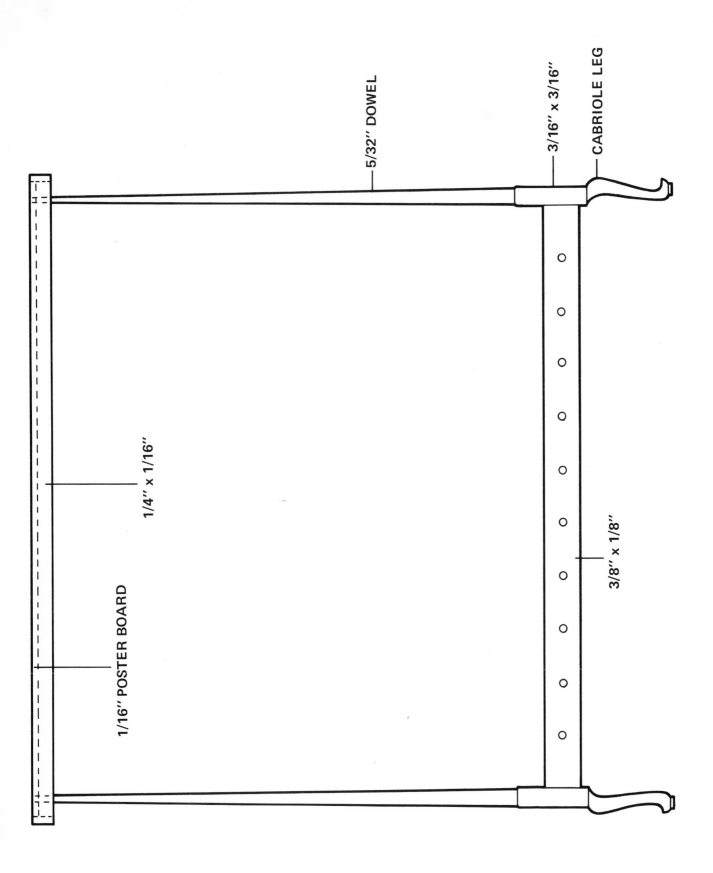

QUEEN ANNE BED

SCALE 1″ = 1′

PLATE 42A

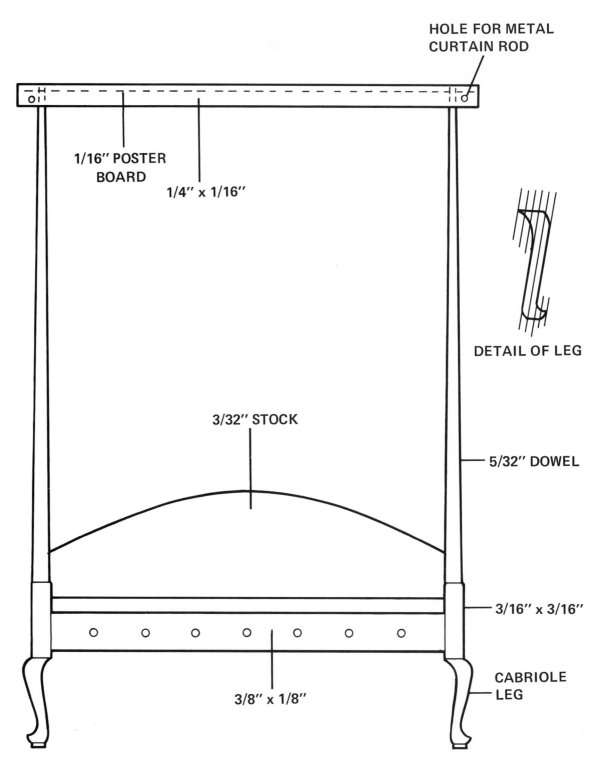

HOLE FOR METAL
CURTAIN ROD

1/16" POSTER
BOARD

1/4" x 1/16"

DETAIL OF LEG

3/32" STOCK

5/32" DOWEL

3/16" x 3/16"

CABRIOLE
LEG

3/8" x 1/8"

SCALE 1" = 1'

PLATE 42B

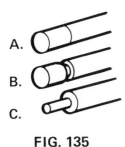

FIG. 135

a bit of wood at the mark (Fig. 135B). Continue carving away wood to form the insert (Fig. 135C). Round off the insert with an emery board.

c. Taper the dowel. To do this, carve the dowel to the general shape. Holding sandpaper curled in the palm of one hand, rotate the dowel inside the sandpaper. This keeps the dowel round as it is being smoothed. Finish smoothing with sandpaper and fine steel wool.

d. Glue the leg, $\frac{3}{16}'' \times \frac{3}{16}''$ piece and the tapered dowel together with inserts into the prepared holes. Bevel the tops of the $\frac{3}{16}'' \times \frac{3}{16}''$ pieces slightly with an emery board.

3. Framework.

a. Drill $\frac{1}{16}''$ holes in the end and side pieces of the bed frame. Glue the bed posts and end pieces together to make the head and foot of the bed. It is helpful to tape the glued pieces to the plans while the glue dries to assure proper position. For extra strength, when the glue is dry, drill $\frac{1}{16}''$ holes through the bedposts and into the end pieces. Insert a carved-down toothpick, with glue. Break off the toothpick and sand smooth, flush with the bedpost.

b. Trace the shape of the headboard on paper. Transfer the shape to the wood with carbon paper. Cut it out. Round off the top edges with sandpaper. Carve the headboard at the sides to fit the bedposts. Glue the headboard in place.

c. Glue the head- and footboard assemblies together with the bed sides. Add toothpicks for strength as before.

d. For the canopy, glue $\frac{1}{4}'' \times \frac{1}{16}''$ wood strips to the poster board top. Drill $\frac{1}{32}''$ holes for the wire curtain rods. Cut the wire

to size with wire clippers. Insert the curtain rods, with glue. Drill holes to receive the top ends of the bedposts. Glue the canopy top to the bedposts.

4. Finishing.

a. Give the bed a coat of shellac, mixed half and half with denatured alcohol to seal the wood. Sand lightly. Paint the bed a light wood tone, using acrylic tube paints. Apply antiquing ink. Rub off for a soft, blended effect to accentuate the shapes or brush off with a dry paintbrush for a wood-grained effect. When the antiquing is dry, give the bed two thin coats of semi-gloss oil base varnish. Smooth the headboard with extra fine steel wool and finish with a coat of paste wax.

b. Weave string in and out of the holes in the end and side pieces, in an over and under pattern to form a base for the mattress.

c. Mattresses can be made of three or four layers of art foam glued together. Dot on the glue rather than cover the entire surface. For the mattress cover, sew two pieces of lightweight cotton together on three sides, right sides together. Trim the seams closely. A bit of glue prevents raveling of the seams. Turn the cover right side out. Stuff the cover with the art foam mattress. Turn under the edges of the open side of the cover and sew closed. Pillows are made the same way, but smaller.

Bed covers, side curtains, and valances are made as desired.

PAINTING FURNITURE

Furniture pieces can be painted and antiqued to give a wood color and wood-grained effect to pieces which are meant to be wood. Pieces which are meant to look like painted pieces are given a color and antiqued to accent the construction and carving details.

The basic painting is done with acrylic tube paints, slightly thinned down with water, using a soft brush. Too thick paint tends to build up in the carved details, too thin does not cover well. Two thin coats may be needed. For wood pieces, many people like water base furniture stains, which are heavy enough to cover the varied

1/2 OAT BEAD

THREAD WRAP

5mm BEAD

5/32" DOWEL SLICE, EDGES ROUNDED

PIN

DETAIL A.

5mm BEAD

THREAD WRAP

5/32" DOWEL SLICE, EDGES ROUNDED

SAND HERE

PIN

DETAIL B.

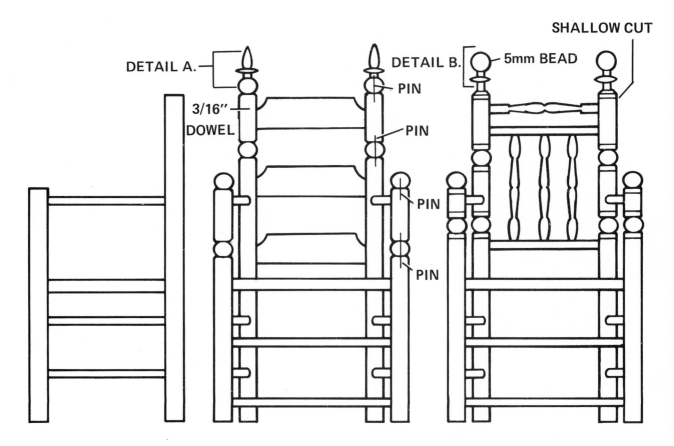

SHALLOW CUT

DETAIL A.

3/16" DOWEL

DETAIL B.

5mm BEAD

PIN

PIN

PIN

PIN

POSTS CAN BE CARVED OR
3/16" DOWELS AND
5mm BEADS, FLATTENED
RUNGS: TOOTHPICKS
SPINDLES: CARVED TOOTHPICKS

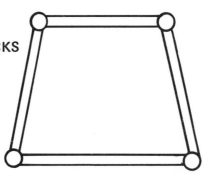

TWO CARVER CHAIRS

SCALE 1" = 1'

PLATE 43

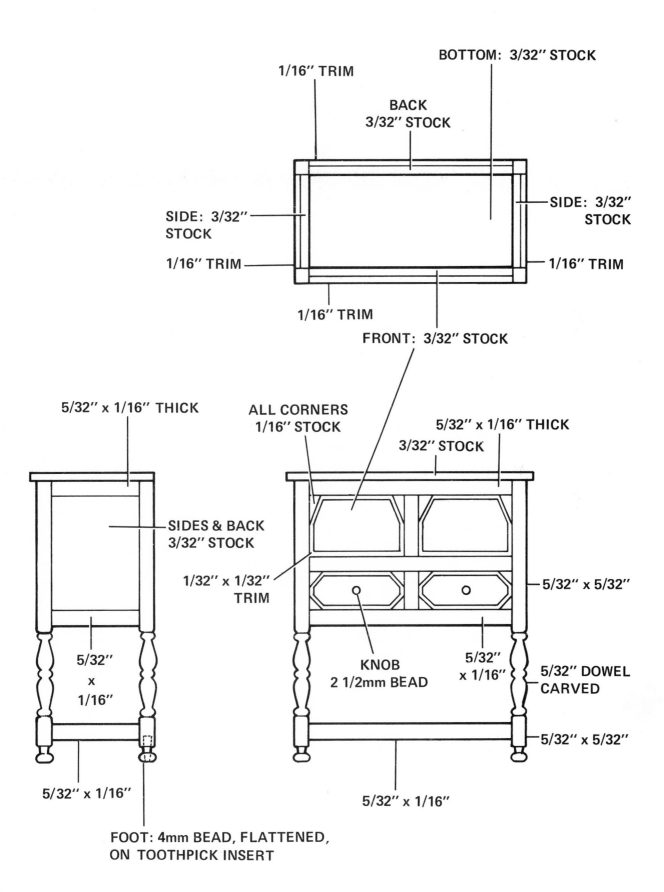

BOTTOM: 3/32″ STOCK

1/16″ TRIM

BACK
3/32″ STOCK

SIDE: 3/32″
STOCK

SIDE: 3/32″
STOCK

1/16″ TRIM

1/16″ TRIM

1/16″ TRIM

FRONT: 3/32″ STOCK

5/32″ x 1/16″ THICK

ALL CORNERS
1/16″ STOCK

5/32″ x 1/16″ THICK

3/32″ STOCK

SIDES & BACK
3/32″ STOCK

1/32″ x 1/32″
TRIM

5/32″ x 5/32″

5/32″
x
1/16″

KNOB
2 1/2mm BEAD

5/32″
x 1/16″

5/32″ DOWEL
CARVED

5/32″ x 5/32″

5/32″ x 1/16″

5/32″ x 1/16″

FOOT: 4mm BEAD, FLATTENED,
ON TOOTHPICK INSERT

SCALE 1″ = 1′

CHEST ON FRAME

PLATE 44

FOR DETAIL OF LEG ASSEMBLY SEE FIG. 78

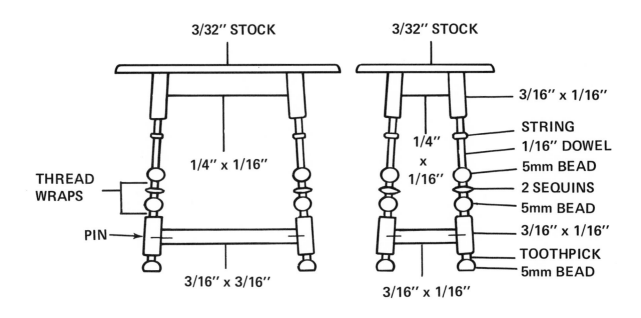

3/32" STOCK

3/32" STOCK

3/16" x 1/16"

STRING

1/16" DOWEL

5mm BEAD

2 SEQUINS

5mm BEAD

3/16" x 1/16"

TOOTHPICK

5mm BEAD

1/4"
x
1/16"

THREAD
WRAPS

1/4" x 1/16"

PIN →

3/16" x 3/16"

3/16" x 1/16"

JOINT STOOL

SCALE 1" = 1'

PLATE 45

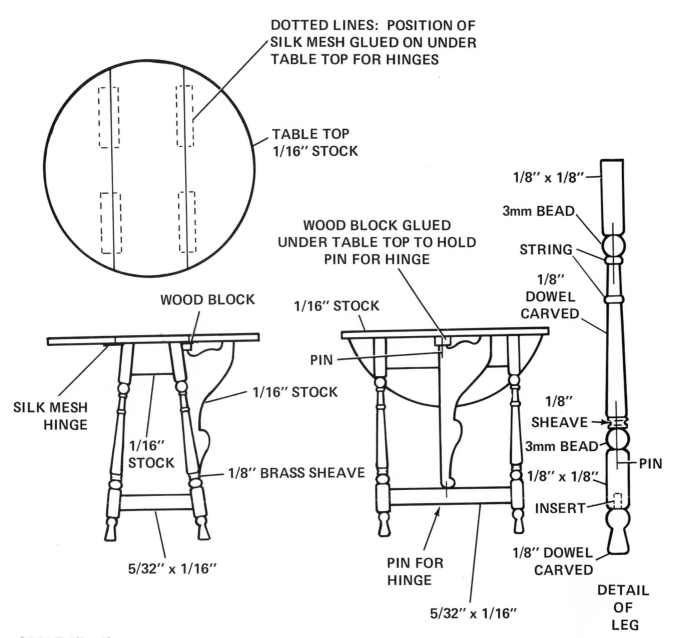

DOTTED LINES: POSITION OF SILK MESH GLUED ON UNDER TABLE TOP FOR HINGES

TABLE TOP 1/16" STOCK

WOOD BLOCK GLUED UNDER TABLE TOP TO HOLD PIN FOR HINGE

WOOD BLOCK

1/16" STOCK

PIN

1/16" STOCK

SILK MESH HINGE

1/16" STOCK

1/8" BRASS SHEAVE

5/32" x 1/16"

PIN FOR HINGE

5/32" x 1/16"

1/8" x 1/8"

3mm BEAD

STRING

1/8" DOWEL CARVED

1/8" SHEAVE

3mm BEAD

PIN

1/8" x 1/8"

INSERT

1/8" DOWEL CARVED

DETAIL OF LEG

SCALE 1" = 1'

BUTTERFLY TABLE

PLATE 46

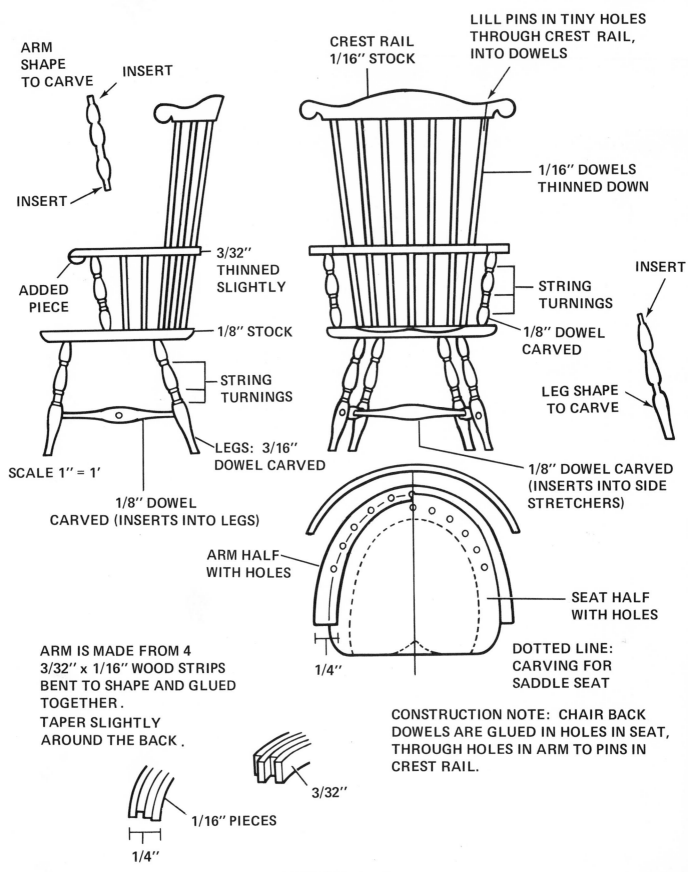

ARM
SHAPE
TO CARVE

INSERT

INSERT

ADDED
PIECE

SCALE 1" = 1'

1/8" DOWEL
CARVED (INSERTS INTO LEGS)

3/32"
THINNED
SLIGHTLY

1/8" STOCK

STRING
TURNINGS

LEGS: 3/16"
DOWEL CARVED

CREST RAIL
1/16" STOCK

LILL PINS IN TINY HOLES
THROUGH CREST RAIL,
INTO DOWELS

1/16" DOWELS
THINNED DOWN

INSERT

STRING
TURNINGS

1/8" DOWEL
CARVED

LEG SHAPE
TO CARVE

1/8" DOWEL CARVED
(INSERTS INTO SIDE
STRETCHERS)

ARM HALF
WITH HOLES

SEAT HALF
WITH HOLES

1/4"

DOTTED LINE:
CARVING FOR
SADDLE SEAT

ARM IS MADE FROM 4
3/32" x 1/16" WOOD STRIPS
BENT TO SHAPE AND GLUED
TOGETHER.
TAPER SLIGHTLY
AROUND THE BACK.

CONSTRUCTION NOTE: CHAIR BACK
DOWELS ARE GLUED IN HOLES IN SEAT,
THROUGH HOLES IN ARM TO PINS IN
CREST RAIL.

3/32"

1/16" PIECES

1/4"

WINDSOR CHAIR

PLATE 47

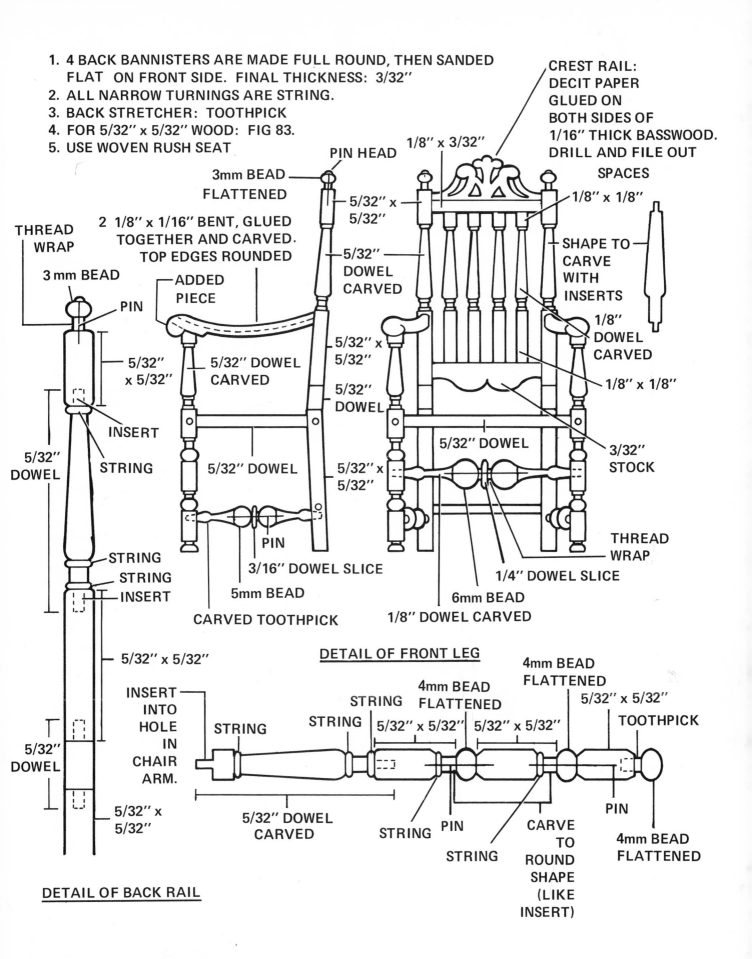

1. 4 BACK BANNISTERS ARE MADE FULL ROUND, THEN SANDED FLAT ON FRONT SIDE. FINAL THICKNESS: 3/32"
2. ALL NARROW TURNINGS ARE STRING.
3. BACK STRETCHER: TOOTHPICK
4. FOR 5/32" x 5/32" WOOD: FIG 83.
5. USE WOVEN RUSH SEAT

CREST RAIL: DECIT PAPER GLUED ON BOTH SIDES OF 1/16" THICK BASSWOOD. DRILL AND FILE OUT SPACES

1/8" x 3/32"

PIN HEAD

3mm BEAD FLATTENED

5/32" x 5/32"

5/32" DOWEL CARVED

1/8" x 1/8"

SHAPE TO CARVE WITH INSERTS

1/8" DOWEL CARVED

1/8" x 1/8"

3/32" STOCK

THREAD WRAP

3 mm BEAD

PIN

2 1/8" x 1/16" BENT, GLUED TOGETHER AND CARVED. TOP EDGES ROUNDED

ADDED PIECE

5/32" x 5/32"

INSERT

5/32" DOWEL CARVED

5/32" x 5/32"

5/32" DOWEL

5/32" DOWEL

STRING

5/32" DOWEL

STRING

STRING INSERT

5/32" DOWEL

PIN

3/16" DOWEL SLICE

5mm BEAD

CARVED TOOTHPICK

5/32" x 5/32"

5/32" DOWEL

THREAD WRAP

1/4" DOWEL SLICE

6mm BEAD

1/8" DOWEL CARVED

5/32" x 5/32"

INSERT INTO HOLE IN CHAIR ARM.

DETAIL OF FRONT LEG

4mm BEAD FLATTENED

4mm BEAD FLATTENED

5/32" x 5/32"

TOOTHPICK

STRING

STRING

5/32" x 5/32"

5/32" x 5/32"

STRING

STRING

PIN

STRING

CARVE TO ROUND SHAPE (LIKE INSERT)

PIN

4mm BEAD FLATTENED

5/32" DOWEL CARVED

5/32" x 5/32"

DETAIL OF BACK RAIL

SCALE 1" = 1'

BANNISTER BACK CHAIR

PLATE 48

building materials. Use whichever you like: they both dry fast. If you use water base stain, seal the stain with one or two coats of vinyl spray or latex varnish before antiquing.

For antiquing furniture, a water base antiquing can be done. It is a thin wash of mixed black and brown acrylic paint. I much prefer, personally, the oil base antiquing ink for doing furniture; nothing else really moves around, accents, can be controlled like an oil base, or gives the same rich look.

Antiquing softens the general effect and accents carved details at the same time. For furniture which is to look painted, start with a strong bright color or a clear light one. Antiquing is meant to dull and soften the color so it is wise to start with brighter, clearer colors than are wanted for the final result.

Wood effect pieces are first painted a light wood tone: orangy tan for maple, yellowy tan for pine and oak, reddish tan for cherry, reddish tan slightly darker for mahogany, and goldy tan for walnut.

The antiquing ink comes in several shades; each shade over a color or wood tone produces a slightly different effect. Old Masters, shade no. 3 is my standby.

Antiquing can be thinned with turpentine for lighter or heavier application. For all furniture pieces, it is best applied with a soft paintbrush. For painted pieces, it can be applied thinly, allowed to flow into carved details to accent them, and then rubbed off with a bit of cloth or cotton swab, or brushed off with a dry paintbrush. This will soften the overall effect, accent details, and generally give the piece a soft, blended look.

For wood pieces, the antiquing can be applied more heavily with a brush. It can be rubbed off, as before, for a soft look or you can let it set up a bit (5 or 10 minutes) and brush it off with a dry paintbrush, lightly. This will give you an effect of wood grain. A nice touch is: After this first "wood-graining" coat is dry, a second, thinner, blended coat softens the effect. For wood effects you just have to play with the base colors, antiquing shades and techniques, to find what you like. One of the nice things about antiquing ink is that it stays wet and workable for a while so you *can* play with different effects. If you do not like any of your efforts, wash off the antiquing ink with turpentine and start over. Antiquing is a fun medium.

When you have achieved the effect you want, let the antiquing dry at least 24 hours. It will lose some luster as it dries but varnish will bring it back. Brush on two thin coats of polyurethane varnish, flat, semi-, or high-gloss. (You may prefer latex varnish. This does not have as much natural luster as the oil base varnish and is most suitable for informal furniture.) Latex varnish should not be used over the oil base antiquing, though I often do it. Here, you might prefer to use a water base antiquing. For large flat areas such as tabletops, apply two or three coats of varnish, sand lightly with #600 Wetordry sandpaper and .0000 steel wool, and then apply a final varnish coat or two.

This is the basic technique, but there are many wonderful other effects to try. One friend of mine paints on his pieces a curly maple wood grain. Can you believe that? Another does delicate gold striping on some formal pieces. Still another does wonderful Pennsylvania Dutch birds, hearts, flowers, and hex designs. And one does decoupage on tabletops. The possibilities are vast and exciting.

Chapter 16

Accessories

DRAPERIES AND CURTAINS

Draperies can be made of most lightweight materials, cotton, dacron, silk, etc. (I particularly like men's striped shirts.) They can be hemmed, fringed at the edges, or lined. If you fringe the drapery panel, machine stitch a row of tiny stitches about ¼″ in from the edge. Then pull out the material threads up to the machine stitching. Hem the unfringed edges. You can sew the hems or fold them over, press with an iron, and glue them in place. The method of gluing hems works on most curtains and draperies. Use white glue, as sparingly as possible. On some fabrics, however, the glue may ooze through on the right side of the fabric and discolor it. For these, you have to sew the hems.

To line draperies, sew the drapery panel and the lining, with the right sides together, on both sides and at the bottom. Trim the seam very closely. Some glue will prevent the seam from raveling. Turn the panel right side out and press. The top edge can be closed with tiny slip stitches, or if you plan to use a cornice (Fig. 136) leave the top edge unfinished.

A cornice is made from ¹⁄₁₆″ thick wood pieces as shown in Fig. 136A. It can be covered with matching drapery fabric stretched over the cornice and glued on the inside. Slash the fabric to follow the curves as shown in Fig. 136B.

To attach the drapery to the window, if you are not using a cornice, make pleats at the top just as for real draperies and glue the panels to the window molding. You can also sew the drapery to tiny metal rings (see Model Shipways in the Source List) and hang the drapery on a ¹⁄₁₆″ dowel, or sew the pleated panel to a ¹⁄₁₆″ × ¹⁄₁₆″ wood strip or ¹⁄₁₆″ dowel for a curtain rod. If you are using a cornice, glue the drapery panel to the window molding folded in pleats.

The cornice is then glued to the wall to hide the glued pleats.

Whatever method you use, secure the drapery, rod, or wood strip firmly to the window molding with glue. Arrange the drapery in folds as you like, straight or tied back.

A twisted cord of embroidery floss makes a good tie back (see "Chippendale Sofa," upholstery). For a matching tie back simply fold a piece of fabric in thirds, trim the last fold so the edges will not show on the front side and glue it on the back side (Fig. 137).

Pin the folds lightly in place on the baseboard or window molding. You can press the draperies lightly, right on the wall, to set the folds. Remove the pins. It is often good to secure the folds at the baseboard with dots of glue to keep the draperies from billowing out.

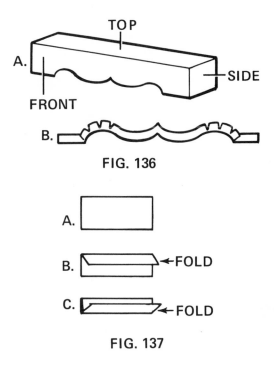

FIG. 136

FIG. 137

155

Hem-stitched handkerchiefs are perfect for making curtains or a rolled or glued hem is also attractive. Cut out the curtain panels. The un-hemmed edges can be finished simply by folding the material over about ⅛″ and gluing the hem. Fine lace glued to the handkerchief hems makes a lovely, light, airy-looking curtain. The curtain panel is then gathered with tiny stitches and sewed to a ¹⁄₁₆″ × ¹⁄₁₆″ wood strip. Secure the wood strip to the window molding firmly with glue. Now you can arrange the curtains in folds. Use tie backs and secure the curtains with dots of glue at the bottom, just as for draperies.

If you want to have the curtains hang straight, arrange the folds and pin them lightly in place. Now cover the wall, window, and moldings, everything but the curtains. Give the curtains 4 to 8 coats of Krylon clear plastic spray. When this is dry, remove the pins. The curtains will hold their shape and the plastic spray keeps them clean. The spray sinks into the fabric and does not give it a hard look. Valances can be done the same way. The tie-back curtains and the draperies described above can also be sprayed to help them to hold their shape.

MATTRESSES AND BEDSPREADS

Mattresses are made of several layers of art foam glued together in spots. A cover for the mattress is made by sewing two pieces of thin cotton fabric, right sides together, on three sides. Trim the seams very closely. Glue on the seams will prevent raveling. Turn the mattress cover right side out. Roll up the mattress, insert it into the cover and unroll it inside the cover. Fold over the raw edges of the mattress cover and close the seam with tiny slip stitches. Pillows are done the same way but smaller.

Bedspreads can be made from any lightweight material, the edges hemmed or fringed. They can be lined or unlined (see "Draperies"). To fit the bedspread around the legs of the bed, the end of the spread is cut as shown in Fig. 138. For any spread, when placed on the bed, it may be necessary to take a few small stitches or tucks at the corners and where the spread covers the pillow, to make the spread hang nicely.

Formal bedspreads can be done with crewel embroidery or cross stitch, using one thread of

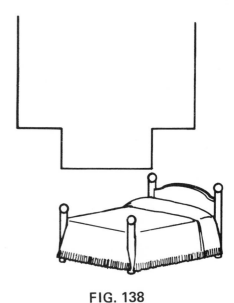

FIG. 138

a six-thread strand of embroidery floss. Fine homespun material is good for doing cross stitch on. There are many cross stitch patterns available which are suitable. Crewel work can also be painted on fabric with fabric paints.

A quilted bedspread can be made from checked gingham fabric. Various squares can be colored with indelible magic marker or fabric paint in patterns or at random for a patchwork look. The gingham is then lined with a thin layer of cotton batting and backed with a thin cotton fabric. The quilting is done by making long running stitches, catching the corner of each square. The edge of the quilt can be finished with narrow bias tape.

NEEDLEPOINT RUGS

There are many books on needlepoint to help you with details, but generally you can use any size canvas you like. 10/20 penelope (using the 10 canvas split to 20) or 20 mono canvas is about the biggest to use. It is really somewhat large in scale, but for farsighted people like me, it is large enough to see comfortably and still produce an acceptable looking rug. 20 mesh and some smaller meshes can be worked with one strand of crewel wool or one ply from a three-ply strand of persian wool.

There are many mesh sizes (see Woolcraft Ltd. in the Source List), all the way down to 40 mesh silk gauze which is worked with one thread

CONTINENTAL

	6	4	2
5	7	3	1	11
		9		
8	10	12	

HALF CROSS

	2	4	6
1	11	3	9	5	7
12	10	8	

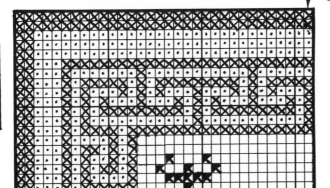

← CENTER ROW- DO NOT REPEAT

COLOR KEY

☐ OFF WHITE
🗷 DARK ROYAL BLUE
⊠ MEDIUM BLUE
⊡ LIGHT BLUE

CHINESE STYLE

← CENTER ROW - DO NOT REPEAT

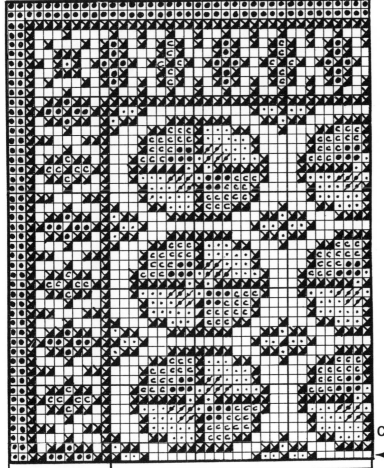

COLOR KEY

🗷 BLACK
⊙ DARK RED
🄲 LIGHT RED
🗷 BROWN
⊡ WHITE

BACKGROUND

☐ BORDER
⊡ FIELD

RUG CAN BE EXTENDED
TO DESIRED SIZE

BOKHARA STYLE

← CENTER ROW- DO NOT
REPEAT

BORDER   FIELD

PLATE 49

BORDER

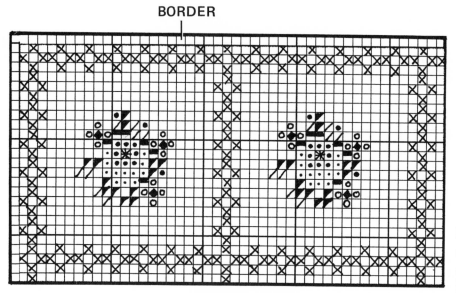

COLOR KEY

⬓ DARK BROWN
◪ MEDIUM GREEN
◿ LIGHT GREEN
⊡ RED
⊙ WHITE
◈ GOLD
⊡ PINK
▦ DARK RED
⊠ BEIGE

BACKGROUND SQUARES
ALTERNATE BROWN
AND MAROON.
BORDER IS BROWN

BORDER

REPEAT PATTERNS

SIZE OF RUG DEPENDS ON NUMBER
OF PATTERNS USED.

COLOR KEY

⊠ DARK BROWN
⊡ RED
☐ ORANGE

PLATE 50

BORDER

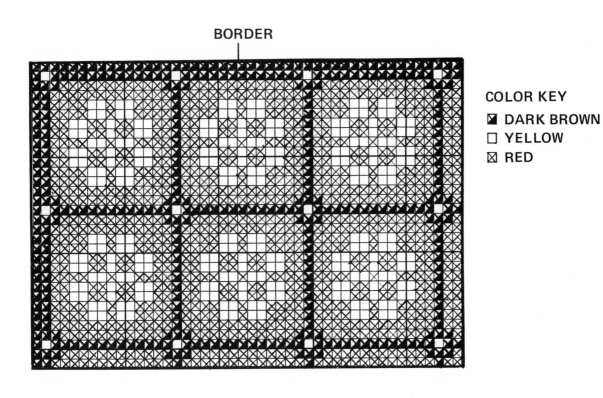

COLOR KEY
☒ DARK BROWN
☐ YELLOW
☒ RED

BORDER

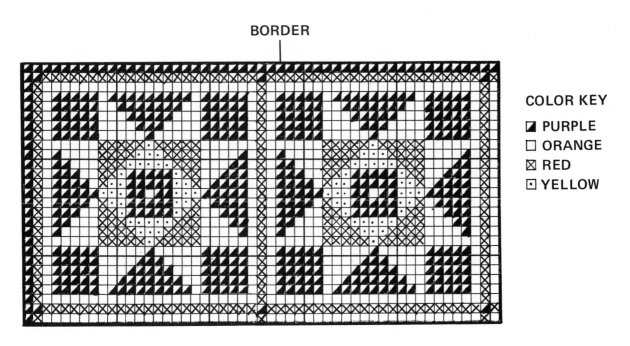

COLOR KEY
◪ PURPLE
☐ ORANGE
☒ RED
⊡ YELLOW

REPEAT PATTERNS

SIZE OF RUG DEPENDS ON NUMBER OF PATTERNS USED

PLATE 51

of a six-thread strand of embroidery floss. You really have to experiment with the canvas size and wool or floss to see what effect you like best.

As for stitches, two are most popular. The continental stitch (see Plate 49) can be used and most people are familiar and comfortable with it. To work this stitch, the needle is brought to the front of the work through hole 1 in the mesh, to the back through hole 2, to the front through hole 3, etc. Most instructions tell you to turn the work upside down to do the next row. You can, but do not have to, especially working in miniature. The disadvantage to this stitch is, because it is a diagonal stitch on both sides of the canvas, it tends to pull the canvas out of shape a bit. The finished work can be blocked back into shape, so if you like this stitch, use it.

The second stitch to use is the half cross (see Plate 49). In this, start at the upper left corner bringing the needle to the front of the work through hole 1, to the back through hole 2, to the front through hole 3, etc. When the first row is done, turn the work if you want to (or do not) and do the next row. Although this stitch is diagonal on the front side (as is the continental) it is straight on the backside which helps to prevent the distortion of the canvas as with the continental. I like to work the designs in continental and the backgrounds in half cross, but only for my comfort, not for any special reason.

Before starting your work, cut a frame (Fig. 139) of heavy illustration board, with the inside space about ½″ to 1″ larger all around than the finished work will be. Staple or tape your canvas to the frame. This frame will help keep the work from being pulled out of shape.

To finish the edges of the rug, see the section on oriental rugs for one method (my favorite). You can also trim the excess canvas to ½″ all around, turn under the edges and whip stitch around the entire edge. Or, you can line the rug much like for lined draperies (see "Draperies"). The last two ways do tend to produce a thicker rug, however.

BRAIDED RUGS

Braided rugs are made of twisted cord, using two long strands of crewel wool yarn or two single plys from a three-ply strand of persian yarn. To twist long strands (15–20 feet or more), tie two yarn ends to something stable, like a doorknob. Tie the other two ends to one beater of an electric mixer. Start the mixer and the beater will twist the cord for you. You can do this by hand of course, but it takes forever. When the cord begins to twist or knot up on itself, hold the cord in the middle (or loop it around a chair) and tie all four ends together at the doorknob. Release the cord at the middle and it will twist tightly on itself. You can make as many colors or combinations of colors as you like using two strands of the same color or two different colors.

With white glue, glue the cord to a paper backing in circular, oval, or square shapes. To change colors, put glue on the cord and let it dry before cutting it to prevent raveling. Start the new color with its cut end butted up next to the old color (Fig. 140).

These are fun rugs. They look marvelously complicated but only take about one day to make.

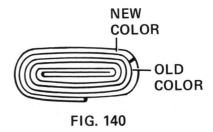

NEW
COLOR

OLD
COLOR

FIG. 140

WOVEN RUGS

Simple variegated handwoven rugs can be made. First cut a frame from ⅛″ thick illustration board (Fig. 141). Next, stick many pins (lill pins are good here) in the ends of the frame. For the

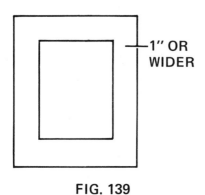

—1″ OR
WIDER

FIG. 139

warp, I used buttonhole and carpet thread. Wind the warp back and forth around the pins. All the warp threads are on the *front* of the frame.

Using single-strand wool yarn threaded on a tapestry needle, weave over and under the warp threads, back and forth, taking care not to pull the weaving strand too tight. Pack the weaving down with a pin as you go. When you want to change colors, lead the end of the old color under the weaving on the wrong side of the rug. Cut off the excess. To start a new color, thread it on the tapestry needle, lead it under the weaving on the wrong side of the rug and start the over and under weaving again. Change colors at the edges of the rug. When the weaving is complete, coat both ends of the rug with glue on the wrong side to secure the weaving. Cut the warp threads from the frame. Next cut a piece of 10/20 penelope canvas a bit less wide than the rug, but longer. Lightly glue the woven rug to the canvas in a few spots. With a small crochet hook, pull the warp threads through the canvas on the backside and secure with glue. To make fringe for the ends of the rug and finish it, see the section on oriental rugs.

The method given is the one I used but I think you could use embroidery floss for the warp threads. That way, when the warp is cut from the frame, the embroidery floss threads can be separated to make the fringe. That should work, but I have not tried it.

Oriental Rugs

Oriental rugs are worked in fringe stitches on 10/20 needlepoint canvas as shown in Plate 52. The technique will be discussed more fully later. 10/20 penelope canvas makes a good strong base, but the finer weaves can also be used. 20 (or smaller) mesh nylon mono canvas is also excellent but sometimes hard to find in stores.

You can use the designs in Plates 53 and 54 or design your own. To make your own design pick a photograph of a rug with fairly simple motifs; Caucasian, Chinese, and Central Asian rugs are good. The design is drawn on 13-squares-to-the-inch graph paper. This is a good size because the squares are large enough to see, but small enough to see the design as a whole. If you are using 10/20 penelope canvas, figure 20 graph

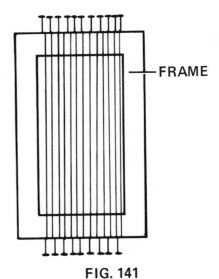

FRAME

FIG. 141

FIG. 142

squares equals one foot in real size or 1″ in miniature. So if you want a rug 4″ wide by 6″ long, design your rug on 80 squares by 120 squares. Mark the outside dimensions of the rug on the graph paper. Now begin to draw in the major areas of the design, the field and borders. It is helpful at first to place your photograph several feet away and draw what you see. This helps the tendency to get too involved in details in the beginning. Next make the drawing conform to the graph squares. Now you can work in the smaller designs and details.

When you are satisfied with the design, work on the color. Darken the lines on the design. Lay tracing paper over the design and with colored pencils, watercolors or magic marker, work out the colors on the tracing paper. This allows you to make many color combinations without redrawing the design each time.

To make the individual stitches, three or four threads of a six-thread strand of embroidery floss are used, fringed with a small crochet hook (see

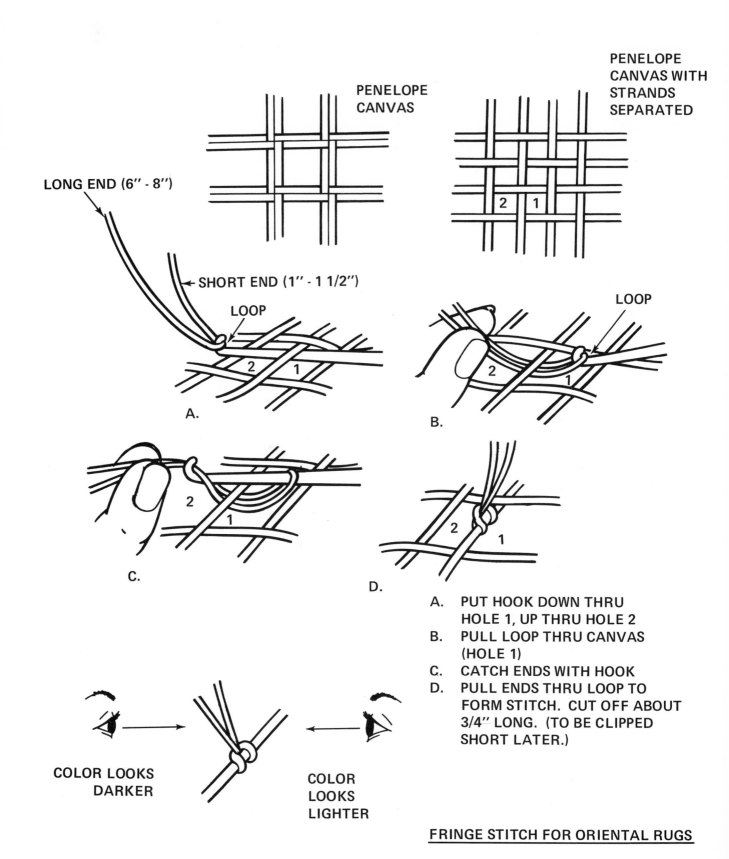

PENELOPE
CANVAS

PENELOPE
CANVAS WITH
STRANDS
SEPARATED

LONG END (6'' - 8'')

SHORT END (1'' - 1 1/2'')

LOOP

LOOP

A.

B.

C.

D.

A. PUT HOOK DOWN THRU
    HOLE 1, UP THRU HOLE 2
B. PULL LOOP THRU CANVAS
    (HOLE 1)
C. CATCH ENDS WITH HOOK
D. PULL ENDS THRU LOOP TO
    FORM STITCH. CUT OFF ABOUT
    3/4'' LONG. (TO BE CLIPPED
    SHORT LATER.)

COLOR LOOKS
DARKER

COLOR
LOOKS
LIGHTER

FRINGE STITCH FOR ORIENTAL RUGS

PLATE 52

CENTER ROW - DO NOT REPEAT

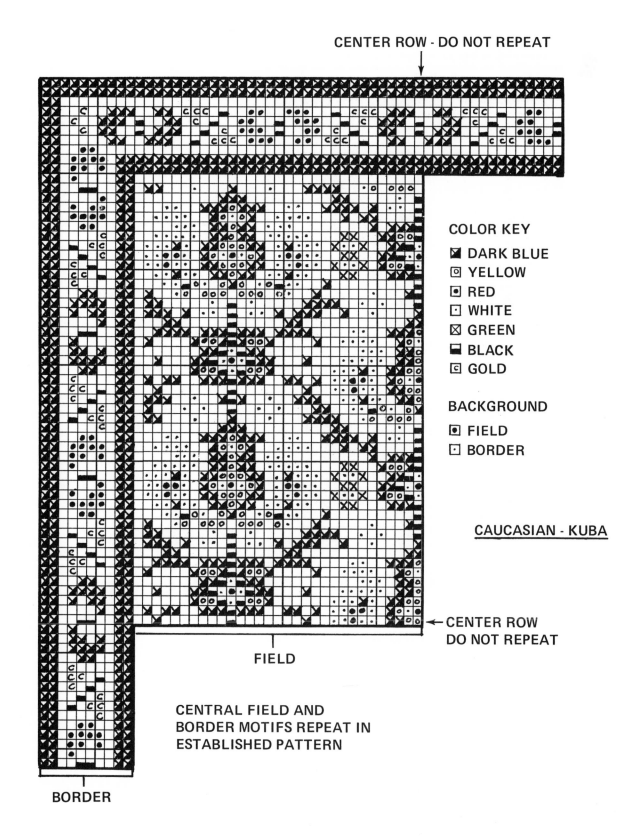

COLOR KEY
▨ DARK BLUE
◙ YELLOW
▣ RED
⊡ WHITE
⊠ GREEN
▬ BLACK
C GOLD

BACKGROUND
▣ FIELD
⊡ BORDER

CAUCASIAN - KUBA

← CENTER ROW
DO NOT REPEAT

FIELD

CENTRAL FIELD AND
BORDER MOTIFS REPEAT IN
ESTABLISHED PATTERN

BORDER

NOTE: BECAUSE THE CENTRAL FIELD AND BORDER
PATTERNS DO NOT REVERSE, THIS PATTERN SHOULD
BE COMPLETELY CHARTED BEFORE WORKING.

PLATE 53

CENTER ROW - DO NOT REPEAT

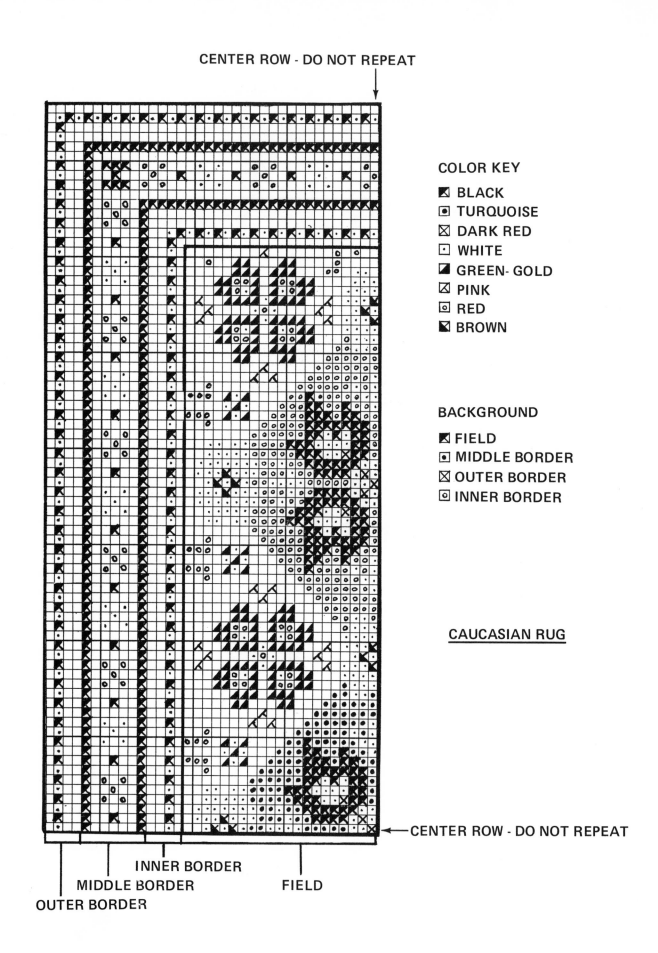

COLOR KEY

◪ BLACK
▣ TURQUOISE
⊠ DARK RED
⊡ WHITE
◨ GREEN- GOLD
⧅ PINK
◙ RED
◩ BROWN

BACKGROUND

◪ FIELD
▣ MIDDLE BORDER
⊠ OUTER BORDER
◙ INNER BORDER

CAUCASIAN RUG

CENTER ROW - DO NOT REPEAT

INNER BORDER

MIDDLE BORDER

FIELD

OUTER BORDER

PLATE 54

Plate 52). By using two or three different colors in each three-thread fringe stitch, almost any shade can be obtained. For instance, a nice turquoise can be made from one thread of bright turquoise, one green, and one grey. Two dark green and a brown make a good black. To work out your colors, hold many threads in a clump and cut the ends (Fig. 142). The color of the cut ends is much deeper and richer than the thread itself. One strand of crewel wool can also be used for a different look.

Before starting your rug, cut an illustration board frame and mount the canvas on it as for needlepoint rugs (see "Needlepoint Rugs").

To make the rug, follow your chart and, starting at the bottom, do one row of fringe stitches (see Plate 52). The thread used for the fringe stitch is used with a short end, 1″ to 1½″, and a long end, 6″ to 8″ or more. In this way, once the fringe stitch is made and both ends cut off short (about ¾″), you still have almost the whole long end intact for the next stitch. This saves greatly on thread. The ¾″ long stitch will be clipped to 1/16″ later.

The size of crochet hook used depends on what is comfortable for you. A size five is what I used. The hook will probably push the canvas strands of the next row out of position. This is normal and these strands will be pushed back later.

Put white glue over the completed row on the back of the rug. Let it dry. (To replace stitches now or later, soften the glue with water, pull out the mistaken stitch and replace it.) Pull all the fringes straight up, lay a 1/16″ thick strip of wood on the canvas and using it as a guide, cut off the excess fringe with sharp scissors. The finished stitches are now about 1/16″ long.

Do the next row. With a pin, push this row close to the first row. Glue and clip as before. As you work you will find that the space between rows may keep increasing. This is because the stitches are wider than they are long. Do not worry, just keep packing the rows close together as you work.

When the rug is done, brush up the nap and clip the high spots. This technique gives you a rug with a smooth, velvety texture. It will change colors according to which way the nap lies (see Plate 52) just as real orientals do. If your design has a definite top and bottom as the one in Plate

53, you will have to plan for this color change depending on whether you want lighter or darker colors.

Fringe Ends and Finishing

Now work fringe for the ends of the rug just like the other fringes except make them lie flat instead of standing up. Next, with a pin, push one strand of canvas up tight to each side of the rug and two or three strands at the ends. Give all these one or two coats of glue and let it dry completely.

Now cut away the excess canvas. The "binding" strands of canvas at the sides of the rug can be colored with indelible magic marker to match the rug border. The binding strands under the fringe at the rug ends will not be seen.

Steam and press the rug very lightly so it will lie flat and brush up the nap again.

Pictures and Mirrors

You can find many small prints in "art" books sold at art museums. Magazines are a good source. Mini-prints used for decoupage can also be used. Postage stamps of famous art treasures are sold. Needlework catalogs provide pictures of their merchandise which can be used as Colonial samplers or crewel work pictures. The Sears and Penney's catalogs have small pictures of American Primitives which they sell in full size. Keep your eyes open, small pictures are all around.

Glue the picture to 1/32″ thick balsa (Fig. 143A). Two coats of gel medium can be brushed over the picture, first crosswise, then up and down to give a "canvas" texture and the look of an oil painting.

Make a strip of molding (see Chapter 4) for a picture frame. Figure 143B gives you one example. The frame can be painted brass, gold, or given a wood finish.

Miter the corners of the frame (Fig. 143C). To miter a corner, lay two picture frame pieces at a 90° angle, overlapping them, and cut through both pieces at once for a perfect miter.

Glue the frame around the picture, on the balsa base. Cut away the excess balsa and bevel the balsa backing, with sandpaper, to blend with the frame (Fig. 143D). Paint the balsa backing and the outside edges of the frame to match the front

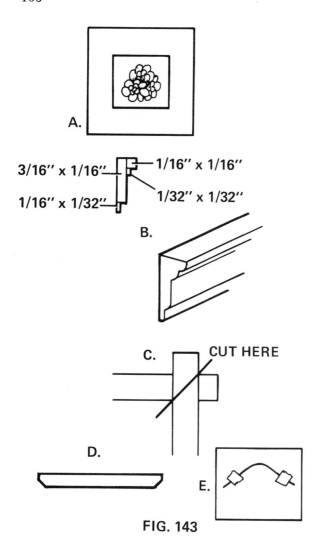

FIG. 143

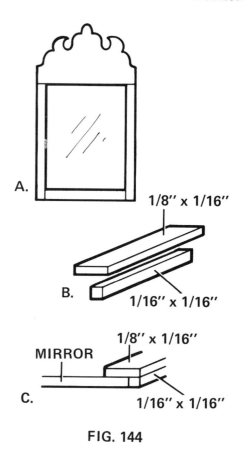

FIG. 144

of the frame.

The picture can be glued flat to the wall or you can make a picture hanger (Fig. 143E). This is just a piece of string glued on. Bits of paper glued over the ends of the string help hold it in place. Drill a pin hole in the wall. Clip off the sharp end of the pin. Push it in the wall. The pin head holds the picture hanger.

If you want "glass" over your picture, after you have glued the print to the balsa backing, lay thin acetate over the picture and glue it to the balsa backing just around the edges of the print. Be sparing with the glue if you use white glue or it might squish out onto the print. Trim the acetate close to the edges of the print and proceed as before with the framing.

For the mirror in Fig. 144, select a small mirror,

from a cosmetic case or mascara case, etc. The frame is then built around the mirror (Fig. 144A) with wood strips glued together to form a groove to hold the mirror (Figs. 144B and C). The carved top shown in Fig. 144A can be shaped as shown in Fig. 86A and B and used at the top in place of the $\frac{1}{8}'' \times \frac{1}{16}''$ piece.

The frame is then fitted around the mirror and glued together. Paint and finish the frame. Glue in the mirror. Glue a paper backing over the whole back to help hold the mirror in place.

For different mirrors, instead of the $\frac{1}{8}'' \times \frac{1}{16}''$ pieces shown in Fig. 144B, use picture framing as shown in Fig. 143B with added wood pieces on the backside to form a groove. Miter the corners around the mirror.

CANDLESTICKS

Candlesticks are made basically from various brass ship fittings (see A. J. Fisher in the Source List). Some fittings, such as ship stanchions, are

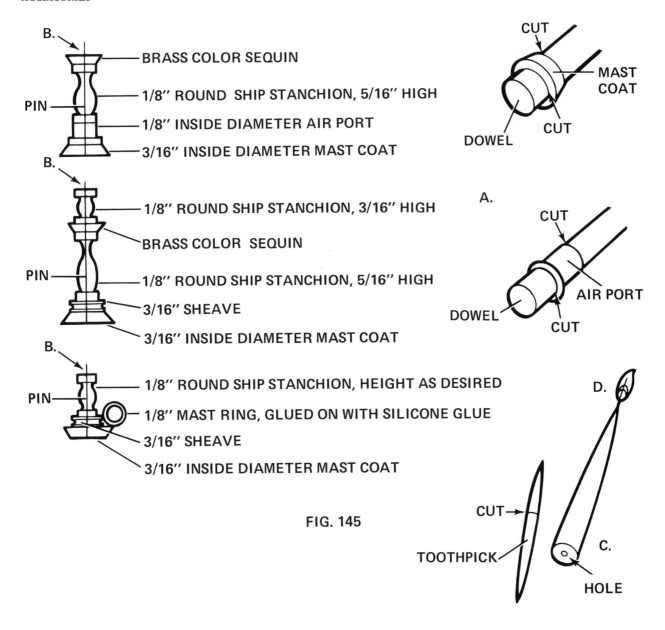

FIG. 145

solid with a pinhole drilled through. Some, mast coats and air ports, are hollow. These need to be filled. To do this, glue the brass part on a dowel which fits its inside diameter (Fig. 145A). Then with a razor saw, cut off the excess dowel as closely as possible to the brass piece. Sand off any excess wood, flush with the brass piece. The candletick pieces are then put together with glue, holes drilled through pieces with wood centers and a pin (with the head clipped off) inserted so that the sharp end extends out the top of the candlestick (Fig. 145B). A candle is then cut

from a round toothpick and a hole drilled in the fat part (Fig. 145C) to fit on the pin. You can also drill a tiny hole in the other end (Fig. 145D) and insert, with glue, a very fine wire for a wick. Cut to desired length. To simulate a flame, dip the wick in glue, the kind used for plastic models. Dip two or three times.

To make candlesticks into hurricane lamps, drill a hole in the bottom of a medicine capsule and glue it in place before adding the candle (Fig. 146).

FIG. 146

Fireplace Accessories

Andirons can be built up of various materials as with furniture (Fig. 147A). To make the legs (Fig. 147B), hammer the ends of solder wire flat, then cut the desired shape for the foot and bend to shape (Fig. 147C). Drill a hole through the andiron structure (Fig. 147D) and glue the legs in.

Paint the andirons brass using brass Treasure Jewels, a bit of varnish and a touch of Testor's enamel, yellow. For added shine, when dry, varnish with high-gloss varnish.

Fenders can be made from brass banding, which can be purchased through catalogs, bent to shape, straight or serpentine (Fig. 148A). Two bands can be laced together with wire for a higher fender. The ball feet (Fig. 148B) are simply pins with round plastic heads. Clip off the excess pin, sew or glue them in place, and paint the feet brass color.

Miscellaneous Accessories

There are myriads of accessories which can be bought but making them from bits and pieces is fun and saves incredible amounts of money. All it takes is imagination. Here are a few examples.

Books can be made of wood pieces of various sizes and thickness (Fig. 149A). The back edges are rounded slightly and the "book pages" part

painted metallic gold. The outside is covered with construction paper or leatherette textured paper for the cover. Trim the cover close to the book. The decorative trim (the dark lines in Fig. 149B) is metallic gold, done with Gold Mark tape, which is available at craft stores. To use it, you lay the tape on the book and with a sharp pencil, print what you want. The gold from the tape transfers on to the book, under the pressure of the pencil. Added color on the binding is done with magic marker. Two coats of latex varnish gives the book cover a finished look.

Fruit to put in a bowl can be made from various sizes of beads. Push the bead on a toothpick, paint the bead, and push the toothpick into a chunk of balsa till it dries (Fig. 150A). With Testor's enamel paint, beads can be painted orange for oranges, a darker orange first and then a lighter, almost yellow stroke for a highlight. For apples, I start with a darkish red, then use a stroke of yellow-green on one side near the top and another stroke of light red near the top for a highlight. These look remarkably like McIntosh apples. Plums are purple with a highlight of blue.

Bunches of grapes can be made by putting three or four 2mm beads on thread with glue (Fig. 150B). The threads, glued together, form a base and more beads are glued on to form the grape bunch (Fig. 150C).

The holes in the beads are left as is for oranges, apples, and plums to look like the natural indentations in the real fruit. For grapes, however, you can fill in the holes with white glue before painting the bunches grape color: green, purple, or red. The finished fruit is then arranged in a bowl and secured with glue.

For bowls there are available hollow metal beads (Fig. 151A) which make marvelous vases (see Miniature Mart in the Source List). Also there is a copper pudding mold available. To this you can add a mast coat (see A. J. Fisher, Source List) to make a footed bowl (Figs. 151B and C). This can be put together with glue or "stickum."

In one of the catalogs is a copper frying pan (Fig. 152A). You can clip off the handle, file down the pouring edges, and use this as the cover for a bed warmer (Fig. 152B). The warmer part is carved balsa, painted black, the handle, a carved $\frac{1}{16}''$ dowel done in wood color. A bit of copper sheeting (see Model Shipways, Source List) is

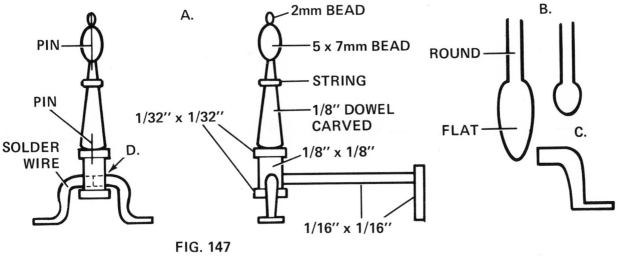

A.

PIN

PIN

SOLDER WIRE

D.

1/32″ x 1/32″

2mm BEAD

5 x 7mm BEAD

STRING

1/8″ DOWEL CARVED

1/8″ x 1/8″

1/16″ x 1/16″

B.

ROUND

FLAT

C.

FIG. 147

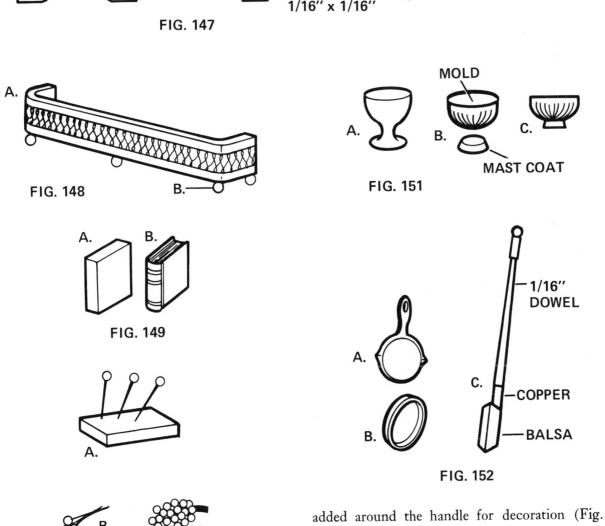

A.

B.

FIG. 148

MOLD

A.

B.

C.

MAST COAT

FIG. 151

A.   B.

FIG. 149

A.

B.   C.

FIG. 150

A.

B.

C.

1/16″ DOWEL

COPPER

BALSA

FIG. 152

added around the handle for decoration (Fig. 152C).

A wood basket can be made from brass grating, wire, and ship stanchions (see Model Shipways and A. J. Fisher, Source List). The grating is cut to shape and bent (Fig. 153A). The legs are small brass ship stanchions and a bead threaded together (Fig. 153B) and sewn to the grating. The carrying handle is bent brass wire and a bit of toothpick with a hole drilled through (Fig. 153C). The logs are tree twigs.

A bucket with the same handle is made from a round basswood piece for the bottom (Fig. 153D) and wedge-shaped ¹⁄₁₆″ thick basswood pieces for the sides (Fig. 153D). On two of these pieces carve a small extension (arrow) and drill a hole in it to hold the handle. The "metal" bands around the bucket are black construction paper (Fig. 153E).

Tiny flower arrangements can be done with dried material: star flowers, stattice, baby's breath, and moss for leaves. Soak the dried material to make it more flexible. The starflowers will close up when wet but will open again as the arrangement dries. Make the arrangement and bind it at the bottom with fine wire. Cut off the excess stems. When the arrangement dries, and the starflowers open, you can add more material, gluing it on, or cut away some. The arrangement can be secured in a bowl with "stickum." Ferns can be made from dried moss. Soak the moss in water and pull off the fronds you want with tweezers. Bunch the "fern" fronds, bind them with wire, trim the excess and secure in a bowl. "Ferns" tend to loose their color over several months. To prevent this, they can be soaked in fabric dye. They will soak up the dye and retain it or better still, when the ferns dry out after several days, paint them with a thin wash of artist's oil colors and turpentine.

Chair seat pads can be cut from ¹⁄₁₆″ poster board. A layer of art foam is glued on (the dotted line in Fig. 154A). Fabric is placed over the seat, trimmed to shape and glued on the back side. You can make tufts by sewing through the fabric, art foam, and poster board, securing the thread on the back side (Fig. 154B). Next cut a piece of fabric to fit the bottom of the chair pad and glue it on. The edges can be decorated with a twisted cord of embroidery floss (see "Chippendale Sofa," upholstery). Glue it around the edges of the pad and at the back to make ties to hold the pad to the chair (Fig. 154C).

Pitchers, bowls, plates, etc., can be done with self-hardening clay. It is easy to shape, fun to

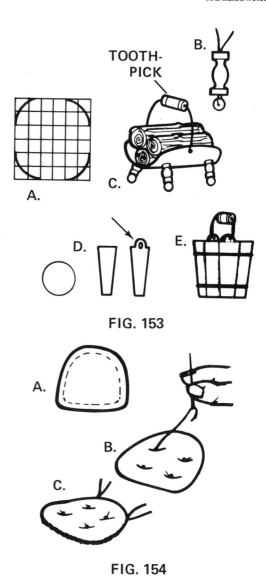

FIG. 153

FIG. 154

work with and dries hard in the air, no baking. Painted with Testor's enamel, the pieces have the look of glazed, fired ceramic.

Wonderful things can be done with "bread dough" and "play clay." I have not done them myself, but the ingredients to make "dough" and "clay" are available in many craft magazines. I have a friend who makes the most terrific vegetables from bread dough; beets with the leafy tops, and lettuce heads you just would not believe, each lettuce leaf individually done and overlapped to make the lettuce head.

The whole field of accessories is so exciting, once you start you just cannot stop. Have fun. Enjoy.

Source List-Catalogs

ACCESSORIES

WOOD
BRASS
MISCELLANEOUS
CRAFT SUPPLIES
ACCESSORIES
DISHES
HINGES
NEEDLEWORK, CANVAS
SILK MESH
MOLDINGS

MODEL SHIPWAYS (WOOD)
39 W. Fort Lee Road
Bogota, New Jersey 07603

A. J. FISHER (BRASS)
1002 Etowah Avenue
Royal Oak, Michigan 48067

LEE WARDS (MISCELLANEOUS
CRAFT SUPPLIES)
1200 St. Charles Road
Elgin, Illinois 60120

CHESTNUT HILL (ACCESSORIES)
Box 38
Churchville, New York 14428

FEDERAL SMALL WARES
(ACCESSORIES)
85 Fifth Avenue
New York, New York 10003

THE MINIATURE MART (DISHES)
883 39th Avenue
San Francisco, California 94121

THE GREEN DOOR STUDIO (HINGES)
517 E. Annapolis Street
St. Paul, Minnesota 55118

WOOLCRAFT LTD. (NEEDLEWORK,
CANVAS, SILK MESH)
#4 Trading Co. Bldg.
Regina, Saskatchewan
S4P OM3, Canada

NORTHEASTERN SCALE MODELS
(MOLDINGS)
Box 425 MM
Methuen, Massachusetts 01844

Index